MW01716627

CASS SERIES: STUDIES IN SLAVE AND POST-SLAVE SOCIETIES AND CULTURES
(Series Editors: Gad Heuman and James Walvin)

SMALL ISLANDS, LARGE QUESTIONS

Also in this series

The Slaves' Economy: Independent Production by Slaves in the Americas
Edited by Ira Berlin and Philip D. Morgan

The Economics of the Indian Ocean Slave Trade in the Nineteenth Century
Edited by William Gervase Clarence-Smith

Out the House of Bondage: Runaways, Resistance and Marronage in Africa and the New World
Edited by Gad Heuman

Unfree Labour in the Development of the Atlantic World
Edited by Paul E. Lovejoy and Nicholas Rogers

Reconstructing the Past: Blacks in Britain, c.1780–1830
Norma Myers

The Human Commodity: Perspectives on the Trans-Saharan Slave Trade
Edited by Elizabeth Savage

The Wages of Slavery: From Chattel Slavery to Wage Labour in Africa, the Caribbean and England
Edited by Michael Twaddle

SMALL ISLANDS, LARGE QUESTIONS

Society, Culture and Resistance in the Post-Emancipation Caribbean

Edited by
Karen Fog Olwig

Routledge
Taylor & Francis Group
LONDON AND NEW YORK

First published 1995 by
FRANK CASS & CO. LTD.

Published 2013 by Routledge
2 Park Square, Milton Park, Abingdon, Oxon OX14 4RN
711 Third Avenue, New York, NY, 10017, USA

Routledge is an imprint of the Taylor & Francis Group, an informa business

British Library Cataloguing in Publication Data

Small Islands, Large Questions: Society Culture and Resistance in the Post-Emancipation Caribbean. – (Studies in Slave & Post-slave Societies & Cultures)
I. Olwig, Karen Fog II. Series
306.097297

Library of Congress Cataloging-in-Publication Data

Small islands, large questions : society, culture and resistance in the post-Emancipation Caribbean / edited by Karen Fog Olwig.
p. cm. – (Studies in slave and post-slave societies and cultures)
Papers originally presented at a workshop held in Magleås, Denmark, in August 1992.
Includes bibliographical references and index.
1. Leeward Islands (West Indies) – Social conditions. 2. Leeward Islands (West Indies) – Economic conditions. 3. Freedmen – Leeward Islands (West Indies) 4. Slaves – Emancipation – Leeward Islands (West Indies) I. Olwig, Karen Fog, 1948– . II. Series.
HN244.A8S6 1995 95-14437
306' .09729–dc20 CIP

ISBN 13: 978-0-714-64576-6 (hbk)
ISBN 13: 978-0-714-64225-3 (pbk)

Contents

Acknowledgement

The editor wishes to express her appreciation to the Carlsberg Foundation for its support of this project.

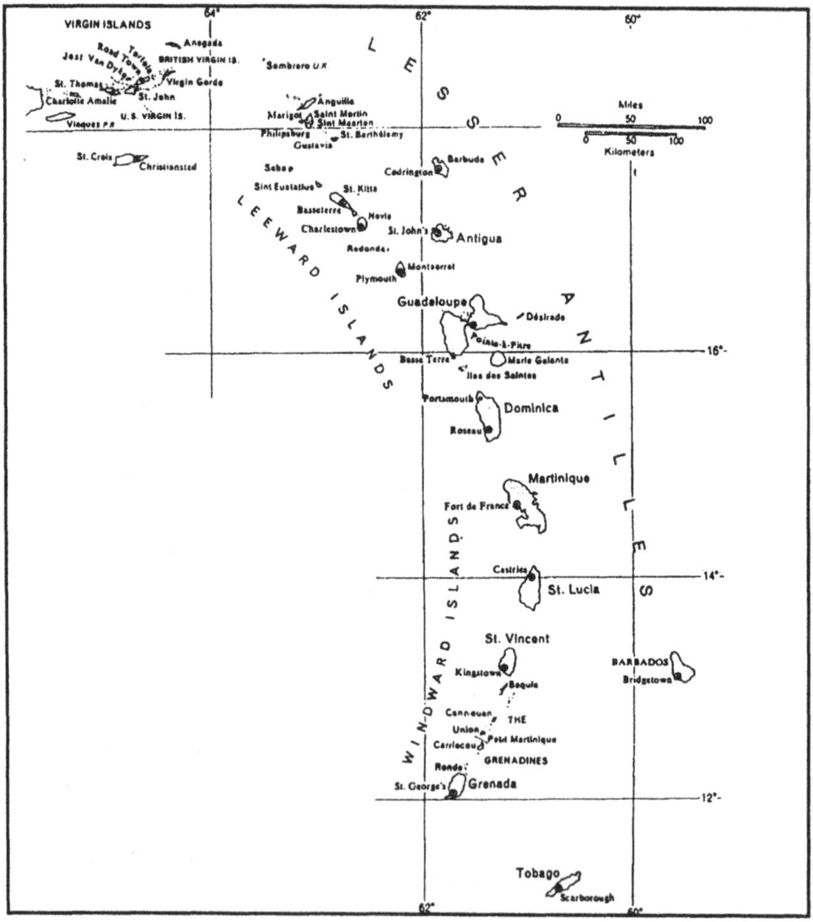

THE WEST INDIES

Part I

Introduction and Historiography

Introduction: Emancipation and Its Consequences

KAREN FOG OLWIG

The post-emancipation era was a formative time for the Caribbean societies of today. Yet it remains little examined: the social sciences have concentrated mainly on present-day societies, whereas historical research has largely been devoted to slavery. The long post-emancipation period, when local societies adjusted to the social and economic conditions of a free labour force and the emancipated attempted to create a new life of their own, has not been subject to similarly extensive and rigorous research.

Small Islands, Large Questions seeks to remedy this gap in Caribbean research.[1] Our particular focus is on the English-speaking Leeward Islands, whose small size makes them especially well suited to case studies of the economic, social, and cultural processes which link the pre-emancipation and the contemporary Caribbean. The regional variation displayed by the individual islands, furthermore, makes them a good starting point for comparative analysis. The authors in this volume, who represent a wide range of disciplines, notably history, geography, and anthropology, have all carried out extensive research in the Caribbean. They share a common interest in discussing their work in a broader regional context and from an interdisciplinary point of view.

Post-emancipation historiography, as Barry Higman suggests, has tended to highlight the transformation of the slave population into a free labour force and to focus narrowly on the social and economic ramifications this change had for the sugar plantations. The freed slaves have thus been largely reduced to the status of workers, and their widespread attempts to acquire land on which to settle have been examined mainly as a threat to the existing plantation systems. The chapters in this book transcend these issues in order to examine the emergence of patterns of life significant for the development of contemporary Caribbean societies.

It is difficult to see how the abolition of slavery gave West Indians of African descent true emancipation, if we take as our point of departure the definition of the verb 'to emancipate': 'to free from restraint, control, or the power of another; esp. to free from bondage' (Webster 1965). As the writers in this volume amply document, the institution of slavery was largely replaced by subjugation that was indirect yet almost as coercive. Access to land was limited throughout the Caribbean, even in islands with considerable uncultivated land, as Riva Berleant-Schiller shows in her chapter on Montserrat. Strict new labour laws on post-emancipation St. Croix in the Danish West Indies, as detailed by George Tyson, drove the emancipated labourers off the plantations and led to the importation of contract workers from abroad. The cultural barriers that commonly restricted social and economic mobility are analysed in Susan Lowes's chapter on Antigua and mine on Nevis.

It is easier to grasp the realities of emancipation, however, if the primary etymological definition of 'to emancipate' is used: 'to release from paternal care and responsibility and make sui juris' (ibid.). With emancipation the former slaves were made legal persons who had to fend for themselves. This book instances numerous examples of the removal of the privileges slaves had previously had under the care of their owners. Tyson and Berleant-Schiller illustrate how emancipation abrogated the customary right to cultivate provision grounds on estate land, removed access to free food and medical care, and curtailed rudimentary support for education.

In summary, the emancipated were expected to have legal capacity as independent citizens while the informal customary rights which they had formerly received now had to be paid for by deductions in wages. Simultaneously they were placed under severe restraint and control by the plantocracy, leaving them with a narrow social and economic base from which to exercise the legal rights of free citizens. The social and economic problems experienced by the freed were exacerbated where contract labourers were imported to replace the native labour force. This was the case on St. Croix, as George Tyson shows, where labourers from the British West Indies were used on the sugar plantations. The presence of a large foreign labour force played an important role in the uprising that broke out there in 1868. Similar forms of violent resistance against the planter regimes occurred in many other West Indian societies at this time; Gad Heuman reviews some of these riots and disturbances in the post-emancipation Caribbean. He concludes that the contradictory expectations of freedom held by the ruling class and by the emancipated were largely responsible for the violence.

The emancipated sought to define a new life for themselves during a period of social turmoil and economic decline characterized by periodic outbreaks of unrest. They did not start from a *tabula rasa*. As Jean Besson notes, the Caribbean peasantries that emerged after abolition built on agricultural traditions developed among slaves since the early days of colonization. To understand how ex-slaves sought to carve out lives of their own, we must look at the strategies for freedom they had adopted during slavery.

Paradoxically, one of the most important avenues toward freedom was exploitation of the 'paternal care and responsibility' owners had extended to their slaves. Many slave 'privileges' – cultivating marginal land on the plantations, selling surplus produce at markets, time off from work to produce subsistence crops and care for children – had been cost-free means of fulfilling owners' legal obligations to their slaves. For the slaves, however, these means became 'interstices' in the plantation system (Mintz 1985), which allowed a modicum of emancipation – that is, release 'from restraint, control, or the power of another'. But ex-slaves' attempts to appropriate such crevices as places where they might establish their own communities were resisted by the planters, who feared that such settlements would expand to engulf the whole plantation system. The nature of the struggle for cultural autonomy and social recognition in the face of restraints and controls imposed by the plantation regimes is an important theme in this book.

The special case of the former free coloured is discussed by Lowes in her article on the non-white elite of Antigua. Their position as privileged intermediaries between the mass of black slaves and the white upper class became untenable after emancipation. Planters, fearing the growing numbers and wealth of the former free coloured, erected economic, political, and social barriers against them. Unwilling to make common cause with the lower classes, the non-white elite finally opted to emigrate, thus imposing voluntary exile upon themselves.

While the plantocracies successfully resisted the threat to their hegemony which they saw emanating from local non-white elites, they were unable to withstand the multitude of strategies devised by the emancipated slaves to establish niches with some measure of cultural autonomy. Most important were the various means by which the emancipated gained access to land as small farmers. As Berleant-Schiller documents for Montserrat, access to land included 'slavery-like' tenancy-at-will agreements where rights to housing and provision grounds were granted in return for labour, *métayer* arrangements where a portion of the crop was exchanged for use of the land, squatting on uncultivated land, and ownership of land acquired through purchase. All these arrangements led to the establishment of a peasantry which in the long run managed to wrest control from the plantocracy. As on most islands, peasant farming did not provide a sufficient economic basis for the growing population, and migration therefore also became an important alternative for the lower classes.

Behind these various patterns of land use and land holdings in late nineteenth century Caribbean societies lay a common desire to establish spheres of autonomy based on kinship and community. Besson focuses on the development of the institution of family land, shared by generations of kinfolk. Since plots were often too small to sustain the large kin networks having rights in them, family land served not primarily as the physical loci of these kin-based communities but as symbolic loci of cultural roots and a sense of belonging, even *in absentia* for far-flung migrants.

In the post-emancipation era, the freed were forced to establish lives of their own by drawing on resources controlled by different segments of the population. Most of the land continued to be owned by the planters; education, and hence access to civil service posts, was in the hands of the church; the more informal social and economic relations of everyday life were embedded in the African-Caribbean communities. The cultural implications of this are discussed in my chapter on Nevis, which delineates three co-existing 'cultural traditions' identified with distinct cultural values and social practices. These cultural traditions were associated with the different segments of the population that controlled the different social and economic resources on the island. Most persons therefore had to deal with several contradictory cultural traditions in various contexts of their lives, leading to cultural patterns of considerable complexity. Such complexity is particularly apparent in cultural institutions, where elements of the various traditions are brought together and reinterpreted.

Frustrated expectations resulting from an emancipation which codified individual independence and responsibility but imposed an array of restraints led to emigration. Elizabeth Thomas-Hope sees in migration a continuation of old patterns of marronage. During slavery, marronage had been the illegal running away from the plantations with no possibility of return. An important result of emancipation, therefore, was the legalization of marronage, so that both movement away and movement back were possible. Migration became central in the Caribbean not as a way of escaping from and abandoning the island of birth with all its restraints and contradictions, but as a means of acquiring the capital needed to realize hopes and aspirations connected with life there.

Most of the themes discussed in this book are relevant throughout the post-emancipation Caribbean. The struggle for improved working conditions, land, and education has been central to popular concerns. However, smallness and marginality make the Leeward Islands particularly poignant cases of the difficulty of exercising newly won freedom in a period of economic decline and increasing external control, as David Lowenthal makes clear in the concluding chapter. The emancipated, of necessity, deployed multiple economic strategies. They developed extensive kin networks and migrated to distant destinations. They also, however, established a tradition of small farming on the islands and formed descent groups rooted in family land which provided the basis for a strong attachment to place.

The post-emancipation era was characterized by a number of different, even contradictory, developments involving the freed in social and economic relations with a local as well as a global dimension. The ability to absorb the contradictions of freedom may well be one of the most important legacies of emancipation for modern Caribbean societies.

REFERENCES

Mintz, Sidney W. 1985. 'From Plantations to Peasantries in the Caribbean'. In *Caribbean Contours*, S. W. Mintz and Sally Price (eds.), 127-53. Baltimore: The Johns Hopkins University Press.

Webster's Seventh New Collegiate Dictionary. 1965. Springfield, Mass.: G. C. Merriam.

NOTE

1. *Small Islands, Large Questions* began as a workshop, organized by Poul Olsen of the Danish National Archives and myself. The seminar, held in Magleås, near Copenhagen, in August 1992, offered an opportunity for scholars from the Caribbean, North America, and Europe to spend three days discussing the post-emancipation era in the Caribbean, with special focus on the Leeward Islands. A generous grant from the Carlsberg Foundation made the seminar and book possible. I would like to thank David Lowenthal, Mary Alice Lowenthal, and Kenneth Olwig for their comments and editorial assistance.

Small Islands, Large Questions: Post-Emancipation Historiography of the Leeward Islands

B. W. HIGMAN

SMALL ISLANDS

The Leewards constitute a true archipelago, a sea studded with islands. Unlike most other parts of the Caribbean, a person on the shore of one island can often see one or more other islands across the water, and from the islands' moderate summits a larger number come into view. This picture of the world carries the possibility of distinctly different readings: one emphasizes the *unity* derived from the encompassing sea, another the *fragmentation* resulting from the separateness of the land masses. These contradictory yet co-existent archipelagic principles have continuing significance for issues of territoriality and sovereignty (Maula 1981:12-13). They also provide metaphors and models for Caribbean history at large (Brathwaite 1974:64), in the same way that the archipelago has sometimes been seen as an allegory for a fragmented Earth (Rand 1981:34-48).

Equally important in defining the primary characteristics of the Leewards is the relative smallness of the islands. In the Leeward zone, defined here to comprise all the islands stretching from Vieques to Montserrat,[1] the largest unit is Antigua (280 km^2), 'a small place' for its own people (Kincaid 1988) and smaller than the smallest of the Windward group, Tobago (295 km^2). Smallness in itself has played a vital role in determining the character of economic and social development for the islands and has done much to ensure a stronger persistence of the colonial relationship than elsewhere in the Caribbean (Royle 1992; Clarke 1971).

The smallness of the islands and their archipelagic pattern are defining characteristics and determining variables in the history of the Leewards, yet they fail to impose homogeneity on the region. Variations in resources resulting from differences in topography, soils, and climate have created a wide range of land-use patterns and settlement types. In other parts of the Caribbean such diversity tends to occur within the bounds of a particular island, but in the Leewards a single settlement pattern often encompasses an entire island. Thus the potential for separate identity, based on geographical insularity, has been strongly supported by unique systems of land use, perceptions of environmental difference, and concepts of community. These sources of variation in historical experience overlap differences in political relationships, particularly in imperial terms (Goveia 1965:52-53; D. Hall 1971:1; Lewis 1972:ix-x). It may be argued that these differences matter less than the variables associated with local physical factors, but the consequences of imperial fragmentation are certainly important for the development of the historiography of the region.

In the broader Caribbean context, the Leewards may be seen as a laboratory within a laboratory, a sample of small-scale experiments in social engineering consequent on the ending of slavery. Contemporaries and later historians attached particular importance to the outcome of emancipation in the Leewards for a variety of reasons, but most obviously because of the presence of Antigua within the region. For the metropolitan powers, from whence came the majority of the historiographers, Antigua (which skipped the apprenticeship and made a direct transition to freedom in 1834) was a test case that mattered more than the consequences of the revolution in St. Domingue.

None the less it must be recognized that the Leewards were quantitatively less significant than the other British and Dutch Caribbean colonies in terms of output, population, and political weight. What happened in Jamaica and in Surinam was always of greater import than the experience of St. Kitts or Saba for policy and practice, and in the longer term for historiography. Only for the Danes did what happened in the Virgin Islands (rather roughly forced into the Leeward zone for the purpose of this analysis) have exclusive importance.

LARGE QUESTIONS

The historiography of the post-emancipation period has tended to focus on a number of central issues, most if not all of which were concerned with the transformation of the ex-slave population into a free labour force. How substantial was the shift from one system of labour domination to another, and what were the factors which determined variations in the pattern? Other questions, such as the extent of political change consequent on emancipation and the reordering of social and cultural life, are important, but these have generally been viewed as products of the larger issue of labour, and the ex-slave as worker fills the centre of the historiographical stage. From a modern perspective, this limited and limiting perception of labour fails to capture the perspective of the ex-slaves themselves.[2] There is no doubt, however, that the behaviour of the ex-slave as worker has been the big question for the historian and the *raison d'être* for some of the grandest theory in Caribbean historiography.

It seems neither necessary nor possible to attempt to outline these theories in any detail; for recent summaries and interpretations are available.[3] The objective here is to consider the historiography of the post-emancipation Leeward Islands within the context of these larger questions and debates, to make some assessment of the use to which the Leeward examples have been put, and to consider what may be learned from a consideration of the historiography.

The large questions and grand theories associated with the ex-slave as labourer have their direct counterparts within the study of slavery itself. Attempts to explain the origins and terminations of slave-labour systems (as well as other forms of labour coercion) are equally central to the economic history of the Caribbean and make use of the same explanatory models, which include the land–labour ratio, the existence of open or closed resources, and the dialectics of domination (Nieboer 1900; Domar 1970). Critiques of the validity of such theories for slavery parallel critiques for the post-emancipation period (Patterson 1977). The basic questions span many stages of Caribbean development.

The post-emancipation historiography of the Leewards, as for the non-Hispanic Caribbean generally, can be divided into three principal periods (Waddell 1966:344; Goveia 1956; Marshall 1975). The first period, to about 1900, was dominated by amateurs, both insiders and outsiders. The second, covering the first half of the twentieth century, saw the ascent of the newly professionalized historians, most of whom were metropolitan Europeans and North Americans. In the third period, since about 1950, West Indian professionals joined metropolitan historians of the academy. These shifts in the origins of the history writers, together with fundamental changes in perspective and method, affected the content of their histories, their interpretations of the post-emancipation period, and their definition and use of sources. In terms of theoretical orientation, however, continuity has been an equally important motif.

HISTORIOGRAPHY: 1834–1900

To date the beginnings of a post-emancipation phase in historiography from 1834, the year of abolition in Antigua and the commencement of the apprenticeship in other British Leeward Island colonies, may seem strange. In fact, the roots of the macro-systemic interpretations of emancipation must be sought in the predictive views that abolitionists and planters had advanced earlier during the debate over slavery. Although abolitionists and planters were antagonists, they both believed that the maintenance of the plantation system after emancipation would ensure prosperity and civilization, and that the ex-slaves needed to be guided or compelled to continue as plantation workers (Eltis 1982:198-205; Ward 1988). These beliefs permitted the compromise over apprenticeship and the master-servant and police legislation advanced by the planter-controlled Assemblies in the British colonies. To some extent the expectations of abolitionists and planters were the product of racial and class perceptions of blacks and workers, but the predictions were also based on knowledge of Haitian developments (for instance, the Jamaican Assembly's call during the apprenticeship for a rural code), and, for the Danish, direct observation of the British Leeward experience (Eltis 1982:205; N.A.T. Hall 1992:54).

Two important strands of thought running through the abolition debate sought to explain the expected reluctance of the ex-slave to continue as a plantation worker. One, which can be traced to ideological justifications of slavery (N.A.T. Hall 1992:34-55), referred ultimately to racial characteristics. The other related to the ease with which subsistence could be obtained within the tropics. These themes became central features of the historiography in the nineteenth century.

Local histories of the British Leeward colonies are scarce. Vere Langford Oliver's *History of the Island of Antigua*, published in three massive volumes between 1894 and 1899, was the most significant, but he had a strong antiquarian preoccupation and said little of the post-emancipation experience (Goveia 1956:107-34, 181). Usually, the islands appeared only in histories which dealt with all the colonies or treated more theoretical issues. Works of the latter kind were, interestingly, some of the first to locate contemporary commentary within the context of history.

One of the most influential of these analytical histories was Herman Merivale's *Lectures on Colonization and Colonies*, published in 1841, and derived from 'a course delivered at the University of Oxford in the years 1839, 1840, and 1841', when he was Professor of Political Economy. His objective was to consider the relationship between capital and labour in the context of colonization (Merivale 1861:xi). The first part of his work was devoted to an 'historical account of the progress of the colonies of modern Europe', the second to the economic effects of colonization on the 'parent state', and the third to the 'progress of wealth and society in colonies'. In this final part Merivale discussed the methods used to secure a supply of labour and considered the impact of emancipation on the relationships among land, labour, and capital.

Following Adam Smith, and with the current colonial land settlement theories of Edward Gibbon Wakefield and Robert Torrens firmly in view, Merivale noticed the apparent paradox that the sparsely populated fringes of imperial expansion tended to be characterized by extremes of both liberty and slavery (Merivale 1861:253-76; Curtin 1977:7-8). What mattered, he concluded, was not simply the land–labour ratio but also the relative importance of export staples in a colony's economy. Although his theory was inadequate as a complete explanation of the origins of particular labour systems, it contributed substantially to the development of the staple theory of economic growth which was, in turn, a great advance on crude climatic and racist conceptualizations. Merivale's ideas feature prominently in Eric Williams' classic work *Capitalism and Slavery* and in Elsa Goveia's *Slave Society in the Leeward Islands at the End of the Eighteenth Century*, most significantly in her view that the density of the slave population in Antigua, St. Kitts, and Nevis had become so great that emancipation was inevitable (Merivale 1861:303; Williams 1964:4-7; Goveia 1965:329-30).

Merivale made a further contribution to post-emancipation historiography by classifying the British sugar colonies according to the ratio of land to labour. This ratio, measured in simple population density terms, was affected by the age structure of the population and correlated with the profitability of labour. Labour profitability was measured at the macro level by slave prices, as averaged for compensation purposes. These data provided Merivale with the quantitative basis for his classification, and he did not in fact calculate population densities *per se*. The correlations among slave population density, productivity, profitability, and prices have been influential in Caribbean historiography.[4] His classification of colonies has been equally important, and the failure to acknowledge Merivale as the source, noted by Marshall, reflects the extent to which his concepts have come to seem natural and intuitive (Marshall 1991:3; cf. Higman 1984:43-71).

The first category of Merivale's tripartite model comprised the oldest British colonies in the 'smaller Antilles'. Some were depressed, others flourishing, but the features common to all were that 'the land was nearly all occupied, population extremely thick, cultivation ancient, and capital accumulated' (Merivale 1861:313). Barbados and Antigua were his primary examples.[5] Such colonies 'were less injured than any others by the immediate effect of emancipation', by which Merivale meant that 'no serious interruption at all, either in [sugar] production or the ordinary course of social life', occurred. The reasons for this stability or continuity were that 'the negroes had no resource except in continuing to work; there was no unoccupied land for them to possess, no independent mode of obtaining a subsistence to which they could resort, still less of obtaining those luxuries which habit had rendered desirable to them'. For Merivale, the argument was confirmed by the planter's 'bold experiment' in Antigua, namely the rejection of apprenticeship, which resulted in an appreciation of the value of property and full employment for the ex-slaves 'at very moderate wages'. The only threat to the maintenance of the system was emigration, and Merivale believed that would prove 'no loss in the end' (Merivale 1861:314).

Merivale's second class of colonies consisted of those 'in which the fertile or advantageously situated soil was all cultivated, and becoming exhausted; but there remained much unoccupied soil, of a less valuable description, and the population was not dense in proportion to the whole surface'. This was most obvious in Jamaica. Merivale said it also applied to 'some of the smaller Antilles' but gave no examples. In these colonies, the attractions of the provision ground and life independent of regimented work on the plantation were strong and spelt doom for the system in the long run. The seeds of that destiny, thought Merivale, had been sown long before 1834 (Merivale 1861:315-16).

The third set of colonies in Merivale's classification comprised territories with large amounts of fertile land; none of them was in the Leewards. What this type of colony needed, Merivale argued, was an inflow of labourers. Some labour could come from 'the thickly peopled Antilles', but Merivale looked more hopefully towards the free coloured people of the United States. Once 'the artificial fabric' of protectionisn had been stripped away, the East would come to supply Europe with its tropical commodities (Merivale 1861:322-24). This last point, Merivale recognized, would not sit well with the planters, and he was torn between accepting the possibility of fresh forms of civilization springing from the ashes of the plantation and a deep fear that the end of the plantation system heralded a return to barbarism and the loss of a new class of consumers (Merivale 1861:319-20, 330-32).[6]

Merivale's analysis contributed fundamentally to the historiography of the post-emancipation period and influenced studies beyond the British territories. For the Leeward Islands, however, he was generally vague and sometimes misleading in allocating colonies to his classificatory model. Only Antigua is mentioned explicitly, and we are left to guess where he would have placed the other colonies. Equally important, Merivale and most who followed him focused their attention on the sugar-producing colonies, omitting islands with alternative economies (such as Anguilla and Barbuda), which have much to tell about the meaning of freedom and other paths of Caribbean development. The preoccupation with sugar must be traced to a plantocratic/imperial perspective that persisted well into the twentieth century.

Parallel to Merivale's historical and theoretical studies were contemporary observations of the British Leewards from a Danish West Indian perspective. Once again, the models created before emancipation appear to have influenced both the transition to freedom and the historiography of the process. The most important Danish commentator was Louis Rothe, High Court Assessor and Judge of Probate in St. Croix, who in 1845 was appointed by the government to investigate the impact of emancipation on sugar production and social relationships in British islands whose physical and land-use patterns most closely resembled those of the Danish colonies (N. A. T. Hall 1983). The islands he visited all belonged to the first or third group of Merivale's classification; Jamaica was ignored. Rothe judged Antigua, which he visited twice, to be the most fascinating case and at the end of 1846 submitted a massive report on that colony. He also prepared extended reports on the effects of emancipation on the British West Indian colonies and on the state of the population of the Danish West Indies (Rothe 1846a, 1846b, 1846c).[7]

Rothe found Antigua and St. Croix similar in terms of their physical environments, and he also pointed out the common influence of Christian missionaries, particularly the Moravians. In general, Rothe painted an optimistic picture of the impact of emancipation on Antigua, noting the maintenance of sugar production levels and the rationalization of plantation land use. Immediately after emancipation in 1834, he said, many ex-slaves withdrew from estate labour and poured into the towns but lack of employment in the urban areas sent them back.

> Since all available cultivable land belonged to the plantations and the island had neither forests nor uncultivated land, they were forced out of necessity to return to the plantation negro houses for shelter and to the fields as the only source from which they could make a living. Any desire, which many of them were already demonstrating, to obtain small plots on which to build houses and live independently of the plantation was difficult of fulfilment (Rothe 1846a:42-43).

Rothe wrote in detail on his view of the ex-slaves' understanding of freedom, which matched the opinions of British planters and abolitionists. Equally, like Merivale, he showed an appreciation of variations in the impact of emancipation, determined in large part by differences in resources and opportunities related to population density, but he confined his analysis almost exclusively to the sugar economies.

One of the first histories to be produced following the Danish emancipation was *A Historical Account of St. Thomas*, published in 1852 by John P. Knox, pastor of the Dutch Reformed Church in that island (Knox 1852). Knox noted that 'whilst the torrid zone is wonderfully adapted to the development of the animal and vegetable kingdoms, it is not prolific in books, nor distinguished for cerebral activity'. He bemoaned the lack of histories of the islands and regretted his own inability to examine the public records in Copenhagen (Knox 1852:v-vi). As to the recent emancipation, Knox referred readers to the Labour Act of 1848 and observed that as a result of this law 'the cultivation of their estates is still enjoyed by the planters'. He believed also that the 'country negroes' had benefited by emancipation, but argued that in the long term

> much will depend upon the wisdom of the Government in maintaining labor, and maintaining it at a fixed price. If the laws should be relaxed

> on this point, idleness and vagrancy must inevitably ensue, to be followed by all that train of vices so destructive of everything good and sacred. The laborers themselves would soon fall back into comparative barbarism and the island in a measure be ruined.
>
> The principle that labor should command its price is correct, but there are exceptions under certain circumstances. Those just set free from slavery are unable to judge of the value of labor, and government establishing its price is a merciful law to guard against evils of the very worst character (Knox 1852:123).

Vagrancy, said Knox, was a problem on most of the British West Indian islands, but here he failed to make the subtle distinctions of a Merivale or a Rothe. Knox did, however, notice significant differences between the experience of town and country, contrasts which must have been highly visible in St. Thomas (Knox 1852:123-25).

Two years after the appearance of Knox's history came the work of John Davy, based on his experience as inspector general of army hospitals in the British Windward and Leeward Islands between 1845 and 1848 and on his reading of Parliamentary Papers, Blue Books, and other material in the library of the Colonial Office (Davy 1854:i-ii). More explicitly than Knox, Davy saw his task as a vindication of 'the negroes of African descent and the people of color of mixed races'. He believed 'that the low and degraded state in which they were sunk and from which they are but slowly emerging, has been owing not to any inherent inferiority of nature or of mental capacity, but to the dire circumstances of their former condition in the state of slavery' (Davy 1854:ii; cf. Knox 1852:127-30).

Although Davy did not style his book a history, he set out to compare the colonies before and after emancipation, and the material covered is similar to most descriptive-historical compilations of the time. He had praise for both the ex-slaves and the planters of Antigua, observing that except for Barbados 'not one of our West Indian colonies has had a better supply of native labour (there being about as many labourers as there are arable acres) or at a more moderate cost, or more continuously, and with more content, and consequently with less need if any, of immigrant aid' (Davy 1854:400; cf. Baird 1850:36-37). Davy was aware of differences among the individual Leeward Islands, placing St. Kitts and Nevis close to Antigua in terms of productivity and labourer–planter relations, with Montserrat in a relatively bad state.

For the remainder of the nineteenth century, the literature which can be considered contributory to the historiography tended to be slight. In part, this resulted from a waning of interest in the outcome of emancipation and the growth of a metropolitan–plantocratic perception of failure. This perception occurred parallel to the development of a more intense racism and to the emergence of social Darwinism. The Leeward Islands also became relatively minor components of the European empires, dropping from sight in the midst of a burgeoning world economy.

James Rodway, in *The West Indies and the Spanish Main* (1896), bemoaned the fact that 'the West Indies have sunk into neglect by Europe' and 'except for the difficulties of the planters their history is almost a blank sheet'. The islands were still as beautiful as they had been four hundred years before, and the forests were as grand as ever, but 'ruin and desolation have fallen upon them since the peace of 1815 and the emancipation. Even the negro – the *protege* of the benevolent – is no longer the object of interest he once was' (Rodway 1896:xiii). Goveia identified in the writings of Rodway 'a tendency towards authoritarianism, reinforced by quite marked racial prejudice', which gave his historical interpretation elements 'strongly reminiscent of the older planter histories'. Rodway came close to racist justifications of both slavery and post-emancipation developments, describing the ex-slaves as 'naturally lazy' (Goveia 1956:130-34).

Rodway was an English druggist who emigrated to British Guiana in 1870 and became interested in history as well as botany. He was appointed librarian of the Agricultural and Commercial Society in 1888 and was put in charge of the museum in 1903 (Cruickshank 1920). The connection between his botanical and historical interests points to an application of ecological determinist models, which were to be particularly influential in the twentieth century, and which served to link climatic theories of the plantation to population-density interpretations of post-emancipation labour dynamics (Higman 1988). Rodway's first piece of nature writing was 'The Struggle for Life in the Forest', published in *Timehri* (the journal of the Royal Agricultural and Commercial Society) in 1891. This was followed by 'The Struggle for Life in the Swamp', and in 1894 by a book titled *In the Guiana Forest: Studies of Nature in Relation to the Struggle for Life* (Cruickshank 1920). Thus the social Darwinism apparent in Rodway's histories is not surprising.

Rodway seems not to have travelled much within the West Indies, and most of his writing had to do strictly with British Guiana. *The West Indies and the Spanish Main* (1896) did, however, range widely. He argued that indentured immigration was needed in the thinly peopled British colonies and contended that 'without healthy competition with other races, the negroes [of Jamaica] sunk back, until they became even more degraded than those of British Guiana and Trinidad.' In Barbados, however, 'the population was so dense that the freedman must either work or starve'. Using the ecological analogy, Rodway held that 'the compulsion of the whip gave way to the force of circumstances, and the struggle for existence which ensued has made the Barbadian negro the most industrious in the West Indies.' Rodway said nothing in particular about the British Leeward colonies but praised the post-emancipation labour laws of the Danish islands, which he believed ensured a quicker recovery. He added the curious comment, 'Possibly, however, the British freedman would not have borne coercion, for even the Danes resented it' (Rodway 1896:328-29). To demonstrate this last statement, Rodway devoted several pages to the Frederiksted riot of 1878, 'because it exemplifies the character of the negro and is a type of such disturbances in other colonies' (Rodway 1896:334).

Rodway's history belongs to a series called 'The Story of the Nations', published in London by T. Fisher Unwin and in New York by G. P. Putnam's Sons. Just three years later, in 1899, Amos Kidder Fiske produced *The West Indies*, which was incorporated into the same series (Fiske 1911). The books by Rodway and Fiske were similar in concept and coverage, but Fiske admitted no knowledge of Rodway's work and believed the recent penetration of the Caribbean sphere by the United States required 'a new point of view, in consequence of the sudden facing of the nation in a new direction' (Fiske 1911:iii). Fiske's book, an American rather than a local or European account of the area, heralded a new force in the historiography of the Caribbean (Higman 1976). Fiske had harsh words for European absentee planters and noticed how the different experiences of the various territories related to their patterns of land tenure and population densities (Fiske 1911:112-13). His racism was less explicit than Rodway's, and he had a less sanguine view of labour relations in St. Croix, saying that 'the insurrection of blacks in 1878 . . . was caused by the hard conditions under which they were bound to labour by yearly contracts after emancipation' (Fiske 1911:300). Fiske provided brief descriptions of Anguilla, St. Martin, St. Bartholomew, Barbuda, Saba, and St. Eustatius but did not include any interpretation of their post-emancipation experiences. St. Kitts, he said, 'has a great deal of history in proportion to its size', but this history ended in 1782 with Rodney's victory over DeGrasse (Fiske 1911:312-13).

HISTORIOGRAPHY: 1900–1950

Historical writing on the Caribbean was affected in the first half of the twentieth century by a growing professionalization and an increasing dominance by United States historians. This trend, however, was not strongly marked for studies of the post-emancipation Leewards. The Americans Pitman (1917) and Ragatz (1928) produced vital work on the period of slavery, but the most important studies of the post-emancipation British West Indies were by the Englishmen Mathieson (1926, 1932) and Burn (1937). The work of the American Westergaard (1917) on the Danish West Indies, was focused on the pre-emancipation period as was the seminal work of Eric Williams, *Capitalism and Slavery* (1944). These books were the products of academia, approved in one way or another by the newly emerged professional guilds, and most of them derived from the newly established apprentice test, the doctoral dissertation.[8] The publishers were all metropolitan. Local histories, locally published histories, and amateur efforts were few and far between. How much did this matter for interpretation of the post-emancipation period in the Leeward Islands?

Westergaard's study really stopped in 1754, but he was encouraged by contemporary interest to include a summary chapter that continued the story to 1917. In this chapter he found space for only a sentence saying that the decline of sugar plantations in the Lesser Antilles in the nineteenth century was due, in part, to 'the demoralization of the labor market by the abolition, first of the slave trade, and later of slavery itself' (Westergaard 1917:253).[9] He noted, too, that emancipation brought the plough and competition between people power and machine power. He ignored the events of 1878 in St. Croix, however, and offered no comparative interpretation of the Danish West Indian experience.

Mathieson employed a comparative methodology, though he limited his analysis to the British sugar-producing colonies. He returned to the tripartite classification based on land–labour ratios associated with Merivale. Burn similarly focused on the British sugar-plantation economies but restricted himself to the legislation underpinning emancipation and apprenticeship 'in order to see how far the result corresponded with the intention of the legislator' (Burn 1937:7).[10] Thus Burn had a theoretical question in mind, believing that such enquiry was the most useful service a historian could provide. Essentially, it was a question of imperial policy, and Burn stated explicitly that he was

> dealing primarily with a small number of the people of the West Indies, with the minority of whites and the tiny group of special magistrates. Beyond these was the great mass of the population, habitually docile, occasionally savage, lazy, improvident, pitifully cheerful, the prey of fears, superstitions, desires, suspicions, which I cannot know. (Burn 1937:9)[11]

Beyond these admitted conceptual limitations, Burn concentrated on the Jamaican case in his study. For the Leeward Islands, he concluded that all might reasonably have followed the example of Antigua in foregoing apprenticeship. He stated variously that the 'comparatively small amount of undeveloped land kept the majority of the negroes dependent upon the plantations', that 'the negroes were sufficiently advanced in civilization', and that 'the dominance of the white man and his economic system had become so precarious that it was not worth while to bolster it up longer'

(Burn 1937:373). The first two conditions applied in Antigua and St. Kitts, said Burn, and the third in Montserrat.

It may be argued that the professionalization of historical studies added relatively little to the understanding of the post-emancipation period in the Leeward Islands. What it did achieve was a degree of rigour in the use of primary documentary sources and systems of citation. The sources, however, tended to be official/state documents bearing the message of imperial policy, and this is how they were read. Significantly, the material was located almost exclusively in metropolitan archives, and the historians rarely travelled to the West Indies. The ex-slaves appeared only as a plantation labour force, and the fortunes of the planter continued to matter most in assessments of the post-emancipation experience (cf. Pares 1950:319, 332).

HISTORIOGRAPHY: 1950–94

Since 1950 historical writing about the post-emancipation Leewards has increased significantly, and, more important, new subjects and perspectives have been introduced, all accompanied by a rapidly developing sophistication of argument, interpretation, and debate. Professionalization facilitated the entry of West Indian historians and encouraged new approaches (history from below, social science history, women's history, mentalities, cliometrics, and psychohistory), and provided the means for their communication (journals, associations, conferences) (Higman 1985–86; Hamerow 1987). An international community of scholars was created and encouraged to labour in their own special areas. Historians were joined by anthropologists with a fresh perspective on the past. These academic developments occurred in the context of post-imperial political change, at a time when several of the Leeward territories moved from colonial to independent status. A thorough survey and assessment of the considerable historical literature produced in the period is not possible here. Only a few general points can be made to suggest the major lines of advance, the barriers to progress, and the way forward.

Continuity in the historiography has been most obvious in the persistence of the land–labour ratio model and Merivale's three-level classification of colonies, which are implicit in most of the literature. William Green expressed the ratio in density terms (slaves per square mile in 1834); Stanley Engerman calculated a land–labour ratio (square miles per thousand total population c.1840) (Green 1976:193; Engerman 1982:196; 1984:142). Engerman added to his table of ratios indexes of slave prices and changes in sugar production, thus bringing together the concepts and data of Spedding (1838), Martin (1839), and Merivale (1861). All of these ratios and indexes provide useful indicators, but further refinement is essential to any attempt at statistical analysis in a field undistinguished thus far by its application of quantitative methodology (Marshall 1991:1). A more substantial series of quantitative data relating to the experience of particular islands, regions, and plantation communities must be developed as a necessary first step. These data must in turn be subjected to more sophisticated statistical exploration, with special attention to their spatio-temporal relations.

Simple formulations of the land–labour ratio, as argued by Green (1976:192-94; 1984), have been criticized by Nigel Bolland (1981; 1984) as determinist and reductionist. Bolland has advanced a more complex analysis, which focuses on the interplay between policy and land tenure, consensus and conflict. This debate is closely tied to interpretations of the emergence of post-emancipation peasantries. In essence, did the ex-slaves flee the plantations immediately following emancipation wherever the opportunity existed or were they pushed off by planters hostile to the maintenance of an internal plantation community?

The argument that the ex-slaves were pushed off the plantations is a new feature in the historiography since 1950 and is the focus of continuing controversy. It is intimately connected with another central issue, the question of how far the post-emancipation peasantry can be seen as an outgrowth of patterns of land use and labour relations established during slavery. Again, this is an issue new to the historiography.[12] Reconnecting with Merivale's schema, Bonham Richardson (1980, 1983, 1984) has proposed a tripartite typology of post-emancipation adaptations based on geographic influences: 'the *highland adaptation* (Jamaica and the Windwards); the *lowland adaptation* (Guyana and parts of Trinidad and Jamaica); and the *migration adaptation* (the Leewards and, to a lesser extent, Barbados)' (1984:166).

With the exception of Richardson's contributions, the recent debates have not focused on the Leeward Islands. The islands do not feature, for example, in Douglas Hall's re-interpretation of the 'flight from the estates' (Hall 1978). So-called marginal territories, which were not traditional sugar-producing plantation economies, have come to feature in the discussion, but thus far most of the examples have been drawn from outside the Leewards. Bolland's use of the case of Belize to argue his interpretation of post-emancipation labour domination has, however, introduced the non-sugar colonies into the mainstream of the historiography.

Douglas Hall included a chapter on Barbuda in his 1971 book *Five of the Leewards*, which was concerned specifically with the post-emancipation period, though he omitted the (British) Virgin Islands from the same work. Isaac Dookhan helped to make good this gap by providing a fairly detailed account in his general history, where he argued that 'the Virgin Islands were probably unique among British West Indian colonies in that although they possessed little unfettered land and a relatively large labour force, they nevertheless realized the establishment of an independent peasantry' (Dookhan 1975:142; cf. Harrigan and Varlack 1975). Karen Fog Olwig's detailed study of St. John has helped broaden understanding by bringing in another marginal case (Olwig 1985).

Full, specialized studies of the post-emancipation experience remain to be written for Anguilla, St. Thomas, St. Croix (cf. Dookhan 1974, chapter 13), and the Dutch and French islands. Equally important, the ecological/economic history of all the islands needs to be supplemented by much more work on their social history (family and religion, for example) and their political history (at the community level) (Olwig 1987; 1990). In these ways the rich diversity of experience in the Leewards can contribute substantially to the developing historiography of post-emancipation societies.

WHOSE HISTORY?

This account of the post-emancipation historiography of the Leeward Islands reflects the interests and concerns of scholars or, perhaps, just one scholar. Whereas the earliest historical writing on the period comfortably includes accounts produced by amateurs outside the professional guild, the establishment and articulation of history as a profession have tended to deny the significance and interest of other public representations of the past. At the same time, an element of continuity connects the early theorizing of non-guild historians with the academic theorizing of more recent times. It seems, therefore, worthwhile to consider briefly what the post-emancipation period looks like to West Indians outside the academic network and to ask what a comparison of public and professional readings of the past may have to offer.

These questions open up an extensive and largely untouched field of investigation. Here it is possible only to throw out a few clues as to the lines it might follow and to provide a small sample of potential examples. The examples are all drawn from Antigua, which is particularly interesting in terms of its central place in the post-emancipation history of the Leeward Islands.

ORAL HISTORIES

Caribbean oral traditions and oral histories rarely become published texts. An important exception is the life history of an Antiguan sugar worker, Samuel Smith (1877–1982), transcribed from audiotaped interviews recorded by his grandsons towards the end of his life (Smith and Smith 1986). Samuel Smith recounted what his family knew about slave kin back into the eighteenth century and what happened at emancipation.

> You know, it's a strange thing, but I heard that when slavery was over the slaves at Old Road [Plantation] didn't even get drunk. I heard there was no great happiness among them. They didn't know what would happen, so them give assurances that they will not leave the plantation, that they will continue on working for the old owners. The old slave massas let them continue to work the ground and grow food for themselves.
>
> But though assurances was given, the young slaves wanted to know what the land was like. So most of the young ones didn't stay at Old Road after slavery end. Some drift from plantation to plantation; others settle down in one place (Smith and Smith 1986:28-29).

Smith gave much attention to family networks (possibly as a function of the context and immediate objectives of the interviews), and to the desire among ex-slaves to reunite kin sold during slavery: 'Them wipe foot from Old Road. They hate the old plantation where they used to live. They hate the people that sold them loved one' (ibid. 32). At the same time, Smith painted a picture of subservience.

> Bakkra always say, 'Manners maketh the man.' Well, let me tell you, not in Antigua, maybe somewhere else, I don't know. It maketh us slaves instead. We suffer privation after slavery because we was dotish [subservient], plenty dotish.
>
> From what I know, the life was worse, and that always make me wonder just how was it that the slaves survive (ibid. 38).

The worst thing that could happen to an ex-slave was to be driven off an estate, since 'the kind of gang-up that took place by the Bakkra against the nega-house people' meant that a 'nega-house man could not live on another estate if he offend even one planter' (ibid. 39). Freedom in post-emancipation Antigua was merely a new form of slavery. Such an interpretation, of course, is not particularly at odds with modern academic accounts.

ARTIFACTS

According to one observer, the proudest artifact of Antigua and of the Museum of Antigua and Barbuda is a cricket bat once used by Vivian Richards.[13] The museum which occupies the old court house in St. John's is, however, mostly devoted to displays concerned with the pre-history of Antigua and the period of slavery. Only two of the twenty-eight main bays deal with the immediate post-emancipation period. The first, entitled

Emancipation, mentions that Antigua experienced no apprenticeship and that this was to the advantage of the planters. Life was hard for the ex-slaves. The second bay, Antigua Settlement Patterns at Emancipation 1834, displays a map of the villages with short histories of each, surrounded by objects: a cane bill or knife, clay smoking pipes, ceramic shards (cf. Henry 1985:50-51). The emancipation display also mentions that Carnival is held every August in commemoration of abolition, and an extensive exhibition of masks follows.[14] The museum visitor is left with the task of fitting the elements into a larger interpretation.

POPULAR HISTORIES

Artifacts take on meaning only within their contexts, including those supplied by labels and tour guides. Thus the Museum of Antigua and Barbuda has produced a booklet 'to give background to its displays which interpret the story of the nation from its geological birth through political independence to the present day'. Its account of emancipation meshes with, and at the same time contests, that offered by Smith:

> There was no drinking or even dancing! Gratitude was the emotion of the day. Over the weekend a release from work was proclaimed. On the following Monday most labourers, as they were now called, turned up for work, but they wanted to know the 'bargain' first. The Antiguan slaves were the first to be emancipated in the British West Indies, for Antigua was the only island in the Leeward Islands to by-pass the four year apprenticeship period suggested by Britain. . .
>
> Though the transition from slavery to freedom was a revolution in the people's condition, the life of the black people on Antigua was not made any easier after emancipation. They were legally free, but also legally bound to their former owners, and consequently their labour was exploited (Nicholson 1991:12-13).

The booklet also describes the post-emancipation history of Barbuda, which builds a more textured picture than the museum's artifacts seem capable of supplying. It might be worthwhile to study the images carried away by readers and viewers and to compare them with other elements of popular culture and with the island's collective memory.

WORDS AND MEANINGS

These few examples of public and popular representations of the post-emancipation past of Antigua are intended to be suggestive rather than comprehensive in their scope. It must, of course, be recognized that oral and artifactual accounts do not emerge from a vacuum and that they can be affected directly and indirectly by knowledge of academic interpretations.

Thus the oral record and the material artifact do not come to the historian as unblemished pieces of evidence any more than the imperial texts do.

An analysis of the words used to label people and things might prove particularly revealing, by exposing the roots of cultural dominance and the essence of the historiographical process. As Michel-Rolph Trouillot (1989:714) has argued, 'Denominations used in scholarly or official discourse to delineate social reality are themselves part of this reality.' The history of the word 'peasant' in the post-emancipation Caribbean context, for example, illuminates clearly the relationship between official vocabulary of the early nineteenth century and continuing scholarly debate on the term, a debate that rarely takes cognizance of the words and meanings understood by the people so described (Trouillot 1989; Mintz 1990). Study of the labels used in museums, popular texts, oral accounts, and professional histories might well provide the foundation for revolutionary change in the historiography, a means of re-thinking the meaning of emancipation.

NOTES

1. Definitions vary, and there is no rational basis for distinguishing the Leeward from the Windward islands of the Lesser Antilles according to the trade winds. The term Leeward is essentially a British imperial one, rooted in administrative expediency and shifting over time. The Dutch refer to Saba and St. Eustatius, which lie in the middle of the group, as Windwards. See West and Augelli (1976:194-95).
2. For attempts to consider the ex-slaves' perceptions and expectations see Mintz (1992:245-56), Eltis (1982), and Marshall (1990). For the emphasis on work during slavery see Berlin and Morgan (1991).
3. The most useful recent accounts are Craton (1992) and Marshall (1991). See also Bolland (1981, 1984), Green (1984, 1986), and Trouillot (1984).
4. Some of Merivale's ideas can also be found in contemporary commentaries, and this makes it difficult to identify the originators of specific models. See, for example, [James Spedding] (1838), who produced a table for all the British colonies, relating changes in the output of sugar to annual average sugar production per slave (1827-33). Spedding concluded that decline in output was greatest where resources were most niggardly and that 'the various degrees of prosperity attained, and of ease in the attainment, may be, for the most part, accounted for by varieties of soil, climate, laws, or customs'. He also noted that 'the points in which the test fails with regard to the thickly inhabited Barbados are obvious enough' (513). Robert Montgomery Martin, particularly in his *Statistics of the Colonies of the British Empire* (1839) also made data compilations.
5. Merivale says 'possibly, also, St. Vincent's, Dominica, and one or two more' (1861:313). The inclusion of St. Vincent and Dominica is difficult to explain or justify and seems wrong. Marshall (1991:3) adds St. Kitts to Barbados and Antigua in this class, but Merivale does not make this attribution.
6. For the persistence of these themes in the historiography see especially Green (1976:404-5).
7. Part of Rothe's Antigua report (1846a) has been translated and published by N. A. T. Hall (1983). Neville Hall has translated all three of the reports, and the full report on Antigua will be published by the Social History Project, Department of History, University of the West Indies, Mona, Jamaica.
8. For discussions of the implications of the professionalization of history in this period see especially Hamerow (1987) and Novick (1988).

9. Not much more is found in the later amateur work of Larsen (1950:191-92, 221-22).
10. Burn was Barrister-at-Law of the Inner Temple and lecturer in Colonial and American History at the University of St. Andrews.
11. Burn's stereotype matches closely that described by Pitman and Ragatz with whom he discussed his work.
12. See the references in note 3 above.
13. The cricket bat was used by Vivian Richards in Antigua in 1986 when he hit the fastest ever Test century. It forms part of a larger display of cricket artifacts dating back to 1913. The text in Richards (1991:182) is by Mick Middles.
14. These observations are based on the author's visit to the Museum of Antigua and Barbuda, 6 January 1993. The author thanks UNESCO for its assistance in making the visit possible.

REFERENCES

Baird, Robert. 1850. *Impressions and Experiences of the West Indies and North America in 1849.* Philadelphia: Lea and Blanchard.

Berlin, Ira, and Philip D. Morgan (eds.). 1991. *The Slaves' Economy: Independent Production by Slaves in the Americas.* Special Issue, *Slavery & Abolition* 12(1).

Bolland, O. Nigel. 1981. 'Systems of Domination after Slavery: The Control of Land and Labour in the British West Indies after 1838'. *Comparative Studies in Society and History* 23:591-619.

______. 1984. Reply to William A. Green's 'The Perils of Comparative History'. *Comparative Studies in Society and History* 26:120-25.

Brathwaite, Edward. 1974. *Contradictory Omens: Cultural Diversity and Integration in the Caribbean.* Mona: Savacou Publications.

Burn, W. L. 1937. *Emancipation and Apprenticeship in the British West Indies.* London: Jonathan Cape.

Clarke, Colin G. 1971. 'Political Fragmentation in the Caribbean: The Case of Anguilla'. *Canadian Geographer* 15:13-29.

Craton, Michael. 1992. 'The Transition from Slavery to Free Wage Labour in the Caribbean, 1790–1890'. *Slavery & Abolition* 13:37-67.

Cruickshank, J. Graham. 1920. 'James Rodway, F.L.S.' *West India Committee Circular* 35:360-61.

Curtin, Philip D. 1977. 'Slavery and Empire'. *Annals of the New York Academy of Sciences* 292:3-11.

Davy, John. 1854. *The West Indies, before and since Slave Emancipation.* London: W. & F. G. Cash.

Domar, Evsey D. 1970. 'The Causes of Slavery or Serfdom: A Hypothesis'. *Journal of Economic History* 30:18-32.

Dookhan, Isaac. 1974. *A History of the Virgin Islands of the United States.* Epping, Essex: Caribbean Universities Press in association with Bowker, Publishing Company for the College of the Virgin Islands.

______. 1975. *A History of the British Virgin Islands 1672 to 1970.* Barbados: Caribbean Universities Press.

Eltis, David. 1982. 'Abolitionist Perceptions of Society after Slavery'. In *Slavery and British Society 1776-1846*, James Walvin (ed.). London: Macmillan.

Engerman, Stanley L. 1982. 'Economic Adjustments to Emancipation in the United States and British West Indies'. *Journal of Interdisciplinary History* 13:191-220.

______. 1984. 'Economic Change and Contract Labor in the British Caribbean: The End of Slavery and the Adjustment to Emancipation'. *Explorations in Economic History* 21:133-50.

Fiske, Amos Kidder. 1911. *The West Indies: A History of the Islands of the West Indian Archipelago, together with an Account of Their Physical Characteristics, Natural Resources, and Present Condition.* New York: G. P. Putnam's Sons. First published 1899.

Goveia, Elsa V. 1956. *A Study on the Historiography of the British West Indies to the End of the Nineteenth Century.* Mexico: Instituto Panamericano de Geografia e Historia.

______. 1965. *Slave Society in the British Leeward Islands at the End of the Eighteenth Century.*

New Haven: Yale University Press.
Green, William A. 1976. *British Slave Emancipation: The Sugar Colonies and the Great Experiment 1830-1865*. Oxford: Clarendon Press.
______. 1984. 'The Perils of Comparative History: Belize and the British Sugar Colonies after Slavery'. *Comparative Studies in Society and History* 26:112-19.
______. 1986. 'The Creolization of Caribbean History: The Emancipation Era and the Critique of Dialectical Analysis'. *Journal of Imperial and Commonwealth History* 14:149-69.
Hall, Douglas. 1971. *Five of the Leewards 1834-1870*. Barbados: Caribbean Universities Press.
______. 1978. 'The Flight from the Estates Reconsidered: The British West Indies, 1838-42'. *Journal of Caribbean History* 10/11:7-24.
Hall, Neville A.T. 1983. 'Louis Rothe's 1846 Report on Education in Post-Emancipation Antigua'. *Caribbean Journal of Education* 10:55-62.
______. 1992. *Slave Society in the Danish West Indies*. Mona: The University of the West Indies Press.
Hamerow, Theodore S. 1987. *Reflections on History and Historians*. Madison: University of Wisconsin Press.
Harrigan, Norwell, and Pearl Varlack. 1975. *The Virgin Islands Story*. Epping, Essex: Caribbean Universities Press/Bowker Publishing Co.
Henry, Paget. 1985. *Peripheral Capitalism and Underdevelopment in Antigua*. New Brunswick: Transaction Books.
Higman, B. W. 1976. 'American Influences on the Development of British West Indian Historiography'. Unpublished seminar paper, Department of History, University of the West Indies, Mona.
______. 1984. *Slave Populations of the British Caribbean 1807-1834*. Baltimore: The Johns Hopkins University Press.
______. 1985-86. 'Theory, Method and Technique in Caribbean Social History'. *Journal of Caribbean History* 20:1-29.
______. 1988. 'Ecological Determinism in Caribbean History'. Elsa Goveia Memorial Lecture, University of the West Indies, Cave Hill, Barbados. Unpublished paper.
Kincaid, Jamaica. 1988. *A Small Place*. Harmondsworth: Penguin Books.
Knox, John P. 1852. *A Historical Account of St. Thomas, W. I., with Its Rise and Progress in Commerce; Missions and Churches; Climate and Its Adaptation to Invalids; Geological Structure; Natural History, and Botany; and Incidental Notices of St. Croix and St. John's; Slave Insurrections in these Islands; Emancipation and Present Condition of Laboring Classes*. New York: Charles Scribner.
Larsen, Jens. 1950. *Virgin Islands Story*. Philadelphia: Fortress Press.
Lewis, Gordon K. 1972. *The Virgin Islands: A Caribbean Lilliput*. Evanston: Northwestern University Press.
Marshall, Woodville K. 1975. 'A Review of Historical Writing on the Commonwealth Caribbean since c.1940'. *Social and Economic Studies* 24:271-307.
______. 1990. '"We be wise to many more tings": Blacks' Hopes and Expectations of Emancipation'. In *The University of the West Indies 40th Anniversary Lectures*, F. R. Augier (ed.). Mona: The University of the West Indies.
______. 1991. *The Post-Slavery Labour Problem Revisited*. Mona: Department of History, The University of the West Indies.
Martin, Robert Montgomery. 1839. *Statistics of the Colonies of the British Empire*. London: William H. Allen.
Mathieson, William Law. 1926. *British Slavery and Its Abolition 1828-1838*. London: Longmans, Green and Co.
______. 1932. *British Slave Emancipation and Apprenticeship in the British West Indies*. London: Longmans, Green and Co.
Maula, Erkka (ed.). 1981. *The Archipelago as a Focus for Interdisciplinary Research*. Karachi: Hamdard Foundation Pakistan.
Merivale, Herman. 1861. *Lectures on Colonization and Colonies*. London: Longman, Green, Longman and Roberts. First published 1841.
Mintz, Sidney W. 1990. 'The Peasantry as a Sociohistorical Category: Examples from the

Caribbean Region'. In *Agrarian Society in History: Essays in Honour of Magnus Mörner*, Mats Lundahl and Thommy Svensson (ed.). London: Routledge.

______. 1992. 'Panglosses and Pollyannas; or Whose Reality Are We Talking About?' In *The Meaning of Freedom: Economics, Politics, and Culture after Slavery*, Frank McGlynn and Seymour Drescher (eds.). Pittsburgh: University of Pittsburgh Press.

Nicholson, Desmond V. 1991. *Antigua, Barbuda and Redonda: A Historical Sketch*. Antigua: The Museum of Antigua and Barbuda.

Nieboer, H. J. 1900. *Slavery as an Industrial System*. The Hague: M. Nijhoff.

Novick, Peter. 1988. *That Noble Dream: The "Objectivity Question" and the American Historical Profession*. Cambridge: Cambridge University Press.

Oliver, Vere Langford. 1894–99. *The History of the Island of Antigua, One of the Leeward Caribbees in the West Indies, from the First Settlement in 1635 to the Present*. London: Mitchell and Hughes.

Olwig, Karen Fog. 1985. *Cultural Adaptation and Resistance on St. John: Three Centuries of Afro-Caribbean Life*. Gainesville: University of Florida Press.

______. 1987. 'Village Culture and Identity on St. John, V.I.' In *Afro-Caribbean Villages in Historical Perspective*, Charles V. Carnegie (ed.). Kingston: African-Caribbean Institute of Jamaica Research Review No. 2.

______. 1990. 'The Struggle for Respectability: Methodism and Afro-Caribbean Culture on 19th Century Nevis'. *Nieuwe West-Indische Gids/ New West Indian Guide* 64:93-114.

Pares, Richard. 1950. *A West-India Fortune*. London: Longmans.

Patterson, Orlando. 1977. 'The Structural Origins of Slavery: A Critique of the Nieboer-Domar Hypothesis from a Comparative Perspective'. *Annals of the New York Academy of Sciences* 292:12-34.

Pitman, Frank Wesley. 1917. *The Development of the British West Indies 1700-1763*. New Haven: Yale University Press.

Ragatz, Lowell Joseph. 1928. *The Fall of the Planter Class in the British Caribbean 1763-1833*. New York: American Historical Association.

Rand, W. 1981. 'An Archipelago as an Abstract Time-Space System'. In Maula, q.v.

Richards, Vivian. 1991. *Hitting Across the Line: An Autobiography*. London: Headline Book Publishing.

Richardson, Bonham C. 1980. 'Freedom and Migration in the Leeward Caribbean, 1838-48'. *Journal of Historical Geography* 6:391-408.

______. 1983. *Caribbean Migrants: Environment and Human Survival on St. Kitts and Nevis*. Knoxville: The University of Tennessee Press.

______. 1984. 'Slavery to Freedom in the British Caribbean: Ecological Considerations'. *Caribbean Geography* 1:164-75.

Rodway, James. 1896. *The West Indies and the Spanish Main*. London: T. Fisher Unwin.

Rothe, Louis. 1846a. 'Beskrivelse over Antigua med saerlig Hensyn til Resultater af Emancipation'. Rigsarkivet, Copenhagen: Generaltoldkammeret.

______. 1846b. 'Vigtige Momenter'. (An Account of the Most Important Aspects of the History of British Emancipation and the Effects of this Measure on the British West Indian Colonies.) Rigsarkivet, Copenhagen: Generaltoldkammeret.

______. 1846c. 'Om Populationsforholdene i de Danske Vestindiske Coloner og Fornemlig paa St. Croix'. (The Populations of the Danish West Indies, with Particular Reference to St. Croix). Rigsarkivet, Copenhagen: Generaltoldkammeret.

Royle, Stephen A. 1992. 'The Small Island as Colony'. *Caribbean Geography* 3:261-69.

Smith, Keithlyn B., and Fernando C. Smith. 1986. *To Shoot Hard Labour: The Life and Times of Samuel Smith, an Antiguan Workingman 1877-1982*. Scarborough: Edan's Publishers.

[Spedding, James.] 1838. 'The Negro Apprenticeship System'. *Edinburgh Review* 66:477-522.

Trouillot, Michel-Rolph. 1984. 'Labour and Emancipation in Dominica: Contribution to a Debate'. *Caribbean Quarterly* 30:73-84.

______. 1989. 'Discourses of Rule and the Acknowledgement of the Peasantry in Dominica, W. I., 1838-1928'. *American Ethnologist* 16:704-18.

Waddell, D. A. G. 1966. 'The British West Indies'. In *The Historiography of the British Empire-Commonwealth: Trends, Interpretations and Resources*, Robin W. Winks (ed.). Durham, N. C.:

Duke University Press.
Ward, J. R. 1988. 'Emancipation and the Planters'. *Journal of Caribbean History* 22:116-37.
West, Robert C., and John P. Augelli. 1976. *Middle America: Its Lands and Peoples*. Englewood Cliffs, N. J.: Prentice-Hall.
Westergaard, Waldemar. 1917. *The Danish West Indies under Company Rule (1671–1754), with a Supplementary Chapter, 1755-1917*. New York: Macmillan.
Williams, Eric. 1944. *Capitalism and Slavery*. Chapel Hill: University of North Carolina Press. Reprinted 1964, London: Andre Deutsch.

Part II
Society and Culture

'They Couldn't Mash Ants': The Decline of the White and Non-White Elites in Antigua, 1834–1900

SUSAN LOWES

THE CINDERELLA OF THE WEST INDIES

The mid-1890s were years of gloom and loss throughout the British West Indies and of great despondency in Antigua, where the cane fields were reported to be in a pitiable state (Beachey 1957; Watts 1906). Sugar production had dropped precipitously owing to an exceptionally long drought (beginning in 1892 and lasting through 1894), which overlapped with a sudden infestation of cane disease (1894–97). Only 7,219 tons of sugar were shipped from Antigua in 1895, compared to 16,120 tons in 1890, and any chance of recovery after the good crops in 1896 and 1898 was destroyed by bad crops in each of the next three years.

Such poor production would have been problem enough, but to make matters worse, sugar prices declined to a new low of £7/7 a ton in 1895, in part the result of increased exports of bounty-supported European beet sugar to England. Worse still, Antiguan sugar producers, who had turned to the United States market when they found it difficult to compete in the British (by 1894, 76 per cent of Antigua's export earnings came from the United States), suddenly lost that market when the United States moved to protect domestic and Cuban production. The value of exports in 1895 was half that in 1892. The value of imports declined as well, but not enough. The government suffered a drastic drop in revenues and a huge deficit; such deficits continued, although on a lesser scale, for the next ten years. The financial situation was made more dire by the British decision in 1899 to abandon Nelson's Dockyard, a naval station since 1743. Overnight the island was stripped of another source of income (Lewis 1968:119).

The mass of the population of about 35,000 suffered severely from the rapid decline in its living standards. The drought affected food crops as well as sugar, while inflation abroad, due in part to the Boer War, led to an increase in the price of imported foodstuffs. Estates laid off workers and lowered wages. A census of the estates for the period from July to September 1897 indicated that only 2,995 people out of a former total of almost 5,000 remained employed, 1,971, or 40 per cent, having been dismissed in the preceding six months.[1] By 1898 deaths from starvation were reported to be on the increase, as was the number of paupers and beggars. Men began to migrate in large numbers, leaving women and children dependent on their own much lower earnings (women earned half what men received on the estates). Between 1897 and 1898, the number on poor relief increased threefold,[2] and an Anglican clergyman was provoked to write the governor (who passed the letter on to the Colonial Office), that the situation had become so bad that the workers were willing to risk the hazards of gaol where they knew they would be fed.[3] Antigua was truly on its way to becoming, as it was described some years later, the 'Cinderella of the West Indies'.[4]

I open with this grim description of the economic situation in the 1890s not only to emphasize the depth of the crisis – certainly the deepest since emancipation and probably deeper even than the Great Depression of the 1930s – but also in order to highlight that this was a watershed decade in Antigua's history. The very severity of the economic problems made this a critical moment, when a series of forces, germinating since emancipation, came together to transform the island's economic, political, and social landscape. The entire population was affected by this transformation, but I shall focus here on the white and non-white elites – the white planter class and the non-white middle class – as each struggled to achieve the promises of emancipation in the context of forces that originated far beyond the confines of Antigua itself.[5]

BROWN SUGAR

Antigua's sorry economic situation in the 1890s had been some time in coming, and for most of the nineteenth century the Antiguan planters had believed they would be able to survive – as they had throughout the eighteenth century – the multiple problems of growing sugar in a small colony with a dry climate poorly suited to that crop. In the 1760s, at the height of the slave-based sugar regime, Antigua's 32,000 slaves, 2,500 whites, and 1,200 free coloured had produced enough sugar to make Antigua the fourth largest producer in the West Indies (after Jamaica, Barbados, and St. Kitts). Production declined thereafter, but even emancipation, whose results were much feared, did not cause the expected disruption, and production continued high through the 1850s, despite the natural disasters that Antiguan producers had learned to expect: an earthquake in 1843, a hurricane in 1848, a drought in 1849 (Candler 1965:54). One visitor reported that in 1849 Antigua was still the 'most populous, productive, and wealthy' of the Leeward Islands (Davy 1854:379).

The real crisis began in 1846, when the British parliament passed the Sugar Duties Act, which gradually removed the tariff protections that had been given to sugar coming into Britain from its colonies. The resulting influx of cheap foreign sugar spelled the beginning of the end for the West Indian sugar industry. As Sidney Mintz has written, 'It might not be too much to say that the fate of the British West Indies was sealed, once it became cheaper for the British masses to have their sugar from elsewhere, and more profitable for the British bourgeoisie to sell more sugar at lower prices' (Mintz 1985:185). If this was true for planters throughout the West Indies, it was particularly true for the less competitive among them, which included those in Antigua.

For many years the Antiguan planters were able to stave off total disaster, primarily because of their ability to control their labour force. In striking contrast to those islands with abundant uncultivated land far from the plantations, where former slaves could (and did) retreat in large numbers, Antigua (like Barbados and St. Kitts) had little land available for peasant cultivation or even for the creation of independent villages. This, coupled with such repressive measures as a severely restrictive Contract Act, harsh vagrancy laws, licensing laws that kept the former slaves out of urban trades, and regressive taxation policies, all reinforced by a virulent local and metropolitan literature that re-installed the image of the 'idle Negro', obliged the workforce to remain on the estates. There was thus no question of competition from a peasant crop – coffee or bananas, for instance – or even from peasant-based production of sugar. In fact, dependence on sugar was almost total: sugar crystals made up between 80 and 95 per cent of the total value of exports throughout the nineteenth century, and most of the remainder – rum and molasses – was sugar-related. In 1891 sugar production provided direct employment, in field and factory, for well over 50 per cent of the population over the age of 15: there were more than 12,000 agricultural workers out of a total population over 15 of 23,690. This total does not include those in ancillary artisan activities, technicians in the sugar factories, and dockworkers, none of whom would have been employed without the sugar industry,[6] or those who worked for the import-export merchants and were therefore involved in the distribution (packing, loading, shipping) of sugar.

The planters were also able to maintain profitability by shifting the bulk of the tax burden on to the labouring population: both taxes on individuals (donkey and hut taxes, for instance) and import taxes on consumer goods fell disproportionately on the poor. Import duties, which had been eliminated on most goods in 1848, were reinstated in 1850 (Hall 1971:157); by 1894, they provided 50 per cent of revenues. This, along with the lack of land and the almost non-existent transfer of government funds back to the poor (through education or social welfare programmes), meant that the labour force was squeezed and re-squeezed in order to give the Antiguan planters a small advantage over their competitors. The British Colonial

Office, supposedly the guardian of the welfare of the former slaves, was opposed in principle to most of these taxes but was loathe to protest too much, since the need to keep the colony financially solvent was the central consideration. The introduction of imported labour, which in other islands became crucial to the continued profitable production of sugar, was viewed with some reserve by the Antiguan planters, primarily because of their lack of capital. After much discussion, it was agreed to import a few Portuguese from Madeira and the Cape Verde Islands, and the first arrived in 1847 or 1848. The total was only 2,235. Virtually no East Indians or Chinese migrated to Antigua in these years.

In the first half of the nineteenth century the planters had been able to hold their own by keeping labour costs down and improving production as much as possible without making any major investment. Lack of capital investment meant, however, that they continued to produce unrefined muscovado, or brown sugar, when refineries in other islands were turning to the higher quality grey crystals. Then in 1862 the worst drought in fifty years drastically and precipitously reduced production: 1862, 12,920 tons; 1863, 10,124 tons; 1864, 2,613 tons; 1865, 7,906 tons. Prices were low at the time, and the combination created a severe crisis.

To make matters worse, at this point bounty-fed European beet sugar began to compete in the British market. Imports to Britain began in the 1860s and increased rapidly: 80,027 tons of beet sugar were imported in 1865, 305,000 tons in 1878, 559,000 tons in 1884, and 1,362,000 tons in 1900 (Dookhan 1975: 18). Not only does this point to an astonishing English sweet tooth, but it presented the most serious threat to West Indian cane sugar production since emancipation. The United States, which had become an important market, was also affected by beet-sugar competition and was unable to take up the slack. One further result was that the price of cane sugar continued to fall: to 13s per cwt in 1884 and on down through the 1890s.

Production declined steadily, if erratically, after 1862. Visitors for the first time saw signs of depression. Daniel Hart (1866:219) reported large tracts of abandoned land and noted a huge imbalance between exports (£79,533) and imports (£178,786), a fiscally dangerous situation that the sagging economy had little chance of rectifying. Many planters began to feel that the future looked grim and started to sell off their estates and head home to England, or became absentees, leaving their plantations in the hands of local attorneys. Antigua, which had had a large number of resident proprietors in the 1830s and 1840s (Burn 1937: 66), had by the 1890s become an island where absentees were the largest owners.[7]

The move to absentee ownership was aided by the passage of the West Indies Encumbered Estates Act in 1854. Antigua did not vote to come under the act until 1864, but once the act was in place sales were frequent: 73 estates were sold through the court between 1866 and 1892, more than in any island other than Jamaica.[8] Since several estates passed through the court twice, it was not actually 73 estates, but 73 transactions, but these nevertheless encompassed a total of 23,569 acres, or more than 37 per cent of the 63,147 acres in estate land at the time.

The gathering speed of the turnover can be measured through an examination of changes in estate ownership over time.[9] By 1878 only 7 estates still belonged to the families that had owned them in 1843, and all but one of these was an absentee, the plantations having been handed over to resident managers when the owners left the island. One merchant stated that all but eight estates changed hands between 1860 and 1897.[10] By 1901 it was reported that the oldest resident proprietor had only been on the island forty years.[11] This is in striking contrast with Barbados, where a resident planter class had been in place since emancipation.[12]

The result of all the turnover was a major change in the structure of land ownership and a large reduction in the number of whites: where there had been 156 owners with more than fifty acres in cane in 1843, there were only 80 in 1895. Compare this again with Barbados, where 440 of the 500 estates in existence at emancipation were still producing in 1890 (Augier *et al.* 1960:238). In 1891 the white population of Antigua was 1,830 (out of a total of 36,119), down from 2,556 in 1861, and the census counted only 224 planters, compared with 326 in 1861.

The colonial government, which was responsible for a wide range of activities, from administering the government and courts to medical care, the port, the police, the post office, roads and water, raised its revenue primarily from import duties. By 1894 import duties alone (not including port, harbour, and wharfage fees) provided 50 per cent of revenues; the next largest components came from the equally regressive court fees and stamp taxes. The planters had always refused to impose any form of direct taxation on sugar exports (this did not come until 1916), and even when prodded to enact a small tax on land in crop, they repeatedly petitioned that the tax be waived because of one unfortunate circumstance or another – hurricanes and poor crops being the most frequently cited mitigating circumstances.

The economic crisis of the 1890s precipitated a political crisis, to which I will return. But first it is necessary to understand the role played by the upper level of the non-white population – what I call the non-white middle class – and its relationship to the white elite.

THE CLASS CALLED COLOURED

In 1836 Governor Henry Light wrote a dispatch to the Colonial Office in which he discussed at some length the upper level (in wealth and status) of the newly freed population.[13] The highest group – what he called the 'first class' among the non-white population – was distinguishable both economically and socially by its well-established prosperity, education, and respectability. In this group Light included merchants, estate managers and overseers, clerks in public and private office, and shopkeepers. The same group was described by Joseph Sturge and Thomas Harvey, who visited in 1837, as being 'persons of intelligence, education, and true respectability'

TABLE 1
THE POPULATION OF ANTIGUA BEFORE EMANCIPATION

Year	White	Free Coloured	Slave
1707	2,892	18	12,892
1787	2,590	1,230	37,088
1805	3,000	1,300	36,000
1821	1,980	4,066	31,064

Source: The figures for 1707 come from Gaspar 1985a:162; for 1787 and 1805 from Davy 1854:386; for 1821 from Sewell 1861:154.

(Sturge and Harvey 1838:90). Mrs Lanaghan, in her book *Antigua and the Antiguans* (1844), wrote extensively about what she called the 'higher class of coloured persons'. Not one to lavish praise on the majority of the non-white population, she nevertheless waxed enthusiastic about this group:

> These are men who, if not educated in England, have received the best instruction the West Indies could afford, aided by thier own strenuous endeavours for information. Hospitable in the highest degree, with a hand ever open to grasp in friendship that of the strangers whom fate or the winds may lead to their pretty little island; living in an easy elegance of style . . . the doers of high and noble actions . . . of agreeable conversation and polished manners . . . (Lanaghan 1844:II, 170).

'Among them', she wrote, 'are some of the most respectable merchants and planters; and the whites themselves, with but few exceptions, follow no higher occupations' (ibid.:182).

The free-coloured population in Antigua developed gradually at first, but it increased dramatically in the decades before emancipation and by 1821 outnumbered the white population by two to one (Table 1).

Although the commonly held pyramidal view of West Indian social structure places the free coloured in the middle in terms of wealth as well as phenotypic skin colour, by the 1820s the free coloured in Antigua as elsewhere exhibited a wide range of wealth, colour, education, and social status. At the upper levels were those with white or wealthy free-coloured fathers who had been educated abroad and/or set up in business, established in a trade, or left with a substantial inheritance, mostly the land and merchant or artisanal establishments they already worked in.[14] There were a few wealthy free-coloured merchants and more somewhat less wealthy shopkeepers; others were writing clerks in private and public office, and in 1814 two free-coloured men, William Hill and Henry Loving, established the *Antigua Weekly Register* (Coleridge 1826:241), which became the principal paper for the next twenty-five years. A number of free coloured owned slaves who either worked directly for them, as clerks in shops, seamstresses, washers, ironers, or were hired out to others, as porters on the docks, for instance, or as skilled tradesmen.

Visitors to Antigua in the immediate pre-emancipation period all reported that the upper-level free coloured owned considerable property and were doing better than in most of the other islands – the key exception being Grenada (Coleridge 1826:203; Bayley 1833:311). Most free coloured were urban dwellers, since deficiency laws, which required that a certain number of whites be employed on each plantation, effectively reserved the jobs of estate manager and overseer to white men. By the early 1800s only a few free coloured owned property outside of town, and only one owned a large working estate, although after the repeal of the White Servants Act in 1833 increasing numbers of non-whites began to take the post of overseer, at a much reduced salary (Sturge and Harvey 1838:48). Legal restrictions on the amount of land the free coloured could own and a lack of access to credit and labour prevented all but a few from practising small-scale agriculture on their own account (Goveia 1965:225).[15] The wealthiest were merchants, and by emancipation most of the larger retail establishments – those selling dry goods, housewares, women's clothing, haberdashery, cosmetics, and so on – were owned by free-coloured families. The large and extremely profitable import-export houses, however, more closely tied to the plantation economy, remained in the hands of the white population.

For reasons that are unclear, the free coloured in Antigua had more political rights than in most other islands. They had the right to vote in Assembly and vestry elections (Goveia 1965:82, 85, 216; Bayley 1833:311), although in practice this was severely restricted by property qualifications.[16] By 1832 the free coloured made up two-thirds of the militia, although they could not hold a commissioned rank; none, however, had ever been elected to the Assembly.[17] Nor had they made many inroads into the upper levels of the civil establishment: an 1832 dispatch from the governor to the Colonial Office included a list of the official appointments held by 'gentlemen of colour': five of the seven held honourary military posts.

The free coloured were active in the social-welfare arena, particularly in the years immediately preceding emancipation – perhaps, indeed, in preparation for it. They established the first friendly society in 1828 in St. John's, and the next in 1832 in the countryside, and by 1854 these institutions had 12,588 members (Davy 1854:394). They also established beneficial societies and were active in charity fund-raising events. They were concerned about the education of former slaves, and in the late 1820s established the Society for Aiding the Education of Poor Children: its officers were from the upper level of the free-coloured community and included those most active in the struggle for free-coloured civil rights.[18] A free-coloured woman had established a Distressed Females' Friendly Society in 1817, which became the Female Refuge Society and then the Female Orphan Asylum, with establishments in English Harbour and St. John's (Horsford 1856).

Of all the non-whites in Antigua at emancipation, it was this stratum of the free-coloured population that was best situated to take advantage of the opportunities offered – once legal disabilities had been removed – to become a non-white middle class, and according to those who visited at the time, this was their expectation.[19] Although the white population remained firmly in control of sugar production, many of the free coloured were well placed to take over the merchant sector (and thus the towns), and from there move into the political arena.

In the relatively prosperous years immediately after emancipation this did indeed begin to happen. Governor Evan McGregor was sympathetic to non-white demands for government posts, and even before emancipation had made two of his key free-coloured supporters justices of the peace; by 1837 there were three, and by 1844, six. In 1843 a former free coloured was inspector of prisons, and others were police magistrates and visiting justices at the gaol. Former free coloured served on the honourary city boards and commissions (health, water, market, but not roads, which remained a white planter affair).[20] John Candler, visiting in early 1850, reported that 'Many highly respectable men, who were also [i.e. once] slaves now fill the office of Legislators, or are otherwise employed in civil office, owing to their talents and qualifications for public business' (Candler 1965: 52).

The political arena was more difficult, for the planter-dominated Assembly was less welcoming than the governor, and at first those non-whites who were elected were immediately disqualified. The Assembly had only one non-white member in 1844. By 1848–49, however, it had three (Davy 1854), and in 1851 six (out of twenty-seven).[21] McGregor's supporters John Athill and Tyrrell Shervington held a number of titular posts, including Puisne Baron of the Exchequer. Tyrrell's brother Joseph was appointed Deputy Treasurer in 1840, a post he still held in 1851, by which time his son John was a senior clerk in the Treasury Department. Henry Loving, as Superintendent of Police, played a large role in drafting the first (and harshest) Contract Act and was subsequently appointed temporary private secretary to the governor; he went on to be acting Colonial Secretary in Montserrat, Stipendiary Magistrate in Barbados, and finally Colonial Secretary and Registrar in Montserrat; he died in 1850. Daniel Hill, another prominent former free coloured, was appointed private secretary to the governor in 1837 (Sturge and Harvey 1838:20; Horsford 1856:81).

In the twenty years after emancipation it also appeared that some of the social barriers of the slave era were beginning to fall. For the first time, according to his own account, the governor invited members of both militias to dine together, hoping to 'banish forever the objections to the seating of mixed and pure blood on similar occasions'.[22] By 1842 Mrs Lanaghan was noting that 'white and coloured gentlemen walk, and talk, and dine together – drink sangaree at one another's houses, sit in the same juror's box, and are invited, *sans distinction*, at "Government House"'; they also served together as pallbearers at funerals (Lanaghan 1844:II, 181, 189). St. John's Masonic Lodge, established in 1843, included at least one prominent former free coloured among its seven founders and took in a number of others in its first few years; several served as Masters.[23]

But as the economic situation deteriorated in the late 1840s, the white population made a concerted effort to preserve its hegemony, and barriers that had seemed to be falling began to be re-erected. Even those staunch allies of the government – Loving, Shervington, and Athill – found that they were being disdained by the governor. In 1848, when Loving was pleading with the Colonial Office for a new position, he was told stiffly that his request would be 'considered in common with those of other candidates for employment', a far cry from the lavish praise he had received only ten years earlier. John Athill and Tyrrell Shervington met a similar fate: despite repeated requests, neither could get a paid post, and when the latter asked somewhat desperately to be promoted to Provost Marshall 'or any other vacancy, in Antigua or any other colony', he was told that there was little hope; in the end the governor appointed him temporary police magistrate as a 'mark of favour'. At the same time, the local whites mounted a campaign to discredit McGregor for his efforts to reform the elections (Michael Brown, personal communication). By 1860, according to Sewell, the non-white middle class was being excluded from the polls, and the Legislative Council was once again composed entirely of planters (Sewell 1861:151).

The number of non-whites who acceded to high position was not only small but from a narrow circle: all the Assembly members, for instance, originated in the same upper level of formerly free-coloured families. In addition, the free-coloured institutions that continued into the post-emancipation era also remained in the hands of these same families, and the same people created new institutions as well. The St. John's branch of the Female Orphan Asylum, the St. John's City Friendly Society, the Antigua Library Society, the Philharmonic Society, and the Polytechnic Association all still existed in 1851, and, in so far as one can tell from the names of the officers, remained firmly in the hands of this elite. As if to emphasize the difference, several of these organizations had parallel white (and Anglican) institutions with a similar purpose: throughout the 1840s and 1850s there was an Antigua Asylum for Destitute Female Children and a Daily Meal Society, both led by white women and with the rector of the Cathedral as their head.

In two other areas non-whites apparently felt a need to create institutions of their own, again parallel to white institutions: the St. John's Savings Bank was a clear response to the Colonial Bank (established in 1836) and the Bank of Antigua (successor to the West India Bank); its officers in 1851 were Joseph Shervington, Treasurer, and James B. Thibou, Actuary.[24] Similarly, the former free coloured created their own education system, which remained almost entirely separate from those schools attended by the mass of the population or by the children of white planters and merchants.

Not only was the non-white middle class being excluded economically and politically, but it was increasingly being excluded socially as well. Prejudice had never disappeared: the first visitors after emancipation heard bitter complaints from non-whites about the extent of prejudice against them (i.e., Candler 1965:55). Even those, such as Thome and Kimball (1838), who reported a general diminution of prejudice, acknowledged that it continued behind the scenes; Mrs Lanaghan, who also felt that great advances had been made, noted that 'the assertion . . . that prejudice is entirely done away with, is incorrect. It still exists, and that, perhaps, very strongly; but policy forbids, in great measure, its outward show' (Lanaghan 1844:II, 180).

But public displays of such prejudice did diminish, as the descriptions of post-emancipation life cited earlier demonstrated. The difference is that those who wrote of a lessening of prejudice were describing gatherings that were limited in two ways: they were public – in the street, at Government House – and they were all-male, like the Masonic Lodge. Privately – at home – and socially, both in the sense of domestic social life and of those institutions that served the family, the barrier between whites and non-whites remained. Thus the social-service organizations, which were led by women, were confined to either whites or non-whites, while a more public organization like the Antigua Mutual Life Assurance Company, established in 1844, had both white and non-white (male) directors. When Candler 'took tea' at the home of Thomas Thibou in 1850, only non-whites were present. None of the visitors, including the indefatigably sociable Mrs Lanaghan, reported any mixing between whites and non-whites when women were present. Social clubs, which were family affairs, also remained separate, whereas the Masons, a male organization, did not.

Furthermore, the practice of white men having open liaisons with non-white women – and therefore two families – diminished. After emancipation, Mrs Lanaghan wrote, the 'unhallowed custom of concubinage' greatly decreased, such alliances having become generally reprobated (Lanaghan 1844:II, 181). The governor reported that 'no white man of respectability dare now openly violate the laws of morality . . .'[25] This change was possible in part because the sex ratio of white men to women had improved and may also have been linked to the retraction of the economy: maintaining two families is an expensive business (Lazarus-Black 1994:162). In addition, the number of marriageable partners increased as the white population became increasingly homogeneous and social differences among them disappeared. By mid-century their roles had become entirely proprietary, managerial, and professional; practically no white artisans remained.

But while these factors facilitated ending the practice of open concubinage, the need to protect the social hierarchy – and particularly the division between whites and all non-whites – provides the key to understanding the reinforcement of the social divide. Because of pressures from the Colonial Office, a comfortable translation of pre-emancipation legal distinctions into distinctions based on skin colour was not possible. The Colonial Office felt that economic factors should be dominant: as Under Secretary of State for the Colonies James Stephen wrote, 'now that a white skin is no longer a badge of aristocracy, there is no other principle than that of comparative wealth and poverty by which rank is assigned to any one man over his neighbours'.[26] But his point of view was unacceptable to the white population, who knew that as the economy worsened it would not be sufficient to distinguish whites from non-whites: some of the latter might have more wealth than many of the former. The white population had to find what Ann Stoler has called 'cultural criteria of privilege' (Stoler 1989:639). This they achieved by reshaping the content of the cultural component of high status, respectability.[27]

In Antigua neither skin colour nor wealth had ever been sufficient for entry into the elite: both criteria had to be accompanied by respectability. But after emancipation respectability began to have legitimacy, and therefore marriage, as a core component. A careful reading of Governor Light's 1836 dispatch shows this shift at work: he disdainfully described a man who wanted to be his aide-de-camp as the 'illegitimate offspring' of a white man and a non-white woman, although this distinction had not been important for his predecessor, McGregor, who had appointed a number of illegitimate non-whites to government posts. In the same year, Thome and

Kimball were told by the local planters that illegitimacy and occupation, not colour prejudice, were the reasons for the lack of greater socialization among whites and non-whites.

It is in this context that concubinage between white men and non-white women, readily accepted before emancipation, was reported to have declined precipitously. The number of illegitimate children did not necessarily decrease, but they were a less acknowledged part of respectable white family life. Thus by mid-century illegitimate children are seldom mentioned in their father's wills, in striking contrast to both the pre-emancipation and immediate post-emancipation periods. For there to be a racial divide, there had to be a sex divide.[28]

The Anglican Church, which had always disapproved of illegitimacy on moral grounds, played a major role in institutionalizing marriage as the norm and making illegitimacy a barrier to social advancement. As early as 1832, when the bishop embarked on discussions about establishing a grammar school – the first in Antigua – he argued that it should not be open to illegitimate children. Despite strenuous objections from his free-coloured parishioners, he got his way, establishing a rule that would last for more than one hundred years. It hardly seems coincidental that this happened in the same year that the free coloured gained full civil rights. After emancipation, a church wedding became the necessary counterpart to legitimacy, and all ranks of society aspired to it. Only the white upper class and the non-white middle class, however, were able to cement the connection between the two; for the mass of the population, neither was the norm.

Women were central to the enforcement of the revamped definition of respectability. Mrs Lanaghan, ever the astute observer, was quick to catch on to the new discourse: 'It is said, that the white ladies are the strongest upholders of prejudice; but that their refusal to mix with this [i.e., the upper level non-white] group of persons is not occasioned from any shade of colour, but on account of their general illegitimacy.' White women were, to use Stoler's phrase, the custodians of the community:

> Whether or not white women exacerbated racial tensions, they certainly did not create them, as is sometimes implied. On the other hand, we should not dismiss the fact that colonial women were committed to racial segregation for their own reasons and in their own right. . . . it is perhaps not surprising that these women championed a moral order that both restricted their husband's sexual activities and reconstituted the domestic domain as a site demanding their vigilance and control (Stoler 1992:333).

The post-emancipation histories of a number of upper-level free-coloured families show the result of these processes as the nineteenth century progressed.[29] Well situated to take advantage of the new circumstances, members of these families expanded their economic and political presence in the 1830s and early 1840s. But progress did not continue, and in each case the next generation was less prosperous and less prominent than its predecessor. By the 1860s, entire branches of each family had disappeared; those members who remained were from the less prominent branches, were less wealthy, and held far fewer appointed and elected positions. Thus if family members had stayed on the island and had children, and if those children in turn had stayed and had children, their numbers would have increased geometrically. Yet the opposite was the case. While the generation after emancipation was as large as expected, the next generation was dramatically smaller, and the one after was smaller still.

Part of the reason for the decline was obviously economic. The period of post-emancipation prosperity was short-lived, and, as we saw above, in the mid-1850s planter fortunes took a turn for the worse and the number of estates in cultivation declined precipitously. This contraction meant that the former free coloured had almost no chance of moving into planting, and the few non-whites who owned sugar estates had lost them by the 1850s; marginal estates such as the free coloured were able to acquire were undoubtedly the first to be hit by any difficulties, financial and otherwise. In addition, the former free coloured who were retail merchants, lacking capital and entirely dependent on the buying power of the population, were also severely affected. To make matters worse, this niche, which had been the centre of free-coloured economic life, was steadily eroded as a new set of white retail merchants, mainly Scotsmen, began to arrive in the 1850s and 1860s.

The former free coloured responded by either leaving themselves or sending their children away. The occupations of the children who remained were considerably less prestigious than those of their parents and grandparents. A few became civil servants but not of the rank of the first generation of Athills or Shervingtons. A few were merchants, though not so many, and without the same wealth, as their free-coloured forebearers, while many more were reduced to clerking for white merchants. None owned producing estates, and few even managed them. Non-whites no longer served on the honourary policing bodies, as magistrates or prison justices. By 1890 only two non-whites were on the Legislative Council, and only one was in the administrative branches of the Colonial Service; all three were from old free-coloured families.

The economic and political marginalization of the non-white middle class was made easier because it had failed to increase in number. The men in particular left the island, while the women stayed behind. Many of those who remained never married, did not have children, or both. Thus in one generation after another, the majority of the sisters in a family never married: these women are often mentioned in their fathers' wills, both because they remained in Antigua and because special care was taken to ensure them a home and an income, however meagre, to live on. Because respectability, marriage, and legitimacy were so inextricably linked, the women were unwilling to marry those who were not socially suitable. These families never recruited husbands from the class below, no matter how wealthy they might be, since this class – because of its own origins – was mostly illegitimate. They preferred to maintain their social distance, even if the price was the erosion of their numbers.

An indication of the extent to which the former free coloured failed to reproduce – or, more specifically, to produce a next generation – can be found in the rolls of the Antigua Grammar School. In the ten years from 1890 to 1900, only two of the six Antiguan non-whites admitted to the school were from these families; there were none among the twenty-nine admitted between 1900 and 1910.

By the time of the economic crisis of the 1890s, then, it was clear that the expectations of the 1830s had been dashed. The wealthier free coloured and their offspring, who had seemed so well placed to continue to accumulate wealth, property, political power, and social acceptance once the restraints of their status had been removed, had failed to achieve any of these. The white population – both those who remained and those who came as new arrivals – were themselves hard-pressed economically and beleaguered socially and had (with the help of various governors and the Colonial Office) embarked on a path of exclusion: the small opening for non-whites had gradually been plugged. The middle class now followed much the same path as the whites: they too sold off their properties, sent their children abroad, and left themselves. And in a situation where there were not enough 'suitable' men to marry, the women who stayed remained unmarried – whether through choice or social or familial pressure – rather than marry 'beneath' themselves. What was left at the end of the century was a number of elderly men and a host of elderly never-married women of modest means, without political or economic power, and socially isolated from both those below and those above.

THE POLITICKING OF SUGAR[30]

As the economic situation deteriorated in the 1890s, the Antiguan planters used every weapon in their arsenal – from petitions to pleas to threats – to get the British government to come to their aid. They joined with other West Indians in peppering the Colonial Office with petitions demanding that the bounties given by the French and German governments to producers of beet sugar be abolished or that countervailing duties be placed on bounty-supported imports to make prices more equal. They pleaded poverty and warned of the dire social consequences of their demise: if they were to abandon their estates, throwing large numbers of people out of work, disturbances might well follow. They begged for grants to tide them over what they maintained was only a temporarily bad period. They asked for a remission of the already small land tax and threatened that without such relief they would have to curtail, or even refrain from, cultivation; they argued that every shilling exacted in taxes would 'mean so much less to be circulated among the labouring classes in wages'.[31] On the other hand, they rejected Colonial Office proposals to increase import duties, warning that this would lead to lawlessness and pauperism, as well as to an increased burden on the British taxpayer, who would be forced to foot the bill for any relief.

By this point the Colonial Office was displaying a withering contempt for the Antiguan planter class and the Legislative Council it dominated.[32] The planters were seen as impoverished, inept and self-indulgent, perpetual complainers with little commercial sense and therefore unworthy of further investment. Their requests for loans were turned down because their only security was their estates, which the British considered worthless.[33] The Colonial Office heartily agreed with Archibald Spooner, manager of the factory at Belvedere and the representative of a group of overseas investors, when he told them that capitalists 'could never be advised to invest their money in this Island as long as such a body as constitutes the elective side of the Legislative Council have any voice in the administration of the Colony's affairs'.[34] To make matters worse, the decline in the white population made it difficult for the governor to find competent men for the nominated side of the Legislative Council, which was expected to back his initiatives. He reported that many office holders were so aged and yet so determined to hold on to their offices that he was having to devise ways to force them out, using whatever face-saving tactics – letting them keep the titles that accompanied their offices, for instance – that came to mind and did not cost money. The Colonial Office noted that with fewer white men and so many offices, any white man who was not a complete disgrace held office in Antigua.[35]

From the Colonial Office and governor's point of view, the solution was to abolish the elected side of the Council completely. In pressing his case for abolition, the governor argued publicly that the problem was a legislature that refused to act except in its own narrow interests, but he was equally worried about the demands of the non-white population for a larger voice in island affairs. In 1891 he wrote to the Colonial Office that he feared that in the near future an increasing number of non-whites would be elected, and that if this happened the island would be given over to the 'Blacks and coloured population' because whites would not stay to be governed by other races.[36] He believed the elected side should be abolished 'unless there is some better prospect than at present of increasing the white population in these Islands'.[37] The public argument – that the labouring classes had to be protected 'through the restraining influence of the Crown' – was almost entirely disingenuous: that the real issue was racial comes through in the confidential reports to the Colonial Office.[38]

The governor's concern was fully endorsed by the white members of the Legislative Council, who saw their numbers declining and were also alarmed at the prospect of the non-white elected element stirring up the rest of the population. While in 1891 only two non-whites sat on the Council, by 1897 there were four. These men were using their position to exert pressure on the government to extend the franchise and to increase the size of the elected element, two reforms that would have enhanced the leverage of the non-white population.[39] Public meetings were held around the island and were reported in great detail in the non-white newspapers. The spectre of rule by their former slaves certainly helped make the white planters more amenable to the governor's efforts.

Although such fears may have been the stick that pushed the Legislative Council members forward, the carrot was provided by the Colonial Office: unless the elected side of the Council was dismantled, the island would neither receive aid nor be able to attract much-needed outside investment. In March 1898 a resolution proposing a council of eight officials and eight unofficials was introduced by John Maginley, an ageing resident planter and loyal member of the Council for more than twenty years. The vote, which took place in secrecy to forestall any public protest, was carried by an eleven to eight majority.[40]

The non-whites who lost their seats included the last of the upper-level free-coloured families to take part in Antigua's political life. They, along with a few others from their class, had fought hard to retain elected members on the Legislative Council, but by then they had no economic base from which to mount a challenge to a united force of governor and planters, not least because they had failed during the preceding decades to form alliances with those below them economically and socially. By 1898 they were few in number, marginal to the economy, and unable to marshal support from other sectors of society. For the next forty years, the place of non-whites on the Council was strictly controlled; there was one 'slot' for a non-white unofficial (increased to two in 1925), which was usually given to a merchant. Not until an elected majority was introduced in 1937 did non-whites regain the role in political life that they had held throughout most of the nineteenth century.

In the late 1890s, then, the Colonial Office achieved its aim: in the context of a severe economic crisis, the white planters agreed to give up representative government because they feared the consequences of keeping it, and because they believed that this was the only way to save the sugar industry on which their livelihood depended. Faced with an increasingly restive non-white population in Antigua and an increasingly critical and meddlesome Colonial Office in the metropole, they placed their faith in a 'home' government that they hoped would be able to do for them what they were finding too difficult to do for themselves: preserve their economic and social power. The non-white middle class, isolated from the whites on the one side and the rest of the non-white population on the other, was unable to protect its own interests. The distance between the white and non-white elites made any alliance against the colonial authorities impossible, yet neither group alone proved able to 'mash ants', to use a graphic Antiguan phrase: neither was able to stand up for its interests even when its very existence was at stake.

Antigua therefore entered the twentieth century with a class structure severely weakened at the top. Yet the expected aid was not forthcoming: although it was decided, following the recommendations of the Norman Commission of 1897, to invest in Antiguan sugar production by building a central refinery to produce grey crystals, in the negotiations that followed the Antiguans were rebuffed in their attempts to maintain control over the process. Despite their vociferous objections and to their utter dismay, the grant to build the refinery was given to a British company with both capital and the ear of the Colonial Office. Within a few years, Henckell DuBuisson & Co. of London owned most of the producing estates, controlled the Legislative Council, and was setting the tone for social relations.

The 1890s were thus a crucial moment in Antigua's history, a decade in which the economic, political, and social landscape was transformed. Furthermore, the profound restructuring of the organization of production and of political and social life set the terms in which the issues of the twentieth century were framed.

ACKNOWLEDGEMENTS

The research on which this essay is based was conducted between 1980 and 1990 as part of a larger project on the formation of a middle class in Antigua from 1834 to 1940 (Lowes 1994). The initial research was funded by an International Doctoral Research Fellowship from the United States Social Science Research Council and a Dissertation Improvement Grant from the United States National Science Foundation. In addition to the sources specifically cited in the essay, I have made extensive use of the Colonial Office series CO 152/ . . . (Leeward Islands), which is at the Public Record Office at Kew, England, and particularly of the minutes that accompany almost every dispatch, as well as a fairly large but incomplete collection of newspapers which I uncovered in various places in Antigua. Equally important, however, was the information I got from the 'older heads' in Antigua. I would therefore like to thank the many Antiguans who graciously gave their time – whether it was hours and hours over months and months or only a few minutes, whether we talked at length about many things or only briefly to crosscheck one little piece of data. Without their help it would have been impossible to reconstruct this small piece of Antiguan history. They also told me many Antiguan expressions, including the disparaging phrase, 'He couldn't mash ants'. This expression, which is used in other islands as well, refers to a person who is too dainty to even step on something as unthreatening as a tiny ant.

NOTES

1. Public Record Office, Kew, Colonial Office (hereafter CO) 152/222/582, 29 Sept. 1897.
2. CO 152/244/151, 6 March 1899.
3. CO 152/233/312, 8 June 1898.
4. CO 152/351/155, 3 May 1916.
5. I have chosen the term *non-white* in order to avoid such imprecise and inaccurate terms as *brown* and *mulatto*, and such value-laden ones as *black* and *Afro-Caribbean*. I also did not want to use Afro-Caribbean because it obscures the European background of many members of this class. I have used *middle class* because this is what the group was, and is, called locally and because of its structural middle position.
6. Census of the Leeward Islands for 1891. Early nineteenth-century censuses are not readily accessible. The 1821 census appears in summary form in Lanaghan (1844:II, 284), and is also cited in Sewell (1861:154). The 1844 census, also in summary only, is in Great Britain, Sessional Papers, 1845 (426), XXXI:426-427. Unfortunately, no census was taken between 1821 and 1844. The 1861 and 1891 censuses can be found in various places, including on microfilm. A summary of the 1891 census is included in CO 152/263/291, 4 June 1901. After 1891, the next census was in 1911, followed by another in 1921.
7. Absentee ownership has been criticized repeatedly in the West Indies for its negative effects on production as well as on the manners and morals of local society, but in Antigua it was not considered a problem until well after emancipation. Burn noted that in 1838 Antigua was remarkable for the comparatively large number of resident proprietors: according to his figures, 63 per cent of the cultivated acreage (and 55 of 112 estates) were owned by absentees (Burn 1937: 66).
8. For lists see CO 318/282.
9. Tracing ownership of estates may be the ultimate exercise in frustration, in part because properties not only changed hands but also changed size, whether through expansion, amalgamation, or going out of production. Complete lists of estates are only available for scattered years: 1843 *Antigua Almanac and Register*; 1851 *Antigua Almanac; Almanac for 1872; Almanac for 1878.* Douglas Hall (1971) put together lists for 1829 and 1891; incomplete lists can be found for 1902 (CO 152/273), 1907 (CO 152/297/295), and 1924 (Watkins 1924).
10. Great Britain, Royal Commission, West India Sugar Commission [Norman Commission], 'Report . . .' , Appendix C, Pt.1 (1899).
11. CO 152/266, Confidential, 31 Dec. 1901.
12. Indeed, in contrast with Barbados and Nevis (Hall 1971: 167), where families arrived in the 1600s and stayed for generations, a key characteristic of the white population of Antigua since its first members arrived in 1632 was the rate at which they came and went. Richard Sheridan (1960–61) and Richard Dunn (1972) are the only scholars who have done any work on the composition of the early Antiguan plantocracy. While their studies, like that of Pares on Nevis (Pares 1950), focus on continuities, a re-analysis of their material demonstrates that the discontinuities are at least as striking. Dunn's data show that by the late 1600s most of the original 'paltry men' had left, and that only six of the top 29 families of 1678 had direct descendants in the plantocracy of the mid-1700s (Dunn 1972: 131). Even this established plantocracy moved on: by 1829, only thirteen of the 65 leading Antiguan families of the 1730-75 period remained as estate owners, and at least three of these were absentees.
13. CO 7/44, 18 Nov. 1836. Light was actually Lieutenant-Governor of Antigua and Dominica

but was referred to as Governor.

14. Little archival research has been done on the free coloured in Antigua. The lone exceptions are David Barry Gaspar's article on freedmen before 1760 (Gaspar 1985b, as well as his discussions in 1985a), and Michael Brown's unpublished paper, 'Henry Loving (1790?–1850): Freeman, Journalist, "Coloured" Civil Rights and Emancipation Campaigner, Police Chief and Civil Servant' (paper presented to the Postgraduate Seminar, Institute for Commonwealth Studies, University of London, 21 January 1965), from which some of the material on Loving comes. What follows is pieced together from Brown's paper, almanacs, visitors' accounts, and wills. In addition, Brown has kindly supplied me with some material from the Public Record Office in London. The discussion in this section is condensed from Lowes 1994.
15. See also CO 7/44, 18 Nov. 1836.
16. According to Mindie Lazarus-Black (1990:50), the right to vote was a matter of custom before 1822, when it became law.
17. The situation was quite different in St. Kitts, where the free coloured held three seats in the Assembly by 1833 (Cox 1984:108). For a comparison of Dominica, St. Kitts, Antigua, and Grenada see Lowes 1994, Chapter 4.
18. CO 7/34/58, 1 Nov. 1832, enclosing a copy of the Society's 1829 report.
19. Because the white population drew such a strict line between itself and all non-whites, the former free-coloured population, including those whose wealth and education were *greater* than that of many whites, by definition became the 'middle' class. Not all visitors saw it this way, however. Sturge and Harvey (1838:90) reported that the middle classes included whites as well as non-whites. But locally to whites, all non-whites *had* to be of a different class.
20. *Antigua Almanac and Register*, 1843.
21. *Antigua Almanac*, 1851. Six of the names are known to me as former free coloured; there may have been others. Horsford (1856) reported five in 1856.
22. CO 7/44, 18 Nov. 1836.
23. A brochure prepared for the Lodge's centenary celebrations in 1944 lists members for the years 1843 to 1854 (with date of joining and occupation), and Masters from 1834 to 1944, and gives a short history of the lodge (St. John's Lodge 1944). In addition, the Master at the time I was in Antigua kindly read me the names of new members, with date of joining, age, and occupation, from 1890 to 1950. He would not let me see the rollbook because it includes the final disposition of members – for instance, if they have been removed – which he felt was privileged information; unfortunately he did not have time to read the list from 1850 to 1890, although the names are there. I have found references to non-white lodge members who are not on the printed reconstruction of the roll (for instance, Horsford 1856), so it seems possible that the printed list missed some non-whites.
24. The Colonial Bank would not lend money on security of land or property and would only provide personal loans to well-known people (Lobdell 1972); this alone would have made a parallel bank with different standards necessary.
25. CO 7/44, 18 Nov. 1836.
26. CO 152/7/68/60, 7 Aug. 1841.
27. For more on the important issue of respectability see Lowes 1994, Olwig 1993, and Olwig's chapter on Nevis in this volume.
28. Before emancipation, marriage had been a means of exclusion for non-whites because it had been so difficult for them to marry. In terms of the free coloured, marriages between whites and non-whites and between whites and free coloured or slaves were discouraged, and the unbalanced sex ratio made marriage an unrealistic possibility for many free-coloured women (Lazarus-Black 1994:82-3). As Barbara Bush has written, 'No matter how respectable coloured women were, they could never transcend the fact that they were, according to the official norms of white society, concubines, never wives' (Bush 1981:258).
29. The material that follows comes from an analysis of a sample of 24 surnames, twelve chosen at random from a free-coloured petition and twelve held by middle-class families of the 1930s. Genealogical research was carried forward from the 1830s and backward from the 1930s, using a combination of informants and archival material: birth and death registers,

wills, jury and voter lists, school rolls, newspapers, and Colonial Office correspondence. For more on this, see Lowes 1994.

30. From Sidney Mintz's comment in *Sweetness and Power* that 'no single food commodity on the world market has been subjected to so much politicking as sugar' (Mintz 1985:185).
31. CO 152/230/199, 30 March 1898.
32. Antigua was a quasi-Crown Colony with a Legislative Council made up of twelve elected and twelve nominated members. The crisis that led to the imposition of Crown Colony government in Jamaica in 1865 had both fuelled Colonial Office doubts about the ability of other islands to govern themselves and given it the leverage to pursue the institution of Crown Colony government elsewhere (Rogers 1970:228). In Antigua, the production crisis of the mid-1860s made the planter class amenable to Colonial Office proposals to reduce the elected role in the Assembly in return for financial relief (Hall 1971:175-77). In 1866 the fully elected Assembly voted to replace itself with a Legislative Council. In doing this, Antigua followed quickly in the footsteps of St. Kitts and Nevis, which had voted for the same arrangement earlier in the year; St. Vincent followed in 1867, Tobago in 1874, and Grenada in 1875. Similar status had been instituted in Dominica in 1863, in the smaller and more impoverished Virgin Islands in 1858, and in Montserrat, in stages, in 1861 and 1866. Howard Aston Rogers's unpublished doctoral dissertation provides a wealth of fascinating detail on this period (Rogers 1970). In some islands, the move to full Crown Colony status followed quickly, and by 1878 only the legislatures in Antigua, Dominica, British Guiana, and Barbados had any elected members.
33. See CO 152/221, June 1895.
34. CO 152/222/549, 14 Sept. 1897.
35. CO 152/207/356, Aug. 1896.
36. CO 152/181/Confidential, 14 Dec. 1891.
37. CO 152/181/Confidential, 3 Nov. 1891.
38. The issue of race was never discussed publicly but nevertheless runs like a rumbling underground stream throughout Colonial Office correspondence. Virtually any dispatch dealing with race was marked Confidential.
39. It is easy to see why the non-whites wanted the franchise extended: the number of voters had declined from 442 in 1872 (*Almanac for 1872*) to 349 in 1897 (CO 152/223/608, 12 October 1897). An average of thirteen voters elected each representative, although several members from the rural areas were elected by only two or three voters each. The qualifications for voting were high and entirely property-based. These had been steadfastly maintained after emancipation, so that the number of voters as a percentage of the population actually decreased.
40. CO 152/276/J. Maginley, 2 April 1902. A columnist in the Antigua *Sun* newspaper noted some years later that the public at large had been prevented from objecting because the vote had been 'sprung' on them, with only the council members and three others knowing about it (*Sun*, 27 June 1914). The negotiations in 1868 had also been carried out in secrecy until the newspapers got wind of them.

REFERENCES

Augier, F. R., *et al.* 1960. *The Making of the West Indies*. London: Longman.

Bayley, F. W. N. 1833. *Four Years' Residence in the West Indies during the Years, 1826, 1827, 1828, 1829 by the Son of a Military Officer*. 3rd ed. London: William Kidd.

Beachey, R. W. 1957. *The British West Indian Sugar Industry in the Late Nineteenth Century*. 3rd ed. Oxford: Basil Blackwell.

Burn, W. L. 1937. *Emancipation and Apprenticeship in the British West Indies*. London: Jonathan Cape.

Bush, Barbara. 1981. 'White "Ladies", Coloured "Favourites", and Black "Wenches": Some Considerations on Sex, Race, and Class Factors in Social Relations in White Creole Society in the British Caribbean'. *Slavery & Abolition* 2(3).

Candler, John. 1965. 'John Candler's Visit to Antigua', J. Boromé (ed.). *Caribbean Studies* 5(3).

Coleridge, Henry Nelson. 1826. *Six Months in the West Indies in 1825*. London.
Cox, Edward E. 1984. *Free Colored in the Slave Societies of St. Kitts and Grenada, 1763–1833*. Knoxville: The University of Tennessee Press.
Davy, John. 1854. *The West Indies, before and since Slave Emancipation*. London. Reprinted 1971, London: Frank Cass.
Dookhan, Isaac. 1975. *A Post-Emancipation History of the West Indies*. London: Collins.
Dunn, Richard S. 1972. *Sugar and Slaves: The Rise of the Planter Class in the English West Indies, 1624–1713*. New York: W. W. Norton.
Froude, James Anthony. 1897. *The English in the West Indies*. New York: Charles Scribner's Sons.
Gaspar, David Barry. 1985a. *Bondmen and Rebels: A Study of Master-Slave Relations in Antigua*. Baltimore: The Johns Hopkins University Press.
______. 1985b. 'A Mockery of Freedom: The Status of Freedmen in Antiguan Slave Society before 1760'. *Nieuwe West-Indische Gids/New West Indian Guide* 59(3-4).
Goveia, Elsa V. 1965. *Slave Society in the British Leeward Islands at the End of the Eighteenth Century*. New Haven: Yale University Press.
Green, William A. 1976. *British Slave Emancipation: The Sugar Colonies and the Great Experiment, 1830-1865*. Oxford: Clarendon Press.
Greenwood, R., and S. Hamber. 1980. *Emancipation to Emigration*. London: Macmillan.
Gurney, Joseph John. 1840. *A Winter in the West Indies Described in Familiar Letters to Henry Clay of Kentucky*. New York.
Hall, Douglas. 1971. *Five of the Leewards*. Aylesbury: Ginn and Company.
Hart, Daniel. 1866. *Trinidad and the Other West India Islands and Colonies*. Trinidad: The 'Chronicle' Publishing Office.
Horsford, The Rev. John. 1856. *A Voice from the West Indies*. London: Alexander Heylin.
Lanaghan, Mrs. 1844. *Antigua and the Antiguans: A Full Account of the Caribs to the Present Day* . . . London: Saunders and Ottley.
Lazarus-Black, Mindie. 1994. *Legitimate Acts and Illegal Encounters: Law and Society in Antigua and Barbuda*. Washington and London: Smithsonian Institution Press.
Lewis, Gordon K. 1968. *The Growth of the Modern West Indies*. New York: Monthly Review Press.
Lobdell, Richard. 1972. 'Patterns of Investment and Sources of Credit in the British West Indian Sugar Industry, 1838-96'. *Journal of Caribbean History* 4.
Lowes, Susan. 1994. 'The Peculiar Class: The Formation, Collapse, and Reformation of the Middle Class in Antigua, West Indies, 1834–1940'. Ph.D. diss., Columbia University.
Mintz, Sidney W. 1985. *Sweetness and Power: The Place of Sugar in Modern History*. New York: Viking Penguin.
Olwig, Karen Fog. 1993. *Global Culture, Island Identity: Continuity and Change in the Afro-Caribbean Community of Nevis*. Philadelphia: Harwood.
Pares, Richard. 1950. *A West India Fortune*. London: Longmans, Green. Reprinted 1968: Archon Books.
Rogers, Howard Aston. 1970. 'The Fall of the Old Representative System in the Leeward and Windward Islands, 1854–1877'. Ph.D. diss., University of Southern California.
St. John's Lodge of Antient [*sic*] Free and Accepted Masons 1944. *Centenary Commemoration Celebrations, June 1944*, Sydney T. Christian (ed.). Antigua, St. Johns Lodge.
Sewell, William G. 1861. *The Ordeal of Free Labor in the British West Indies*. New York: Harper & Brothers. Reprinted 1968, London: Frank Cass.
Sheridan, Richard. 1960–61. 'The Rise of a Colonial Gentry: A Case Study of Antigua, 1730-1775'. *Economic History Review* 12(1).
Stoler, Ann. 1989. 'Making Empire Respectable: The Politics of Race and Sexual Morality in 20th-Century Colonial Cultures'. *American Ethnologist* 16(4).
______. 1992. 'Rethinking Colonial Categories: European Communities and the Boundaries of Rule'. In *Colonialism and Culture*, Nicolas Dirks (ed.). Ann Arbor: The University of Michigan Press.
Sturge, Joseph, and Thomas Harvey. 1838. *The West Indies in 1837*. London. Reprinted 1968: London: Frank Cass.

Thome, Jas. A., and J. Horace Kimball. 1838. *Emancipation in the West Indies: A Six Months' Tour in Antigua, Barbados, and Jamaica in the Year 1837*. New York: The American Anti-Slavery Society.

Watkins, Frederick Henry. 1924. *Handbook of the Leeward Islands*. London: The West India Committee.

Watts, Francis. 1906. 'The Central Sugar Factory in Antigua'. *West Indian Bulletin* 6.

From Labour to Peasantry in Montserrat after the End of Slavery

RIVA BERLEANT-SCHILLER

'History is bunk to capitalists, not to peasants.'
Frank Kermode

The various transformations of the work force in the plantation economies of the Americas – from indentured servitude to chattel slavery, from slavery to wage labour, from slavery to peasantry – have engrossed researchers for twenty years and continue to be challenging. In the British Caribbean, emancipated slaves became wage labourers or peasants or both, though the transformations were not the same in every colony. Some colonies complained of labour shortage and others did not. The labour force in each colony included different proportions of day workers, job workers, and sharecroppers; some colonies contracted immigrant labour, whereas others did not; each had a different potential for free workers to acquire land and yeoman status. These distinctions were linked to population density, topography, pre-emancipation economies, the condition of the post-emancipation sugar economies, metropolitan and local policies, and other factors.[1] But so long as sugar production and the function of the Leewards in relation to the metropolis and the world economy did not change, the official role assigned to the rural working population could not change easily or quickly.

This population had other important, if unofficial, functions. Food production, marketing and distribution of food, fishing, and small-scale commodity farming are well known. Rural people both used and created tiny niches in the dominant sugar economy and devised a variety of economic roles. When the transition from labour to peasantry was at last recognized and officially sanctioned by the Colonial Office, which had long tried to thwart it, most of the peasant adaptations were already worked out.

The economic activities of small-scale rural producers quickened and constituted the transformation on the island of Montserrat. These producers – an unofficial and unrecognized peasantry – helped to integrate the Caribbean regionally through inter-island trade and to buttress the internal economy of Montserrat by a variety of small-scale productive and extractive activities. They contributed to the process by which social contrivances for making sugar were transmuted into more viable societies, however much they were, and still are, hobbled by their colonial plantation pasts. A half century passed, from 1834 to the mid-1880s, before metropolitan policies, accepting and indeed provoking the collapse of West Indian sugar production, began at last to promote a peasant and small farming economy in the Leewards (Beachey 1957: ch. 8; Great Britain, West India Royal Commissions, 1884, 1897).

Early in the period – from 1834 to about 1850 – the freed people of Montserrat endured unabated misery but managed to initiate a peasant adaptation that developed further from about 1851 to 1886. Squatting, livestock production, land acquisition, and food production for export were essential features in this transformation. By 1886 the Colonial Office recognized that a class of small-scale rural cultivators existed and that one mode of economic development and efficient land use might be to assist and encourage it.

This essay details the transformation of emancipated Montserratians from a plantation labour force to a peasantry growing food crops on small plots for subsistence and market. It is not meant to contribute to debates about the nature and definition of peasantries or to question our understanding that a proto-peasant adaptation had been evolving in the Caribbean since the seventeenth century.

Sugar and slavery had been great levellers of difference among the Caribbean islands. After emancipation local factors fostered island variations on a pan-Caribbean plantation economy and culture. In the Leewards, for example, Dominica had more mountainous and remote crown land available for squatting than did Montserrat or Antigua. Population densities ranged from under 10 per square mile in Barbuda to 345 in St. Kitts. St. Kitts and Antigua remained more firmly dedicated to sugar production than did Montserrat. Barbuda had always been distinctive and continues to be distinguished by its system of customary tenure, which grants all Barbudans equal rights to land for cultivation, grazing, foraging, and woodcutting. Antigua bypassed apprenticeship, whereas Montserrat claimed a full four years. In Montserrat attempts to diversify commodity production began early; in St. Kitts sugar continues to this day. Exploring the nineteenth-century history of these islands discloses their courses toward distinctiveness and their diverse ways of mitigating – without ever erasing – the consequences of a colonial slave and plantation society.

Research on the factors that differentiated islands and colonies – including the transformation of labour and the evolution of peasantry after emancipation – fits well with the burgeoning research on the Leeward Islands. The Leewards are important in themselves and for the contribution their study can make to regional synthesis. Recent historical studies of Antigua, Barbuda, Dominica, Montserrat, Nevis, and St. Kitts have enlivened discussions of the entire region (e.g. Gaspar 1985; Berleant-

Schiller 1978; 1989; Trouillot 1988; Olwig 1990; Richardson 1983). Montserrat's particular complex of factors influenced its course toward peasant emergence. A shaky sugar economy and the economic distress of planters affected the amount and tenure status of land available to labour for independent cultivation. Proprietors resisted selling small plots in times of hardship, and the alternatives they chose – estate abandonment and sharecropping, known locally as *métayer* – pushed rural producers into squatting, which became a fundamental condition of peasant development in Montserrat.

MONTSERRAT

Montserrat is mountainous and small – only 32 square miles in area. Three volcanic structures make up the backbone of the island. Deep volcanic soils and plentiful rain over most of the island in most years were good for sugar cultivation, but Montserrat like other sugar islands suffered from soil erosion and exhaustion. One feature of its physical geography affected the livelihoods and adaptations of rural people after slavery: the island is dissected by deep guts or ravines, often with streams, that parallel the downward slopes of hills.[2] Slave provision grounds had been located on the steep sides of the guts. After emancipation, when some sugar islands turned to new technology to boost production, Montserrat's dissected terrain thwarted mechanization in the cane fields and precluded central mills, because cane could not be transported across the guts. Another physical handicap was the absence of a harbour: supplies and exports had to be transported between ship and shore by small boats, and much of the island's commerce was carried out indirectly through St. Kitts.

Montserrat had always been a small, marginal place in the Caribbean sugar world and in the British colonial world. It was never a centre of Leeward Islands' government as were Antigua and St. Kitts, and its sugar production never reached the levels of those two islands. Although after slavery Montserrat had much less land available for small plot cultivation than Dominica and Barbuda, it had more than St. Kitts and Antigua. Still, in 1848 a report stated that Montserrat 'exhibits the working of the West India system in miniature'.[3] The island can, therefore, enhance our understanding of labour control, land use and distribution, the internal supports of staple economies, and the evolution of peasantries and plantation economies in the Leewards after slavery.

Descriptions of nineteenth-century Montserrat are few. Joseph Sturge and Thomas Harvey left a brief account of their visit to the island in 1837 (Sturge and Harvey 1838), as did John Davy in 1854 (Davy 1854). Douglas Hall's *Five of the Leewards* (1971) contains the most substantial account so far of Montserrat after slavery, but Hall dealt mainly with commercial development and wage labour. Stuart Philpott's work on Montserrat as a migration society includes a brief section on the nineteenth century (1972:19-27). Despite Hall's work, much remains to be discovered about apprenticeship and the development of rural adaptations in Montserrat. Howard A. Fergus's *History of a Caribbean Colony: Montserrat* (1994) will surely enlighten us further. Meanwhile, it is important to understand how the rural dwellers of Montserrat survived the bleakness of apprenticeship and its aftermath, and how from about 1851 to 1886 they began to acquire land to cultivate and new economic niches.

QUALITY OF LIFE FROM APPRENTICESHIP TO 1850

John Cullingford was the Methodist Missionary Society's minister in Montserrat in 1834. We are fortunate that his interests, and those of his immediate successors, ranged further than his duties required. A month before the day of formal emancipation he wrote, 'up to the present time the Island is in a perfect state of tranquillity. The labouring population are peaceable and with a few exceptions attend to their work. That there will be some commotion on the first of August and for some days after is what we must expect.'[4]

His prediction was close enough to the event, so perhaps we may put some faith in his other comments, remembering that they are filtered through his missionary role and meant for an audience of missionary officials in London. Some of his and his successors' comments give us clues about the daily lives and livelihoods of the people and reveal a little about their income, productive activities, land, health, and relationship to government during the apprenticeship period.

Cullingford had expected 'commotion' on emancipation day, but 1 August itself was peaceful.

> On Friday morning all were free. What was to be expected from persons starved, depraved, oppressed? . . . The streets of the town were literally lined for several hours with negroes going to and from the places of worship . . . Not a life has been taken, not a cane burned, not a habitation injured, nor have I heard of any act of violence . . . We have had a great deal of commotion. But I am bold to say without any fear of having it proved contrary, that the fault was the masters.[5]

'Commotion' occurred when apprentices observed that proprietors expected apprenticeship to be hardly different from slavery and refused to work until their rights were assured. No special magistrate arrived until Tuesday, 5 August, but his coming, however late, probably staved off insurrection and bloodshed.[6]

By 1 October, just two months later, the apprentices had gained 'little material advantage' in their new situation and 'the distress of the people was never greater'. Planters asserted control in ways more subtle than slavery. There was, to use an example that concerned Cullingford especially, no gain in educational opportunity. He opened a primary school at Tar River Estate, 'a very ignorant and wretched place', where apprentices were avid for education, but lack of money foiled his efforts there and elsewhere. 'The poor are too poor to give' and 'the rich have no charity'.[7]

A few months later, in March 1835, Cullingford's successor, James Walton, noted the 'abounding poverty of the people'. There was still no support for schools, since the legislature refused either to appropriate or to contribute £50. One member of the legislature, Dr Dyett (whose family had been free persons of colour since the earlier part of the century), succeeded in soliciting his friends for a one-time contribution to education without any likelihood of another.[8]

At various times before 1834, Methodist missionaries had run schools and Sunday schools on individual plantations. But conditions for education had worsened as planters, fearing weakened control over labour, favoured cane fields over classrooms as appropriate places for apprentice children. In 1837 there were no schools at all. Planters refused to give money and space, and the legislature again denied public funds. Whatever educational funds were available came from the Methodist Missionary Society, from the Church of England for its own schools, and from the Ladies' Society for Educating the Children of Negroes in the West Indies. The people themselves were too poor to pay.[9] This disregard for education on the part of individual planters and the legislature may be read as a persisting form of labour coercion and as resistance to establishing even a minimal kind of civil society not directly related to their own needs for sugar production. Antigua, which had rejected the option of apprenticeship, was far ahead in educating freed people. Finally, in 1838 the missionary Jonathan Cadman succeeded in raising enough money to build a school at Cavalla Hill village (which is still a Methodist stronghold), attended by fifty children. This became a government school at the end of 1839, but even after it had been mandated by British law Montserrat officialdom continued to block public education.[10]

Planter domination took other forms as well. At Christmas time in 1834, a season when slaves had always received food, drink, privileges, and a holiday, the planters gave nothing. Yet there were no disturbances, and the apprentices made their own festivities.[11] Planters repeatedly obstructed the autonomous movement of apprentices, even though labour supply was not a problem. In February of 1838, an apprenticed couple sent their son away from the estate to learn carpentry. The manager, who was also an assistant judge, retaliated when the son returned to visit his parents by having him arrested for trespass. One magistrate dismissed the case, but a second sent the boy to prison. A week later a woman was evicted from her home because she had left the estate without permission to attend chapel.[12] Another manager tore the roof from a cottage while children were inside and their parents away from home.[13]

Apprentice life was wretched in other ways. Nothing tempered the consequences of recurrent natural and health hazards, since apprentices did not receive even the minimal care that planters might formerly have given to slave property. In 1836 alone a visitation of yellow fever, a dysentery epidemic that killed hundreds, and a calamitous gale struck apprentices, whose destitution made them all the more vulnerable.[14] A disproportionate number of children died, especially in a yellow fever epidemic that swept off 600 people.

Managers continued to brutalize apprentices bound to the property and sell them illegally to Demerara (British Guiana). Rum seemed to comfort misery (Sturge and Harvey 1838:85-87), and proprietors were happy to pay wages in rum instead of money.[15] The special magistrate could not counter brutal and illegal conditions because his interests were in conflict: not only was he was paid from the island treasury, but he held the prosecuting office of police sergeant at the same time he held the defending office of special magistrate (Sturge and Harvey 1838:88). Only when apprenticeship ended in 1838, and local special magistrates gave way to genuinely disinterested stipendiary magistrates did freed people gain any hope of protection and justice.[16]

Had planters themselves been just, they would probably have had a willing and co-operative labour force. In 1837 potential labour was plentiful, but the wage was only 4½d. sterling a day.[17] Even when apprenticeship ended formally in 1838, there was plenty of labour.[18] By 1840 the agricultural wage had risen to 6d. per day, perhaps because of competition from independent jobbing gangs and an expanding task system, in which workers were paid by the job rather than by the day. Even though a task worker could earn as much as 2s. a day, a pound of coffee cost over a shilling, beef was 9d per pound, and milk over 2d. a quart. If we compare the beef and milk costs to the price of a goat, which was 4s.6d., we see one reason why livestock proliferated and squatting was uncontrollable.[19]

Free labour won one struggle for better conditions when planters capitulated to task work. Task work was actually beneficial to employers as well as to workers, since under this system labour was never in short supply. Workers preferred to stay on their familiar estates if they could work by task rather than by day, and roving task gangs disappeared. Most planters still feared losing labour, however, and balked at giving up the tenancy-at-will arrangements that exacted commitments to work in return for houses and provision grounds.[20]

The end of apprenticeship brought little change in the lives and livelihoods of people who were now fully free in a legal sense. The last day of apprenticeship, 1 August 1838, passed peacefully. Nearly all the newly freed people took the week off. Yet one instance of voluntary labour convinced the Methodist missionary, Jonathan Cadman, that there might be no problems between proprietors and workers, if people were but 'remunerated justly and treated kindly'. In this instance a number of workers had volunteered to work on 1 August when their employer, a drogher captain, feared the holiday would make him miss his ship from Antigua. Cadman further reported that people generally wished to remain on the estates where they had lived and which they considered as home.[21]

But by 1839 a worsening predicament forced many to emigrate. In 1840 only fourteen balls fired illegally at their schooner could stop 'a large number' of workers from defying local law and illegally escaping from Montserrat, even though the firing caused a near-revolt among those on shore.[22] Ten years later emigration began in earnest as wage workers became poorer than they had been as slaves (Davy 1854:420-21). Sunk in want and menaced by drought and smallpox, they lacked basic clothing and food.[23] Their inadequate wages of 4d. or 5d. a day were lower than they had been a decade earlier.[24]

Demographic statistics show the extent of emigration. In 1834 the population had been 7,540. By 1851 it had dropped to 7,053, even though natural increase was so high that half of all people in 1851 had been born after emancipation and were under age 16 – almost double the number in that age group twenty years earlier (Higman 1984:139). Annual births averaged well over 250.[25] Emigration had begun even before the end of apprenticeship, with Trinidad and Demerara as favourite destinations.[26] The sugar economies there were still expanding, their labour needs were acute, and wages were higher. Between 1844 and 1851, 3,741 people emigrated (Great Britain. Colonial Office 1852:130).

THE STRUGGLE FOR LAND

We might suppose that those who stayed were those who had managed to better their own condition, but in fact most freed apprentices were still bound to estates for their livelihoods. The mere presence of a rural population does not guarantee a rural wage labour force unless people cannot acquire land of their own or unless their freedom is qualified (Domar 1979). Montserrat planters refused to sell land to free workers and were notorious for their two principal ways of restricting the freedom of wage labour, tenancy-at-will and métayer. Tenancy-at-will coerced labour by making wage work a condition for the occupancy of houses and provision grounds on the estate. It was the most common land-and-labour arrangement after the end of slavery, but other systems of land occupancy began to gain – squatting, métayer, freehold, and leasehold. Métayer is as much a payment as a tenure system, enabling proprietors to pay in kind rather than in cash and never to risk more than half the value of their crop for labour costs (Shephard 1945:7). Squatting flourished as an effective strategy even when it was prohibited. Freeholds and leaseholds slowly grew in numbers as debt forced proprietors to sell small parcels.

Many factors supported Montserratian planters in their resistence to selling land to freed apprentices. One of the most significant was British colonial policy, which promoted limited access even where land was plentiful, as it was, for example, in Dominica and Demerara (Moore 1987). Glenelg, secretary of state for the colonies, explained to the West Indies governors in 1836 that if staple economies were to prosper, they would have to make 'it the immediate and apparent interest of the negro population to employ their labour in raising them'. This could be done by 'impeding' their acquisition of land and forcing them into estate labour for survival. Crown-land sales were to be carefully priced 'out of the reach of persons without capital' and always sold publicly to the highest bidder above a set minimum. The 'object is not to force the cultivation of the present staples, by depriving the negroes of every other resource for subsistence, but merely to condense and keep together the population in such a manner that it may always contain a due proportion of labourers.' Land was to be priced high enough to keep most people as landless labourers, but not too high to discourage the most industrious workers from saving out of their wages in the hope of purchase. Squatting was to be forestalled (Great Britain 1846:3-4).

These metropolitan policies that blocked access to land accorded with the desires of the Leeward Islands legislatures. Other regional and global factors that allowed planters to keep land out of the hands of workers, in the British colonies as elsewhere in the Caribbean, included taxation, labour coercion short of chattel slavery, world sugar politics, innovations in sugar technology, and labour importation (Rivière 1972; Bolland 1981; Scarano 1989).

In Montserrat, therefore, there was not so much a 'flight from the estates' as a long struggle to acquire land (Sewell 1861; Farley 1964; Paget 1964; Adamson 1972; Rivière 1972; Mandle 1974; Hall 1978; Mintz 1979; Trouillot 1984; Moore 1987). The struggle included coerced, low-paid wage work, willing or unwilling participation in the systems of restrictive tenancy and share-cropping that planters imposed to keep labour on their estates, and overcoming planters' resistance to sales of small plots. Nevertheless, peasant production expanded. Half a century after formal emancipation visiting commissioners noted that 'ground provisions are largely cultivated'

(Great Britain 1884), and by the 1890s there were about 4,000 cultivated acres not devoted to sugar, many of them in small holdings (Great Britain 1897:52).

How did Montserratians begin to acquire the land they needed for a peasant livelihood? Squatting was the *sine qua non* of the successful transition to peasantry because it allowed people to expand their small-plot cultivation and stock keeping despite barriers to the purchase or lease of land. In 1838 stipendiary magistrates were directed to remove squatters from crown lands in the West Indies (Great Britain 1846:5-7). Montserrat had only two acres of crown land, which were occupied by coastal batteries (Great Britain 1828:3). But squatters occupied abandoned estates and plentiful unused mountainous land.

As early as 1835 we hear of 'large tracts of arable and wood lands now lying waste at the north and south divisions of this Island'.[27] Henry Hamilton, President of Montserrat, wanted them turned over to livestock and new commercial crops, such as tobacco, cotton, coffee, and corn, worked by apprentice labour. These 'waste' lands were privately owned, though abandoned, and were almost certainly squattage already. The president described the large and rising numbers of livestock – goats, sheep, pigs – that apprentices owned. Goats and sheep, if not pigs, require large tracts for grazing. Hamilton's scheme appears to have been designed to solve all the island's problems at once: new commercial crops would diversify the economy and relieve the 'embarrassment' of sugar proprietors, while new clearing and cultivation would curb illegal squatting and overcome the 'indolence' of apprentices who owned too many animals.[28] His proposal came to nothing, but his remarks on apprentice-owned livestock in 1835 are telling and show that squatting was an immediate response to formal emancipation in Montserrat.

In 1840, after apprenticeship had ended, two men were prosecuted for keeping provision grounds on land to which they had no right, but by 1846 squatting could not be checked. One significant reason was that Montserratian planters did not pay their workers for periods of six months to beyond two years and were therefore 'hardly in a position to resist encroachment on the part of . . . their creditors'. Who could fault labourers for 'irregularity' and preferring to tend their own gardens, 'the produce of which renders them independent of other employment for precarious wages'?[29]

In 1847 falling sugar prices forced large tracts of cane land out of cultivation. The Leeward Islands were not competitive in the world sugar market and were not protected in the British market (Great Britain 1847). The abandoned lands prompted even more squatting, an evil perceived by planters to shrink the supply of field hands.[30] In 1851 squatting was reported to 'prevail extensively'.[31] The Montserrat statistical report of 1860 claimed that 'squatting does not prevail on private properties but the system prevails to some extent on . . . unclaimed land designated as "Public Lands"'. Since Montserrat had no crown lands other than the two acres occupied by coastal batteries, it is difficult to know what the unclaimed lands might have been if not abandoned estates.

In any case the number of squatters and the area they occupied were certainly not dwindling. The real number was unknown but was estimated for official purposes at 140. The impossibility of stopping squatting is indicated by the *de facto* recognition granted in 1860, when squattage was first taxed.[32] In 1870 eight estates were described as ruined and abandoned but partly cultivated, possibly an oblique reference to squatting.[33] In 1886 the Council resolved to ask the governor of the colony to enumerate the many small squattages scattered around the island with 'a view to utilizing them for public benefit', presumably through taxation.[34]

Squatting was a vital adaptation from apprenticeship onward. Exports that first appeared in 1870 show its results: 107 bushels of arrowroot and 201 bushels of maize, which could have been grown on small plots in any kind of tenure, cattle and horses valued at £1000 sterling. Such livestock, which could only be grazed on open-range squattage, now accounted for 6 per cent of the total value of exports.[35]

Squatting was a reasonable response to the barriers against buying or leasing land. Alan Adamson describes a similar situation in British Guiana, where large areas of unused estate land attracted squatters directly after emancipation. Adamson (1972:35) argues that 'planters now missed a golden opportunity to maintain their labor force by selling land in the heart of their estates'. Montserratian planters missed the opportunity, too. In 1840 Governor Colebrooke conceded that it would be desirable to allow freed people to save money for the purchase of land and to establish villages with schools, but he thought a long time would pass before workers could 'rise above' the need to work for wages.[36] Yet a few freed slaves in Montserrat were settled on land of their own within a year and a half after the end of apprenticeship, and 'appear[ed] to be doing very well'.[37] One supported his household on two acres with the use of household labour and earned enough to send his son to town every day for education.[38] The number of freeholders grew consistently, as Table 1 shows.

In 1983 a 70-year-old woman in St. Patrick's village told me a land story that embodies the elements in the slow growth of freehold tenure. She was the oldest of five living generations of one family who owned about two acres of family land in the village, with additional cultivation land higher on Galways Soufrière. Her mother's mother's father, who had been living at St. George's Hill, heard of a coming estate sale and rode down on his donkey

TABLE 1
FREEHOLDERS IN MONTSERRAT, 1845–1928

Year	Freeholders
1845	150
1846	178
1851	270
1862	400
1928	1628*

Source: Compiled from CO 178/15, 16, 21, 32, Montserrat Bluebooks for 1845, 1846, 1851, 1862, and CO 152/408/4, Report on the Development of Montserrat, 1928.
*Five or fewer acres.

TABLE 2
SUGAR PRODUCTION IN MONTSERRAT, 1807–1925

Period	Average annual production (tons)	High	Low
1807–1835	1154.0	1928 (1810)	520 (1830)
1836–1865	336.5	870 (1842)	0 (1853)
1866–1895	1302.2	2540 (1892)	686 (1867)
1896–1925	307.5	1778 (1896)	0 (1920, 1924, 1925)

Source: Compiled from statistics given in Deerr 1949:II, 196.

several days ahead, sleeping outside, to wait for the chance to purchase the land. She thought that would have been around 1860, since her mother's mother had been born on the newly acquired land around 1863.

Elsewhere in the British Lesser Antilles – St. Vincent, Tobago, and Nevis, for example – proprietors in want of money sold small plots to labourers.[39] In Montserrat proprietors clung to their image of the island as a great sugar colony and sold plots only if they had no other choice (Hall 1971:149). In 1861 some had no choice. After the earthquake of 1843, they had received loans from Great Britain to restore their estates and, defaulting, now saw their estates put to auction by law 'and sold in separate lots'.[40] Perhaps that was when my informant's great-grandfather acquired his land.

Some of these small freeholders became not only peasant producers of subsistence and food crops for the local market but small farmers who grew commodities on a small scale. By 1870 owners of four- or five-acre cane pieces had joined together to build a small works for processing their sugar.[41]

Even though the number of freeholders grew 267 per cent from 1845 to 1862, they were still few in absolute numbers, as proprietors turned to métayer after the drop in sugar prices of 1846. The proprietors of twelve estates, lacking capital, let workers grow cane themselves for a share of a third or a half of the crop. The Leewards governor approved the system: what else could proprietors do when they lacked capital and could not pay wages? If they did not turn to sharecropping, labour would emigrate.[42] The planters could continue to grow sugar without money or credit and were assured of half the proceeds (Hall 1971:114). Perhaps the workers saw an advantage in sharecropping, as they did in Dominica, where proprietors furnished land and tools and sharecroppers controlled their own work organization (Trouillot 1988:84-87).

Métayer was a temporary expedient that proprietors adopted when earnings dwindled and they were short of cash or credit. Thus profitable Montserratian estates that were forcibly auctioned under the Incumbered Estates Act in 1870 had only small areas of métayer. River Head (Weeks Estate) and Upper Streatham each had eight acres 'for the labourers on the half system'; Windward (White's) and Hermitage (Irish's) had fifteen acres each. But by 1885 Upper Streatham, Windward, and Hermitage were failing, and all their cultivated lands were in métayer.[43] The system resurged in the 1890s when the sugar economy was dying.

A few planters recognized alternatives to sharecropping and leased land to peasant cultivators for a modedrate but safe return. Governor Colebrooke favoured this as early as 1839, but only one proprietor established leasehold lots for houses and grounds then. The annual rent for each of his thirteen two-acre leaseholds was £7/16 in current gold and silver money, payable monthly. The lease was renewable so long as both lessor and lessee agreed; pigs and goats were permitted, cattle and sheep banned.[44] The stipendiary magistrate who observed the success of the scheme thought that the higher return of job work over day labour enabled workers to lease land and that leaseholds led to better conditions.[45] Yet most planters clung immovably to tenancy-at-will and when short of cash turned to métayer.

Tenancy-at-will linked the occupation of houses and plots with wage work. It exploited the desire of many newly freed people to keep the houses, gardens, and social ties they relied on and the dearth of other opportunities. Indeed it curbed other opportunities while binding labour to the estate. Apprentices and their descendants may also have feared loss of both house and work if not partnered with proprietors, even though no laws regulated relations between proprietor and worker and tenants could be evicted without notice.[46]

In 1845 Edward Baynes, the uncommonly perceptive and unbiased President of Montserrat, pointed out the 'evil effects' of the system, which he described as a vestige of slavery and a brake on independence. He also pointed out the disadvantage to proprietors: the worker's first care was the provision ground, which returned nothing to the landlord. It is notable that the Colonial Office edited these opinions out of the published version of the

President's report.[47] In 1847 Baynes recommended that the legislature abolish tenancy-at-will and institute higher wages, village settlements, and money rent. He also proposed ridding the island of métayer, that 'rude expedient of agriculture in its infancy'. Predictably, neither the legislature nor the Colonial Office took up these ideas, whose time had clearly not yet come.[48]

CHANGES AFTER 1850

In 1846 Montserrat was a backward, intransigent colony where epidemics, natural disasters, and a depressed sugar market exacerbated an already wretched state.[49] By 1851 the generally desperate condition of the unofficial peasantry had begun to improve. Despite the difficulty of renting or leasing land, peasant production had swelled, as exports of arrowroot, corn, cattle, and horses show.[50] The number of freeholders grew significantly from 178 in 1846 to 270 in 1851 (Table 1), and squatting was widespread and gaining. These trends were promising, even though most small plot cultivators got access to land through tenancy-at-will.

There were other signs of improvement. Villages were propagating and 150 people lived in detached houses in villages built since emancipation. To the colonial eye these villages did not seem to be 'regularly formed', perhaps because they were linear. Some were independent of estates. An 1870 estate map shows two linear villages between estate boundaries on the windward side of the island.[51]

Education and the payment of wages also changed for the better. In 1851 ten day schools, two of which were Wesleyan and eight Church of England, had a total of 727 pupils; nine Sunday schools with 827 pupils provided basic as well as religious education.[52] Apparently the Montserratian plantocracy had begun to see that letting children go to school did not disable the labour force. Drunkenness waned since wages were no longer paid partly in rum.[53]

Other problems persisted, however. Emigration swelled from sixteen in the first half of 1851 to 122 in the latter half, mainly because wages were higher on neighbouring islands and were paid on time. As we saw earlier, the population had dropped since apprenticeship despite a high rate of natural increase. Also, the falling price of sugar led Baynes to urge the Colonial Office to end the sugar economy, although there is no hint that he favoured the promotion of peasant production in its place.[54]

In 1860, a poor sugar year, only 16 tons were exported (Deerr 1949:I,196). But the export list is fat with the variety and value of peasant activity: arrowroot, cattle, cedar logs, cocoa, maize, cotton, firewood, goats, horses, logwood, pigs, sweet potatoes, sheep, preserved tamarinds, eddoes, fish, shells, dried fruits, cassava, hides, groundnuts, ginger, beans, and yams. Muscovado amounted to only 15 per cent of the value of exports; other non-peasant commodities included tiny amounts of sulphur, lime juice, and trans-shipped coal and livestock. But the greatest proportion – 84 per cent – came from the kinds of crops and goods that peasants produce. Who actually produced these exports in 1860 cannot be ascertained, but if we hazard a conjecture about the past from observations of the present, the producers were in all likelihood peasants, whether they occupied freeholds, leaseholds, squattage, or tenancies-at-will.

The non-crop exports offer interesting clues to the range of peasant activities. In the Leewards I have observed rural people cutting cedar wood for boat-building, gathering wild (though not native) tamarinds, and gleaning the beaches for shells and other useable items. In 1860 at least, Montserrat was not a sugar island, but an island of small-scale producers exploiting a variety of resources. The official report stated, all the same, that the island had 'no regular crops . . . other than . . . sugar'.[55]

That does not mean the peasant exports went unremarked. In 1862 export duties newly imposed on such peasant products as sweet potatoes, yams, goats, sheep, and maize noticeably augmented the island treasury. Further, in 1862 there were already 400 freeholders (Table 1), and out of a total of 51 estates in Montserrat, twenty were abandoned and thirteen were in métayer. Yet the report reiterates, 'No regular crops . . . save sugar'.[56]

New imports signal waxing peasant prosperity. In 1839 and 1842, for example, such new items as books, glassware, hats, paint, ribbons, shoes, and sugarplums show up on the import list. The appearance of these amenities in 1839 may have a compound explanation: the altered status of former apprentices and the doubling of sugar income in 1838 over that of 1837. The Bluebook for 1839 explains the change in the nature and value of imports as a consequence of 'the altered condition of society'.[57] By 1840 the imports reflected both the increased earning that followed the proprietors' acceptance of job work and the incipient peasantry 'making themselves more comfortable'.[58] After 1840 the import lists are basic and repetitious, which accords with the general backsliding into misery we have already seen in the decade. It also accords with a shortage of circulating money on the island and shop sales that were low in proportion to the total of what workers earned.[59] Presumably working people were saving their wages while they occupied squattage or tenancies-at-will or both and hoped for the chance to buy land.

After about 1860, with more people engaged in peasant production and with increasing exports of food crops and livestock, a market for new goods and comforts developed again. The import list for 1860 registered greater amounts of ale, beer, ham, and porter; new items included bottled lemonade and soda water. Just under half the value of imports for the year (£9,900 out of £20,060) comprised linens, cottons, and other unspecified manufactured goods from Britain. In 1870 there were notable numbers of unspecified manufactured goods, glass tumblers, and new imports of cocoa, biscuits, and cherry cordial. The 1882 list is remarkable for its musical instruments, jewellery, books, 'fancy articles', earthenware, boots and shoes, perfumery, 'sweetened spirits', 'groceries and confectionery', haberdashery, hats, tea, and more than £6,000 worth of cotton, linen, and woollen goods. The value of the imports, higher in 1882 than at any time since 1840, might be partly attributable to a significantly larger population (10,083), but the nature of the imports surely points to money for many goods beyond subsistence, both from a revitalized sugar economy and expanded peasant production.[60]

Peasant production had another important effect: it quickened economic exchanges within the Caribbean. Of Montserrat's total exports of £17,043/7/0 sterling in 1860, only £2,622 went to Britain, and that was mostly muscovado. All other exports were traded within the Caribbean, principally with Antigua, Barbados, and St. Kitts, but also with Bermuda, Tortola, and foreign colonies.[61]

During the period from 1848 to 1865 inclusive, Montserrat's sugar production was at a low, averaging only 160 tons a year. In ten of these eighteen years it was under a hundred tons, and in seven of these ten under forty tons. Table 2 shows the general decline and resurgence of sugar in Montserrat from 1836 to 1895. The sugar economy revived just as the unofficial peasantry had begun to prosper, and in 1866 Montserrat entered a period of sugar production even greater than before emancipation.

Despite the resurgence of sugar production in the British Caribbean colonies, some questioned the official support for sugar. In 1873 William Walker, the former Lieutenant Governor of British Guiana, argued that planters throughout the British Caribbean had erred in trying to 'mix up' the separate matters of rent and labour by insisting on tenancy-at-will and refusing to lease secure allotments. He urged the encouragement of smallholders who cultivated 'immense diversities of useful products available . . . with comparatively little labour or capital': cassava, bananas, arrowroot, tous-les-mois, maize, tobacco, cocoa, coffee, coconuts, and useful plants for fibres and dyes (Walker 1873:9-11). He argued that sugar alone could not fund the future, even though it could not be immediately withdrawn (Walker 1873:19). Only later, in the 1890s, did this view come to predominate in the Colonial Office.

In Montserrat, meanwhile, peasant cultivation and small farming continued to wax. By 1884 the number of small-scale commodity farmers had grown so much that planters complained of the 'harm' they did through what was perceived as poor cultivation. Their goats also were a nuisance to proprietors. On the other hand, smallholders complained of unremitting control and harassment exerted by planters. The taxes on a two-acre freehold were so high that one owner had to sharecrop additional land to pay them and was forced to agree to sell his sugar to the proprietor, though better prices were offered elsewhere. Other smallholders were forced to sell parts of their plots on account of the taxes. Proprietors refused to allow tenants and sharecroppers to take firewood (Great Britain 1884, III:123-25). Despite these hindrances peasant plots yielded enough vegetables for local needs, and ground provisions were 'largely cultivated' throughout the island (Great Britain 1884, IV:10).

CONCLUSION

A large literature has grown up around the question of whether peasantries in the Caribbean today developed on a foundation established during slavery, arose after 1834, or even exist at all (e.g., Marshall 1968; Handler 1971; Mintz 1974, 1979, 1983, 1990; Fraser 1981; Olwig 1985:ch.4; Berleant-Schiller and Pulsipher 1986). This exploration of the development of a peasantry in Montserrat has not emphasized the pre-emancipation origin of the peasant adaptation, even though the adaptation was well begun in the seventeenth century and shows both continuities and innovations (Berleant-Schiller 1989). At the same time it is also true, as Woodville Marshall (1968) has argued, that the nineteenth-century peasantry was a new development. Innovations then included a range of tenure forms, new relationships to metropolitan policies, the possibility of resistance to plantation hegemony through squatting, commodity small-farming, and intra-regional trade.

But systems of land and labour in Montserrat, and in the Caribbean, have always been tied to a global economy. Outward migration responds to global demands for labour and relieves the pressure of population growth on the peasant economy at home. In Montserrat migration has been sizeable and significant since emancipation (Philpott 1972). Ironically, free Montserratians continue to supply labour to the industrialized world just as their enslaved ancestors did to the industrial labour regime of the sugar plantation. In this situation Montserrat is of course not unique.

Within Montserrat the development of a peasant economy had non-agricultural consequences. It fostered social and economic amenities in a society that, however oppressively colonial and hierarchical it remained, began to include some non-material goods for ordinary people, such as village communities; greater access to education and to health, communication, and transport services; an adequate marketplace building and a savings bank. All these improvements emerged during the 1880s, some after forty years of talk. They were not simply given nor were they simply earned; the emergent peasantry itself was the stuff of a society much fuller than the plantation economy had allowed.

The vitality of the peasant adaptation that had grown between 1834 and the final collapse of sugar after 1895 compelled official recognition of the value of autonomous peasant endeavour. This recognition included land-settlement schemes, debates on tenure, agricultural extension services and experiment stations, and research on crop storage, transport, and marketing. It did not sink the perception of rural people as labour but added to it an appreciation of their peasant character. Even though Montserrat and the other Leewards have never been able to provide livelihoods for all their rural people, the gradual expansion of peasant cultivation improved the quality of life from the misery of apprenticeship and eventually commanded the official recognition so long withheld.

ACKNOWLEDGEMENTS

I thank the University of Connecticut Research Foundation for funding my research in London in 1992 and Nancy Smith Naro for her helpful suggestions.

NOTES

1. For a summary of the issues and an annotated bibliography see Ward 1985. For a comparative analysis of transformation processes see Klein and Engerman 1985.
2. 'Gut' is the correct spelling of the generic geographical term (see *OED*, 'gut', definition 5). When it is part of a proper name in Montserrat, it is spelled 'Ghaut', as in Fort Ghaut or Spring Ghaut. That spelling was not common in maps and documents until after 1900.
3. Public Record Office, Kew, Colonial Office (hereafter CO) 7/89, Merivale's Response to Baynes's Address, 15 Dec. 1847.
4. Methodist Missionary Society (hereafter MMS), Box 135, File 1834, Cullingford's Diary, 1 July 1834. The Methodist Missionary Society papers are held at the School of Oriental and African Studies, University of London.
5. MMS, Box 135, File 1834, no. 2, Cullingford's letter to his parents, 14 Aug. 1834.
6. CO 177/22, Minutes of the Meeting of the Montserrat Council, 28 Nov. 1835.
7. MMS, Box 135, File 1834, no. 1, Cullingford to the Society, 1 Oct. 1834.
8. MMS, Box 136, File 1835, no. 83, Walton to the Society, 17 March 1835.
9. MMS, Box 208, File 1837, no. 33, Cadman to the Society, 12 Sept. 1837.
10. MMS, Box 208, File 1838, no. 68, Cadman to the Society, 22 Dec. 1838; Box 208, File 1839, no. 66, Railton to the Society, 1 Nov. 1839.
11. MMS, Box 135, File 1834, no. 67, Addition of 5 Jan. 1835 to Cullingford's letter to the Society, 13 Dec. 1834.
12. MMS, Box 208, File 1838, Cadman's Journal, 9 Feb. 1838.
13. CO 7/64, Warner to Colebrooke, 1 Dec. 1839, enclosing the Sixth Report of the Stipendiary Justice of the Island of Montserrat.
14. MMS, Box 138, File Jan.-May 1836, no. 17, Walton to Bunting, undated.
15. CO 7/100, Mackintosh to Grey, 14 Feb. 1852, enclosing Montserrat no. 13, Report of the Stipendiary Justice for the Half Year Ending Dec. 31, 1851.
16. W. L. Burn (1937:8-9) distinguished stipendiary magistrates from special magistrates. Special magistrates were island residents whom the Colonial Office appointed to temporary posts in the first year of apprenticeship. They were withdrawn at the end of apprenticeship because of their conflict of interest and replaced with stipendiary magistrates, who exercised 'a concurrent jurisdiction with local justices'.
17. CO 178/7, Montserrat Bluebook for 1837.

18. MMS, Box 208, File 1838, Cadman to the Society, 22 Dec. 1838.
19. CO 178/10, Montserrat Bluebook for 1840.
20. CO 7/64, Report from the Leeward Islands: Montserrat, Feb. 1840.
21. MMS Box 208, File 1838, no. 50, Cadman's Report on August 1, 1838, dated 16 Aug. 1838.
22. CO 7/64, MacPhail to Shiell, 18 Nov. 1840.
23. MMS, Box 210, File 1850, no. 9, Pearson to the Society, 26 Feb. 1850.
24. MMS, Box 208, File 1839, no. 10, Cadman to the General Secretaries, 5 Feb. 1839; Box 210, File 1849, no. 13, and File 1850, 26 Feb. 1850, Pearson to General Secretaries.
25. This information was compiled from CO 7/100, Report of the Stipendiary Magistrate for the Half Year Ending Dec. 31, 1851, enclosed in Mackintosh to Grey, 14 Feb. 1852, Montserrat no. 13; CO 178/4-21, Montserrat Bluebooks, 1834–1851. Sturge and Harvey 1838:87; Davy 1854:412; Martin n.d. [1851?]:150, 2nd pagination.
26. CO 178/6, Montserrat Bluebook for 1836, p. 118.
27. CO 7/41, MacGregor to Aberdeen, Feb.-Mar, 1835, enclosing President Hamilton's Report on Montserrat.
28. Ibid.
29. CO 7/86, Higginson to Grey, 17 April 1847, Higginson's Report on the Colonies within his Charge.
30. Ibid.; CO 7/86, Half Yearly Report of the Stipendiary Justice for 31 Dec. 1846, 22 April, 1847.
31. CO 7/100, Mackintosh to Grey, 14 Feb. 1852, enclosing the Report of the Stipendiary Justice for the Half Year Ending Dec. 31 1851, Montserrat no. 13.
32. CO 178/30, Montserrat Bluebook for 1860.
33. CO 178/40, Montserrat Bluebook for 1870.
34. Montserrat. Government House Archives, 82-106. Minutes of the Legislative Council, 1886. I thank Dr. Howard Fergus, resident tutor at the University of the West Indies Centre in Montserrat, for this reference.
35. CO 178/40, Montserrat Bluebook for 1870.
36. CO 7/64, Colebrooke to President of Montserrat, 20 March 1840.
37. CO 7/64, Leeward Islands Report, July 1840.
38. CO 7/64, Warner to Colebrooke, 1 March 1840, 9th Report of the of the Stipendiary Justice of Montserrat.
39. CO 441/3/15, Estates to Be Sold under the Incumbered Estates Act, no. 15, 1864; no. 23, 1865; no. 54, 1870; no. 99, 1874.
40. CO 177/29, Montserrat House of Assembly Memorial to Newcastle, 30 Aug. 1861.
41. CO 178/40, Montserrat Bluebook for 1870.
42. CO 178/16, Shiell's letter, enclosed with Montserrat Bluebook for 1846; CO 7/83, Cunningham to Gladstone, 11 March 1846.
43. CO 441/3/15, Estates to Be Sold under the Incumbered Estates Act, no. 54, 1870; no. 152, 1885.
44. CO 7/64, Hamilton to Colebrooke, 3 Aug. 1839.
45. CO 7/64, Warner to Colebrooke, 1 Dec. 1839, enclosing the Sixth Report of the Stipendiary Justice of the Island of Montserrat.
46. CO 7/64, Report from the Leeward Islands: Montserrat, Feb. 1840; CO 7/83, Cunningham to Gladstone, 11 March 1846, enclosing the Montserrat Bluebook for 1845, which contained Baynes's Report on Montserrat for 1845.
47. CO 7/83, Cunningham to Gladstone, 11 March 1846, enclosing the unpublished version of Baynes's Report on Montserrat for 1845.
48. CO 7/89, Baynes's Address to the Council and Assembly, 15 Dec. 1847.
49. CO 7/83, Cunningham to Gladstone, 11 March 1846, enclosing Baynes's Report on the State of the Island.
50. CO 178/21, Montserrat Bluebook for 1851.
51. CO 441/3/15, Estates to be Sold under the Incumbered Estates Act, no. 54, Estates Owned by Hugh Riley Semper to Be Sold in Five Separate Lots, 1870. The map shows 'Perche's Settlement' and 'West Hill Settlement', both of which have short coastlines on the windward side but extend uphill and inland in a linear formation. Linear villages exist in

Montserrat today.

52. CO 178/21, Montserrat Bluebook for 1851.
53. CO 7/100, Mackintosh to Grey, 14 Feb. 1852, enclosing the Report of the Stipendiary Justice for the Half Year Ending Dec. 31, 1851, Montserrat no. 13.
54. CO7/100, Baynes's Report to Grey, 24 Feb. 1852.
55. CO 178/30, Montserrat Bluebook for 1860.
56. CO 178/32, Montserrat Bluebook for 1862.
57. CO 178/9, Montserrat Bluebook for 1839, p. 33.
58. CO 7/64, Reports of Stipendiary Magistrates for Feb. 1840 and July 1840.
59. CO 7/64, Report of Stipendiary Magistrate for March 1840.
60. CO 178/30, 40, 52, Montserrat Bluebooks for 1860, 1870, 1882.
61. CO 178/32, Montserrat Bluebook for 1862.

REFERENCES

Adamson, A. H. 1972. *Sugar without Slaves*. New Haven: Yale University Press.

Beachey, R. W. 1957. *The British West Indian Sugar Industry in the Late 19th Century*. Oxford: Basil Blackwell.

Berleant-Schiller, Riva. 1978. 'The Failure of Agricultural Development in Post-Emancipation Barbuda'. *Boletín de Estudios Latinoamericanos y del Caribe* 25:21-36.

______. 1989. 'Free Labor and the Economy in Seventeenth-Century Montserrat'. *Willliam and Mary Quarterly* 46:539-64.

Berleant-Schiller, Riva, and Lydia M. Pulsipher. 1986. 'Subsistence Cultivation in the Caribbean'. *Nieuwe West-Indische Gids/New West Indian Guide* 60:1-40.

Bolland, O. Nigel. 1981. 'Systems of Domination after Slavery: The Control of Land and Labor in the British West Indies after 1838'. *Comparative Studies in Society and History* 23:591-619.

Burn, W. L. 1937. *Emancipation and Apprenticeship in the British West Indies*. London: Jonathan Cape.

Davy, John. 1854. *The West Indies before and since Slave Emancipation*. London. Reprinted 1971, London: Frank Cass.

Deerr, Noel. 1949. *The History of Sugar*. 2 vols. London: Chapman and Hall.

Domar, Evsey D. 1979. 'The Causes of Slavery and Serfdom, A Hypothesis'. *Journal of Economic History* 30:13-32.

Farley, Rawle. 1964. 'The Rise of Free Village Settlements in British Guiana'. *Caribbean Quarterly* 10:52-61.

Fergus, Howard A. (1994). *The History of a Caribbean Colony. Montserrat*, London: Macmillan.

Fraser, Peter. 1981. 'The Fictive Peasantry, Caribbean Rural Groups in the Nineteenth Century'. In *Contemporary Caribbean, A Sociological Reader*, Susan Craig (ed.), vol. 1, 319-347. Trinidad and Tobago: Susan Craig.

Gaspar, David Barry. 1985. *Bondmen and Rebels: A Study of Master-Slave Relations in Antigua*. Baltimore, The Johns Hopkins University Press.

Great Britain. 1828. 'Return of Crown Lands in the Islands of Antigua and Montserrat'. *Parliamentary Papers*, vol. 23, no. 146.

______. 1846. 'Regulations or Instructions under Which Crown Lands in the West India Colonies and British Guiana are Permitted to Be Put up for Sale'. *Parliamentary Papers*, vol. 30, no. 514.

______. 1847. 'Eighth Report of the House of Commons Committee on Sugar and Coffee Plantations'. In *Select Documents on British Colonial Policy, 1830–1860*, Kenneth Bell and W. P. Morrell (eds.), 437. Oxford: Clarendon Press, 1928.

______. Colonial Office. 1852. *Reports...of Her Majesty's Colonial Possessions, Transmitted with the Bluebooks for the Year 1851*. London: Her Majesty's Stationery Office.

______. West India Royal Commission 1884. *Report of the West India Royal Commission. Part III: The Leeward Islands; Part IV: Supplementary Remarks*. London: Eyre and Spottiswoode.

______. West India Royal Commission 1897. *Report of the West India Royal Commission*. London: Her Majesty's Stationery Office.

Hall, Douglas. 1971. *Five of the Leewards*. Barbados: Caribbean Universities Press.

______. 1978. 'The Flight from the Estates Reconsidered, The British West Indies, 1838-42'. *Journal of Caribbean History* 10-11:7-24.

Handler, Jerome. 1971. 'The History of Arrowroot and the Origin of Peasantries'. *Journal of Caribbean History* 2:43-67.

Higman, Barry W. 1984. *Slave Populations of the British Caribbean, 1807-1834*. Baltimore, The Johns Hopkins University Press.

Kermode, Frank. 1991. 'Vérités Bergères', review of John Berger's *Lilac and Flag*. *London Review of Books* 13 (5) (7 March):18.

Klein, Herbert S., and Stanley L. Engerman. 1985. 'The Transition from Slave to Free Labor'. In *Between Slavery and Free Labor*, Manuel Moreno Fraginals *et al.* (eds.), 255-69. Baltimore: The Johns Hopkins University Press.

Mandle, Jay R. 1974. *The Plantation Economy*. Philadelphia: Temple University Press.

Marshall, Woodville K. 1968. 'Notes on Peasant Development in the West Indies since 1838'. *Social and Economic Studies* 17:252-63.

Martin, Robert Montgomery. [1851?]. *The British Colonies; Their History, Extent, Condition, and Resources*. Vol. IV, *Africa and the West Indies*. London and New York: London Printing and Publishing Co.

Mintz, Sidney W. 1974. *Caribbean Transformations*. Chicago, Aldine.

______. 1979. 'Slavery and the Rise of Peasantries'. *Historical Reflections* 691:215-242.

______. 1983. 'Reflections on Caribbean Peasantries'. *Nieuwe West-Indische Gids/New West Indian Guide* 57:1-15.

______. 1990. 'The Peasantry as a Sociohistorical Category'. In *Agrarian Society in History*, Mats Lundahl and Thommy Svensson (eds.), 31-40. London: Routledge.

Moore, Brian L. 1987. *Race, Power, and Social Segmentation in Colonial Society: Guyana after Slavery, 1838-1891*. New York: Gordon and Breach.

Olwig, Karen Fog. 1985. *Cultural Adaptation and Resistance on St. John*. Gainesville: University Presses of Florida.

______. 1990 'The Struggle for Respectability, Methodism and Afro-Caribbean Culture on 19th Century Nevis'. *Nieuwe West-Indische Gids/New West Indian Guide* 64:93-114.

Paget, Hugh. 1964. 'The Free Village System in Jamaica'. *Caribbean Quarterly* 10:38-51.

Philpott, Stuart B. 1972. *West Indian Migration, The Montserrat Case*. London: Athlone.

Richardson, Bonham C. 1983. *Caribbean Migrants*. Knoxville, University of Tennessee Press.

Rivière, W. Emmanuel 1972. 'Labour Shortage in the British West Indies after Emancipation'. *Journal of Caribbean History* 4:1-30.

Scarano, Francisco. 1989. 'Labor and Society in the Nineteenth Century'. In *The Modern Caribbean*, Franklin W. Knight and Colin A. Palmer (eds.), 51-84. Chapel Hill: University of North Carolina Press.

Sewell, William G. 1861. *The Ordeal of Free Labor in the British West Indies*. 2nd ed. Reprinted 1968, London: Frank Cass.

Shephard, C. Y. 1945. *Peasant Agriculture in the Leeward and Windward Islands*. Trinidad: Imperial College of Tropical Agriculture.

Sturge, Joseph, and Thomas Harvey. 1838. *The West Indies in 1837*. London. Reprinted 1968, London: Frank Cass.

Trouillot, Michel-Rolph. 1984. 'Labour and Emancipation in Dominica, Contribution to a Debate'. *Caribbean Quarterly* 30:73-84.

______. 1988. *Peasants and Capital: Dominica in the World Economy*. Baltimore, The Johns Hopkins University Press.

Walker, William. 1873. *On the Social and Economic Position and Prospects of the British West India Possessions*. [London?]: Royal Colonial Institute.

Ward, J. R. 1985. *Poverty and Progress in the Caribbean 1800–1960*. London: Macmillan.

Land, Kinship, and Community in the Post-Emancipation Caribbean: A Regional View of the Leewards

JEAN BESSON

The post-emancipation era in the Caribbean region was marked by both rooting and uprooting among the former plantation slaves. Some proto-peasants, who had cultivated provision grounds on plantation backlands while enslaved, remained as post-slavery estate-based peasantries in situations of both opportunity and constraint; whereas elsewhere the exodus from the plantations into independent peasant villages paralleled earlier maroon communities of runaway slaves (Mintz 1989:151-54; Besson 1992a). The flight of ex-slaves from the estates was also reflected in migration (Thomas-Hope 1978, 1986, 1992, and chapter in this volume; Richardson 1992:134-38). Within peasant settlements, customary land tenures based on kinship and community provided economic, social, and cultural autonomy and enabled circulatory migration.

Such variations were shaped by many factors, including contrasting rates of plantation development and decline and plantation-peasant interplay. This contrast especially distinguished Hispanic from non-Hispanic Caribbean societies; for large-scale slave plantations proliferated earlier in the non-Hispanic territories and were declining there when the plantation system escalated in the Spanish colonies. These differences in plantation evolution in turn influenced availability of land for peasant settlement (Mintz 1959, 1989).

Topography, ecology, and size also affected the emergence of peasantries and their customary land tenures. Peasants gained a more secure foothold in the larger or more mountainous territories, such as the Greater Antilles, Trinidad, the Windward Islands, and the mainland societies of Guyana and Suriname. Peasant formations were more attenuated or constrained in smaller or flatter islands such as Barbados and Antigua.

The process of emancipation itself also affected land rights, kinship, and community among the ex-slaves and their descendants. The variations in this process were reflected in the different dates of emancipation: 1834–38 in the British territories; 1848 in the colonies of France and Denmark; 1863 in the possessions of the Netherlands; and 1876 and 1886 in the Spanish colonies. The slave revolution of French Saint-Domingue (1791–1804), which forged an independent Haiti, was another variation on this regional theme.

The different dates of emancipation not only affected the emergence of post-slavery peasantries and their customary land tenures but also influenced opportunities for overseas migration among the former slaves and their descendants. Movements of British West Indians within the British Caribbean and to Hispanic Central America established a migration tradition,· and non-Hispanic migrations typified the post-emancipation scene.

Against this regional background, this chapter first contrasts Hispanic and non-Hispanic post-emancipation agrarian relations and highlights how post-slavery peasantries and their customary tenures, originating in the pre-emancipation era, typified non-Hispanic Caribbean societies. A general overview of the interrelation of land, kinship, and community in the non-Hispanic Caribbean, focusing especially on the larger territories, follows. Attention then turns to the Leewards, with their highly developed plantation societies, early slave emancipation, smallness of scale, intense land scarcity, and marked migration traditions. In these islands post-emancipation customary land tenures, rooted in kinship and community and linked to pronounced migration, were microcosmic reflections of the wider non-Hispanic Caribbean scene.

HISPANIC AND NON-HISPANIC TENURE

From the early post-conquest period differences in Hispanic and non-Hispanic colonial control shaped Caribbean peasant communities and their customary land tenures, including those of the post-slavery era. Marshall has argued that the West Indian peasantry 'starts at emancipation in 1838' (Marshall 1968:252), but Mintz has shown that Caribbean peasantries emerged as early as the immediate post-conquest period, in response and resistance to colonialism, slavery, and the plantation system (Mintz 1989:132-33, 146-56; cf. Berlin and Morgan 1991).

Following the Columbian conquest of the Caribbean gateway to Europe's New World in 1492, Spanish control of the Antilles expanded from the first Caribbean colony of Hispaniola and remained unbroken for about a century (Hoetink 1985:59; Mintz and S. Price 1985:3). During this time Spain developed the first plantations in the Greater Antilles with enslaved indigenous populations and imported African slaves. In resistance to these Hispanic plantations, squatter peasantries of mixed physical and cultural origins established themselves on marginal land in the mountainous interiors (Mintz 1989:147-8). In this way the first post-conquest customary tenures were created.

From around 1600 the non-Hispanic European powers, particularly Britain, France, and the Netherlands, challenged Hispanic Caribbean hegemony. Throughout the seventeenth century more highly developed non-Hispanic plantations, based on indigenous and African slave labour and on European indentured labour, were established, beginning in the Lesser Antilles. On leaving these plantations, once-indentured Europeans acquired land in the interstices of the plantation system. These early yeomen peasants were soon eradicated, however, by the escalating plantation system. A similar extirpation of squatter peasants and their customary tenures occurred in British Jamaica and French Saint-Domingue. Meanwhile squatter peasants persisted in the Hispanic colonies of Santo Domingo, Puerto Rico, and Cuba, where the plantation system was stagnating (Mintz 1959, 1978:85, 1989:147-51; Hoetink 1985).

Within the eighteenth-century non-Hispanic plantation systems, proto-peasant slaves cultivated kitchen gardens and provision grounds, especially in territories with mountainous or other marginal land unsuited to plantation agriculture. Planters allocated provision grounds to the slaves to produce a cheap and reliable food supply. The slaves, however, used the land to create a domestic economy well beyond the planters' rationale, producing surpluses for sale in public markets. Moreover, the provision grounds complemented the village yards in providing some economic independence and a degree of social and cultural autonomy within the slave plantation system. The slaves also created customary modes of land transmission, based on kinship and community (Mintz 1960, 1979, 1989:151-52; Brierley 1987; Berlin and Morgan 1991; Besson 1992a).

The maroons, or runaway peasantries, also evolved customary land tenures during the pre-emancipation era. Indeed, 'the aim of runaway slaves was more than flight, it was recognized sovereignty over the land itself' (Lowenthal 1961:4, quoted in Richardson 1992:164). Maroon communities lived under constant threat of war from colonial plantation-military regimes and were, therefore, established in virtually inaccessible areas such as mountains, swamps, forests, and ravines. Some maroon communities were wiped out, while others won freedom and legal rights to land through treaties with colonial governments forced to sue for peace. The maroon reservations were subsequently transformed into sacred landscapes through customary use, tenure, and transmission within kin groups and communities (Kopytoff 1979; Vernon 1989:209; Besson 1995).

Marronage occurred throughout the entire period of New World slavery and was widespread in both Hispanic and non-Hispanic Caribbean societies and elsewhere in Plantation-America. Maroon treaties were made in Brazil, Colombia, Cuba, Ecuador, Hispaniola, Jamaica, Mexico, and Suriname. However, the most significant and longest lasting maroon communities became established in the non-Hispanic Caribbean territories of Jamaica and Suriname, where treaties were negotiated in the eighteenth century (Price 1979; Genovese 1981; Thoden van Velzen and van Wetering 1988).

The treaty between the Leeward Maroons of Jamaica and the colonial government, signed on 1 March 1739, 'marked the first act of collective emancipation for formerly enslaved blacks in the Caribbean' (Richardson 1992:164). Such post-treaty maroon communities, which persist to the present day, were complemented later in the slavery era by the post-revolutionary peasant communities of Haiti rooted in maroon and proto-peasant slave resistance.

With the process of emancipation throughout the non-Hispanic Caribbean in the mid-nineteenth century, new post-slavery peasant communities also evolved from the proto-peasant adaptation especially in the context of the flight of ex-slaves from the plantations (Hall 1978; Besson 1992a). Simultaneously the escalating Hispanic plantation system, based on slave, contracted, and coerced labour, was stifling squatter peasantries and their customary land tenures in Cuba and Puerto Rico (Mintz 1959, 1978:85, 1989:82-94, 148). An attenuated domestic economy did, however, emerge among plantation slaves in Cuba in the mid-nineteenth century, with customary land rights related to kinship and community (Scott 1985:15-19).

Soon after emancipation occurred in Puerto Rico (1876) and Cuba (1886), the establishment of modern plantation *centrales* by the burgeoning imperial power of the United States, following the Spanish-American War when the United States seized these colonies from Spain in 1898, resulted in the consolidation of the post-emancipation Hispanic-American plantation system (Mintz 1968:309-311, 1978:85, 1989:116-25). This consolidation severely constrained the emergence of post-slavery peasants and small-scale customary tenures in the Hispanic Caribbean (Mintz 1959, 1989:132; cf. Scott 1985:255-78). An exception to the encompassing influence of the Hispanic plantation system was Cuba's hilly and mountainous eastern province of Santiago de Cuba, where 'large-scale plantations did not yet have a monopoly of the land' (Scott 1985:259). There proto-peasants evolved into post-emancipation peasantries, and 'slaves and their descendants had the greatest opportunity to obtain access to small plots of land by ownership, rental, or de facto occupation' (ibid:259), that is, through legal and customary tenures.

The non-Hispanic Caribbean, therefore, provided the main arena for the growth of post-emancipation peasantries and for the consolidation of land rights, kinship, and community as bases of economic, social, and cultural autonomy among the former slaves. Such peasant settlements and customary tenures were reinforced by the post-treaty maroon communities, especially in Jamaica and Suriname. A post-emancipation migration tradition also emerged, with migrants retaining land rights in villages and kin groups.

THE NON-HISPANIC CARIBBEAN

The Greater Antillean colonies of British Jamaica and French Saint-Domingue were the two most profitable Caribbean slave plantation societies in the eighteenth century. Proto-peasant adaptations were also the most highly developed in these two colonies (Mintz 1960, 1979, 1989:151-52, 180-213). These adaptations evolved into post-slavery peasantries with customary land tenures in Haiti after 1804 and Jamaica after 1838 and were complemented in Jamaica by persisting maroon societies.

In Saint-Domingue plantation slaves had cultivated provision grounds on the mountainous backlands of estates and provided food for the entire colony through a system of public markets (Mintz 1960). These proto-peasant activities 'continued to flourish during the Revolution itself, and to expand thereafter' (Mintz 1979:227). This post-revolutionary peasant society provided the model for the post-emancipation peasant communities that emerged elsewhere in the non-Hispanic Caribbean. Mintz highlights the economic and symbolic significance of land and the customary system of land use, tenure, and transmission that evolved among the Haitian peasantry, noting the question of possible African or French cultural provenance of the landholding kin group or *lakou* (Mintz 1989:242, 274). For both the Haitian and Jamaican peasantry, Mintz and R. Price raise the issue of the precise nature of the post-slavery landholding kin groups (1976:39, 1992:75).

After Haitian independence, the British colonies were the first to experience emancipation. The 1831 slave rebellion in the western parishes of Jamaica, though ruthlessly suppressed, was a major factor contributing to emancipation from below (Craton 1985). This rebellion was part of a long tradition of slave resistance in Jamaica, including frequent rebellion and pronounced maroon and proto-peasant formations (Patterson 1967; Price 1979; Mintz 1989). The proto-peasant adaptation established by Jamaican slaves, who cultivated kitchen gardens in village yards and provision grounds on the mountainous plantation backlands and sold surpluses in public markets, was the most highly developed in the British Caribbean (Mintz 1989:180-213). The entire free population of Jamaica depended on the slaves for food, and by 1774, at the zenith of Jamaican slavery, the slaves controlled 20 per cent of the island's currency (ibid: 199).

The yards and provision grounds were of economic importance and symbolic significance to the Jamaican slaves. They formed a basis for consolidating kinship and community through co-operative labour, burial, and customary tenure and inheritance (Besson 1992a:189-91). As early as 1793, Bryan Edwards noted a system of customary inheritance among the Jamaican slaves, including the transmission of land rights; in the early nineteenth century Stewart observed that each slave had such rights to land

(Edwards 1793, 2:133, and Stewart 1823:267, quoted in Mintz 1989:187, 207). These reports indicate female as well as male participation in the customary system of land use, tenure, and transmission, especially given the significance of women as field slaves and the matrilateral emphasis in slave yards and communities (Patterson 1967:59, 168-69; Mathurin 1975; Bush 1985; Dadzie 1990). A cognatic (i.e. non-unilineal) descent system was therefore emerging, incorporating both men and women and their female and male descendants, paralleling in part the African concept of landholding kin groups, but departing from the unilineal systems predominant in Africa. In Jamaica this incipient cognatic system would burgeon among the ex-slaves and their descendants in the post-emancipation villages in the context of 'family land'.

The exodus of former slaves from the Jamaican plantations, following apprenticeship from 1834 to 1838 and full emancipation in 1838, originated in the tradition of slave resistance and was triggered by legislation which obstructed customary rights to yards and provision grounds (Besson 1992a:191-92). However, the availability of land for purchase by ex-slaves with capital from proto-peasant marketing was constrained by a virtual veto by planters on selling land to former slaves. In this context the Baptist Church, under the leadership of James Phillippo and William Knibb, played a major role in post-emancipation peasant settlement through the purchase and subdivision of properties to establish church communities. Other free villages and dispersed settlements were also established by some ex-slaves who managed to acquire land through purchase, rental, or squatting. By 1840, two years after full emancipation, Knibb stated there were nearly 8,000 cottages in 200 free villages. By 1845, he estimated that 19,000 ex-slaves had purchased land and were erecting cottages, with Trelawny, with twenty-three free villages, at the centre of these developments (Paget 1964; Besson 1984b, 1987b, 1988, 1992a:192; Mintz 1989:157-79).

The Trelawny villages persist today, hemmed in on marginal land by individually owned estates and corporate plantation centrales. Historical anthropological research in five such villages – Martha Brae, Granville, Refuge, Kettering, and Alps (New Birmingham) – reveals that the kin-based institution of family land is the central mechanism through which these peasant communities have been maintained in the face of the persisting plantation system.[1] The small plots of freehold land acquired in these communities after emancipation were not only of economic and political importance, providing some independence from the plantations and a bargaining position for higher wages, but also of symbolic significance to the former chattel slaves. Before emancipation the ex-slaves had been legally landless and property themselves; afterwards their newly acquired freehold land symbolized personhood and freedom.

An unrestricted cognatic descent system, rooted in the customary use, tenure, and transmission of rights to yards and provision grounds among both male and female proto-peasant slaves, developed in the free villages. Freehold land rights were thereby maximized in a context of continuing plantation-engendered land scarcity. For land rights were passed on to all descendants rather than excluding some as in colonial primogeniture, in unilineal descent, and in a restricted cognatic system based on residence. This unrestricted system, which included all descendants regardless of sex, birth order, legitimacy or residence, also maximized the descent ties of former slaves by creating ever-increasing and overlapping kinship lines.

The symbolism of family land is most clearly manifested in traditional burial patterns, where the identity of kinship lines remains rooted in family burial grounds as it was in the proto-peasant past. Such family land with its burial grounds is regarded as inalienable. Trees planted by ancestors on family land are also viewed as sacred and part of the corporate estate, and all descendants may pick from fruit trees on such land. In the post-emancipation era, therefore, the creation of family land represented a process of rooting in Jamaican peasant communities, a basis of economic, social, and cultural autonomy, and a mode of resistance to colonialism, slavery, the plantation system, and the Eurocentric agrarian legal code.

The unrestricted system at the heart of family land was also linked with the migration tradition that emerged in the post-emancipation period. Former slaves and their descendants migrated to other parts of the Caribbean and to Hispanic Central America in a quest for material improvement, autonomy, and identity. Their destinations included the expanding southern plantations of Trinidad and Guyana immediately after 1838, the trans-Isthmian railway in Panama in 1850, the Panama Canal in the 1880s, and the Costa Rican railway for the American Fruit Company's banana plantations from 1872 to 1892. The tradition continued into the twentieth century with migrations to the expanding Hispanic plantations of Cuba from 1914 to 1919 and to Central America, North America, and Britain. The unrestricted descent system has provided an avenue for such migrants to return.

Jamaican family land has been attributed to African cultural survivals, especially the Ashanti heritage (Clarke 1953, 1966; Carnegie 1987), and Jamaican landholding kin groups have been variously described as bilateral kindreds (Clarke 1953, 1966), joint families (Davenport 1961), and restricted non-unilineal (i.e. cognatic) descent groups in which non-residents are excluded (Solien 1959; Otterbein 1964). As noted previously, however, family land is based on an unrestricted cognatic descent system, which differs from Ashanti matrilineal landholding. Family land is, therefore, a dynamic Caribbean cultural creation.[2] Mintz (1989:xxvii) notes that this reinterpretation, in terms of Caribbean cultural creativity rather than cultural survivals, 'has begun to unravel the mystery of so-called "family land" and kinship in Jamaica'. The rethinking of the Jamaican case also elucidates the post-revolutionary Haitian lakou, with its inalienable family-land burial grounds and ancestral trees. For the lakou is based on unrestricted cognatic descent (Larose 1975; Besson 1979:110, 1984a:60, 1987a:26, 28-29, 34) rather than restricted 'groups of patrikin' (Mintz and R. Price 1976:39; 1992:75) and is therefore a Caribbean institution rather than of French or African origin (Mintz 1989:242, 274).

Simultaneous with the establishment of post-emancipation peasant communities and family land throughout Jamaica, the maroons were evolving customary tenure based on common land in their marginal mountainous reservations (Kopytoff 1979; Besson 1995). With the Maroons Allotment Act of 1842 the colonial government sought to nullify the maroon treaties of 1739, abolish the special rights and duties of maroons, and revest 'the Maroon common lands in the Crown, to be reallocated to individual Maroons' (Kopytoff 1979:53). The firmest resistance to this legislation came from the Leeward Maroons of Accompong, the oldest surviving post-treaty corporate maroon community in Plantation-America (Besson 1995; cf. Richardson 1992:164), and this resistance continued.[3] For example, in 1868, 1870, and around 1880 the Accompong Maroons were involved in tax and border disputes (Kopytoff 1979:54, 57).

Disputes between the maroons and the state have continued up to the present, despite Jamaican independence in 1962. Accompong has been 'the most aggressive in asserting its rights' (Kopytoff 1979:58), and during my fieldwork in 1991 disputes were still occurring. In addition to this defence of common tenure, the maroons are evolving an unrestricted cognatic system of transmission, similar to family land, in relation to yards, provision grounds, and trees. Their evolution of a cognatic descent system within the context of common land is also reflected in the change from early African ethnic burial grounds to a Creole community cemetery and to recent burial in family yards. The sacred Kindah Tree, with its sign 'We are Family', at the heart of Accompong, symbolizes the common kinship of the Creole maroon community reflected in the overlapping cognatic descent lines (Besson 1995).

As with Jamaican family land, customary tenure in Accompong has been attributed to African survivals (Barker and Spence 1988). Accompong's common tenure, however, is a Caribbean cultural creation. The commons originated in a colonial treaty that resulted from Jamaican maroon resistance and differ from African unilineal landholding. The cognatic descent system evolving within the commons, like family land, also differs from African unilineal descent.

Patterns of customary land tenure similar to those of Haiti and Jamaica developed in other post-slavery non-Hispanic Caribbean societies. In Guyana, in the context of a flight from the plantations and of plantation-peasant resource conflict, ex-slaves established two types of communities: proprietary and communal (Despres 1970:279). In the proprietary villages, individuals purchased land; in the communal villages, which were more common, ex-slaves pooled resources to buy land collectively (Farley 1954, 1964).

In the communal villages, two processes of fragmentation evolved. First, to ensure equitable distribution of agricultural land, 'widely separated plots or parallel strips' were allocated; second, 'land fragmentation was further augmented by what Africans call "children's property"', a form of tenure and transmission found in most Guyanese villages (Despres 1970:280). Children's property is based on an unrestricted cognatic descent system in which all descendants have inalienable rights, often in a jointly held undivided estate. Children's property has been attributed to the colonial Roman-Dutch legal principle of joint rights in undivided land (R.T. Smith 1964:311, 316, 1971:253-55) and to 'the African pattern of kinship' (Despres 1970:280). However, as Despres also notes, 'under slavery the traditional patterns of African kinship were destroyed' and replaced by bilateral kinship and the multilineal system of children's property (ibid.). Therefore, children's property reflects Caribbean culture-building in response to Caribbean agrarian relations.[4] The interrelation of community and cognatic descent in customary landholding also parallels Jamaica's Accompong maroon community.

Ex-slaves in the British mainland colony of Belize were more severely constrained than in Haiti, Jamaica, and Guyana, despite the potential availability of land. The mahogany lords maintained a land monopoly by a virtually unique labour-control strategy based on the advance and truck systems, which kept labourers in permanent debt to their employers and stifled the development of a post-emancipation peasantry (Bolland 1981:600-11; Besson 1992a:197-98). Wages were paid in advance to labourers in Belize Town in the hiring season, which was generally at Christmas, on the pretext of enabling them to purchase supplies. As anticipated by employers, such advances were spent on Christmas obligations and celebrations. As a result, 'the labourers then had to purchase their supplies on credit and at exorbitant prices from the employers' stores in the forests' (Bolland 1981:608). Among the Black Caribs, descendants of Caribs and maroons deported from St. Vincent in 1797, however, a cognatic inheritance system similar to those of Haiti, Jamaica, and Guyana evolved in the context of post-slavery land scarcity (Solien 1959, 1971; Richardson 1992:165).

In Barbados the former slaves also faced a situation of severe constraint. Located-labour legislation, land scarcity, and high land values kept most Barbadian ex-slaves on the estates. Barbadians had no provision grounds during slavery, but they established a petty proto-peasant economy based on house-spot gardens and a vibrant huckstering system (Beckles 1991:33). The located-labour laws required a stipulated amount of low-wage labour on the estates as a condition for retaining, through rental, such gardens. Land ownership provided more autonomy and an avenue of escape from located-labour legislation. Therefore despite high land prices, a small peasantry became established in villages on freehold land obtained from some subdivided estates (Greenfield 1960:170; Besson 1992a:196-97; cf. Henshall 1976:38; Marshall 1979:244; Mintz 1979:228-30).

In such Barbadian communities, in resistance to the persisting plantation system, ex-slaves created family land, reinforced by the selective use of English legal principles (the 'settlement' and 'seed to seed' inheritance, which included all descendants in perpetuity regardless of sex or legitimacy), ensuring inalienable freehold rights. A post-emancipation migration tradition also developed with extensive emigration, for example, to Trinidad and Guyana, and a significant incidence of return migration (Richardson 1992:135). The unrestricted system at the heart of family land, which included all descendants, enabled such migrants to return.

Bahamian ex-slaves had more room for manoeuvre; for the Bahamas were at the margins of Caribbean plantation society, with an attenuated cotton, rather than sugar, plantation system. Especially in the absentee-owned, ecologically marginal Bahamian Out Islands such as Great Exuma, an isolated proto-peasantry with customary land rights based on both community and cognatic descent emerged during slavery (Besson 1987a:38-40 n5, 1992a; Craton 1987). After emancipation, when legislation designed to restrict ex-slaves' access to land proved impractical to enforce, slave proto-peasant adaptations evolved into free communities. Former slaves were not entirely free from coercion, however; for credit and truck systems, similar to the advance and truck systems of Belize, were introduced to keep the ex-slaves 'in a position of "practical slavery"' (Johnson 1991:84). An agro-mercantile elite monopolized much-needed credit, provided credit through commodities rather than cash, and paid labourers in the salt, pineapple, and sponging industries with provisions, clothes, or a share of the crop (ibid: 84-109). In this context, customary tenures, merging aspects of generational land and commonage, provided some autonomy. Therefore, rather than being African retentions due to isolation (Craton 1987), these tenures were a variation on Caribbean regional themes with close parallels to the frontier society of Guyana and to Jamaica's Accompong maroon community (Otterbein 1964; Besson

1987a:38-40 n5, 1992a:212 n6, 1995).

In Trinidad, substantial numbers of former slaves left the plantations to establish villages, though on a lesser scale than in either Jamaica or Guyana. A customary cognatic system of land transmission evolved in such post-slavery peasant communities (Rodman 1971:16), where today there is still 'continuing, if increasingly tenuous, security of family land' (Littlewood 1993:177) in the face of urbanization and corporate plantations (Besson 1992b:6). In Tobago, similar villages were established; these communities originated in a proto-peasant adaptation and were often situated around the pre-emancipation church as in Jamaica (Henshall 1976:39; Pemberton 1985; Marshall 1991; Besson 1992a:194). In such villages today attachment to family land persists as a basis of autonomy, a need now exacerbated by the encroachment of the tourist industry.

In the British Windward Islands of Grenada, St. Vincent, and St. Lucia, similar interrelations of land, kinship, and community evolved in the post-emancipation period (Besson 1992a:195-96). The well-established proto-peasant economy had included 'an attachment to the land' (Marshall 1985:205). Small plots of land allocated by planters to both male and female slaves had been worked by family groups, with occupancy bequeathed through customary transmission (Marshall 1991:52, 60). As in Jamaica and the Bahamas, a customary cognatic landholding system was, therefore, evolving as early as the slavery period. During apprenticeship, the continued occupancy of house and ground became a contentious issue, with the apprentices claiming possession of houses, yards, and provision grounds (Marshall 1985:215, 219). However, as planter attitudes, policies, and practices became more oppressive, it became clear to the incipient peasantry that 'an effective stand could not be made on others' ground' (ibid:221). This led, where possible, to an exodus from the estates, to the founding of post-emancipation communities, and to the establishment of legal and customary tenures including family land. The unrestricted inheritance system, as elsewhere in the region, provided a basis for both the perpetuation of peasant communities and circulatory migration (Brierley 1974:90-91; Besson 1984a, 1987a, 1992a; Acosta and Casimir 1985; Rubenstein 1987a, 1987b; Thomas-Hope 1992:5). Among the remaining Caribs of St. Vincent unrestricted cognatic descent also evolved as the basis for land rights within the Carib territory established by the colonial government in 1805 (Gullick 1976:252, 1985:18).[5]

Dominica, the largest and most mountainous of the British Windwards, showed both similarities to, and differences from, the other Windward Islands. Before emancipation a well-developed proto-peasant economy had focused on provision grounds, to which both male and female slaves and their family groups had customary rights (Trouillot 1988:28, 68-75). After emancipation, the ex-slaves did not face obstructive planter legislation, but the coastal estates occupied most arable land which initially curtailed a post-emancipation flight from the plantations (Henshall 1976:38; Trouillot 1988:81; Besson 1992a:196). However, in the later post-emancipation period a peasantry became established through small purchases of land (Trouillot 1988:90, 95-96). By the twentieth century, when peasants had virtually replaced plantations, a significant amount of peasant landholdings were family land, which provided autonomy in peasant communities and enabled circulatory migration (Trouillot 1988:113, 252, 281-82; Honychurch 1991:18-19). In the Carib territory, a cognatic system also evolved within the context of common land (Honychurch 1991:19).

The post-emancipation scenario of land, kinship, and community unfolded in the French West Indies when emancipation came in 1848. During slavery the provision-ground system had expanded, despite attempts to suppress the slaves' economy, and was well established by the 1830s. By the 1840s the French colonial authorities and planters regarded the provision-ground and marketing systems as a means of inculcating concepts of family and property among the slaves. The slaves, however, had long been creating customary Afro-Caribbean systems of kinship and landholding as the basis of some autonomy within the plantation system (Tomich 1991).

The process of adaptive resistance was especially pronounced in Martinique. There a proto-peasant cognatic descent system, reinforced by burial on provision grounds, sometimes merged with the wider concept of community, when childless slaves transmitted garden rights to their nearest kin or friends, and masters had to respect the bequeathing of trees to unborn slaves (Tomich 1991; cf. Besson 1989). After emancipation this cognatic system became established in peasant communities in the hills, such as Morne-Vert. Therefore, rather than being a survival from the Napoleonic code (Horowitz 1992:29-30), such family land is a Caribbean creation (Besson 1984a).

While a post-emancipation peasantry was becoming established in Martinique, a maroon society was forming in French Guiana. The Boni, or Aluku, maroons, who fled from Dutch Suriname to French Guiana in 1776–77, concluded an agreement with the French colonial government in 1860 and continued to consolidate customary matrilineal landholding in the remote interior (Bilby 1989; Hoogbergen 1989).

Customary landholding also evolved in Suriname after emancipation in 1863. In the Para coastal region cognatic systems burgeoned within corporate land-holding communities based on former estates purchased by ex-slaves who had formed cognatic descent groups for ancestral ritual on the slave plantations (Mintz and R. Price 1976:36, 1992:69-70). Meanwhile in the vast forest interior, the largest post-treaty maroon societies in Plantation-America, such as the Saramaka, consolidated matrilineal landholding (Price 1975, 1976, 1979; Thoden van Velzen and van Wetering 1988:9; Bilby 1989; Vernon 1989).

THE LEEWARD ISLANDS

Against this general overview the relationships among land, kinship, and community in the post-emancipation Leewards may be explored and more fully understood. The Leeward Islands included highly developed plantation societies and, with their small size, scarcity of land, and pronounced migration traditions, were microcosmic reflections of the wider non-Hispanic Caribbean scene. Antigua, Nevis, and to a lesser extent Montserrat were significant plantation societies at emancipation (Goveia 1965:103; Hall 1971:2-3), with constrained proto-peasant adaptations.[6] St. John, in the Danish West Indies, was a less profitable plantation society with a well-developed proto-peasantry and later emancipation (1848) (Olwig 1985). Barbuda had no plantations and has therefore been regarded as unique (Berleant-Schiller 1987). But it may also be considered a variant on regional themes, since it served as the backlands for some Antiguan plantations, and the single slave community had developed a proto-peasant life style bordering on marronage (Besson 1987a:38-40 n5, 1992a:204-7).

Full emancipation came to Antigua, the largest of the Leewards, in 1834, four years before emancipation in the rest of the British Caribbean. Antigua's slaves were freed, however, in a context of constraint. With its highly developed plantation system, flat topography, and an area of only 108 square miles,[7] the island provided limited scope for a proto-peasant economy during slavery and a post-emancipation flight from the estates (Mintz 1989:181; Besson 1992a:196-97). As in Barbados, however, a petty proto-peasant cottage-garden and marketing system existed. Some Antiguan plantations allocated small provision grounds to both male and female slaves, although others relied on imported food (Smith and Smith 1988:20; Gaspar 1992). Even without a period of apprenticeship, many Antiguan ex-slaves remained as wage-labourers on the estates, where they were allowed to continue to occupy houses and gardens rent-free on condition of such labour. Their gardens were seldom more than 50 square feet, and the land was not their own (Hall 1971:38, 40).

Some land was available for purchase, however, in small plots beyond the plantations, and Antiguan ex-slaves established the first independent villages in the Caribbean by 1835 (Hall 1971:40-43; Smith and Smith 1988:21). The village system was not favoured by the planters; nevertheless by 1842, Antigua had twenty-seven village communities with 1,037 houses and approximately 3,600 inhabitants (Hall 1971:44). By 1845–46, 9,273 people were living in such villages (ibid:49), and by 1858 sixty-seven such communities had been established with '5,187 houses and 15,644 inhabitants' (Henshall 1976:38; cf. Besson 1992a:197). The attractions of the independent villages, along with the support of Nonconformist churches and friendly societies, and higher wages than in other Leeward Islands such as St. Kitts, Montserrat, and Nevis, were important factors in curbing the migration that developed in a more pronounced form in those other islands (Hall 1971:40-41, 49).

The significance of such village lands and communities as a basis of economic, social, and cultural autonomy in a context of the continuing plantation system in Antigua is well portrayed in the oral narrative of Samuel Smith (1877–1982). A descendant of Antiguan plantation slaves, 'Papa Sammy' was born on Jonas Estate in Antigua forty-three years after emancipation. In 1888, his family moved off the estate and built their own house in Freeman's Ville, Antigua's second post-emancipation village (Smith and Smith 1988:21, 37-70).[8] More than one hundred years later, in 1993, in a context where tourism is now engrossing Antiguan land, I encountered oral histories of family land transmitted in such communities.

In Montserrat, an island with only 39 square miles of extremely hilly land, a microcosmic proto-peasant adaptation was established during slavery. After emancipation the ex-slaves continued use of estate provision grounds on condition of providing labour. However, Montserrat's provision grounds, where a customary system of land tenure and use had evolved, were more extensive and autonomous than the more usual cottage gardens of Antigua. The estate-based peasantry in Montserrat continued as the major mode of small-scale agrarian adaptation in the immediate aftermath of emancipation, since there was no unalienated land which ex-slaves could acquire through purchase, though there was squatting from 1835 (Berleant-Schiller in this volume). By 1845–46 only 25 new titles for small freeholds were recorded, and 108 persons lived in post-emancipation villages. Wages were lower than in Antigua. A pronounced migration tradition was therefore established after emancipation, with Montserratians migrating especially to Trinidad and Guyana where wages for estate labour were high (Besson 1992a:197; Hall 1971: 29, 40-41, 49; Philpott 1973:19-22).

A relatively independent peasantry did, however, emerge in Montserrat in the 1850–70 period when some marginal estates were subdivided and sold. In such peasant settlements as the Methodist communities of Cudjoe Head and The East, customary tenures of family land and generation land provided kinship and community identity and continuity among the ex-slaves' descendants. As with family land elsewhere in the region, an unrestricted descent system enabled migrants to retain inalienable land rights even in the late twentieth century (Philpott 1973:22-25, 74-83, 125-28).

Nevis, with only 36 square miles, is even smaller than Montserrat, but with somewhat gentler mountain slopes. At emancipation it was another significant sugar island, but the stony soil constrained the exodus from the plantations even more than in Montserrat, and by 1845–46 Nevis had no free villages (Hall 1971:3, 49). The stranglehold of the plantations continued until the 1930s, stifling the emergence of a post-emancipation peasantry beyond the estates. Like Montserrat, wages were lower than in Antigua.

Olwig (1987b) shows how a pronounced tradition of out-migration developed in Nevis during the early post-emancipation period (for example, to Trinidad), as a response to these constraints. This migration tradition, maintained with varying destinations to the present day, led Olwig to question an assumed 'innate attachment to the native land' as a basis for nationhood in contemporary Nevis (ibid:153). However, as Olwig shows elsewhere (1990a:100-2), a significant though attenuated domestic economy evolved among the slaves in Nevis, which provided a basis for Afro-Nevisian culture in the nineteenth century. The provision grounds played a central economic and symbolic role in Nevisian slave life; two Sunday markets, in Charlestown and in Gingerland, served as important centres of trade and social intercourse among the slaves (Olwig 1990a:101-2; cf. Olwig 1990b:8-10).

Momsen further shows that after emancipation a sharecropping, estate-based peasantry emerged in Nevis, and a customary mode of land tenure and transmission has been preserved from the proto-peasant past through the post-emancipation era to the present day. In the 1930s, following the decline of plantation agriculture, estates were subdivided and sold, and a peasantry then developed independent of the estates. Government land settlement schemes were also introduced, and subsequently sharecropped estates were purchased by the colony and transformed into land settlements, mostly based on annual rental. Despite the virtual absence of either freehold tenure or long leases, the Nevisian peasantry transformed the externally imposed solution of land settlement into a customary system. Many farmers 'could trace their family's presence on a particular estate back through the period of sharecropping to slave days', and 'even without land ownership settlers have often attempted to ensure that their heirs, resident or absentee, [were] allowed to take over occupance of the settlement plot' (Momsen 1987:63, 65). Momsen, therefore, shows that the Nevisian peasantry 'recreated its traditional attitudes to land within the formal structure of the land settlement' (ibid:65). Some Nevisian migrants were also retaining their settlement land, thus demonstrating a continuing attachment to such land.

The symbolic role of such settlement land in providing a basis for kinship continuity, security, and independence, and its frequent use as a form of common land for grazing livestock, parallels the roles of both customary family land and common land elsewhere in the region (Besson 1992a:207-8; Besson and Momsen 1987:3; Momsen 1987:65-66). Olwig's later work in Nevis also indicates that some family land, to which migrants can return, evolved from limited land acquired in the late nineteenth century in a few small villages (Olwig 1993:97-98, 110-11 n5, 130-31, and Nevis chapter in this volume). Paradoxically, then, the dual role of Caribbean family land as a basis for autonomy among the descendants of ex-slaves and a means of enabling circulatory migration is perhaps most clearly seen in its tenuous foothold on Nevis.

Although Barbuda, with an area of 62 square miles, is larger than Montserrat and Nevis, it had the smallest population in the British Leewards at emancipation. With thin soil and little rainfall, Barbuda was not a sugar island and had only one community, Codrington village. Barbuda's historical ethnography has been perceptively documented by Berleant-Schiller (1977, 1978, 1987, 1991), with complementary analyses by Lowenthal and Clarke (1977, 1979, 1980). Berleant-Schiller (1987) highlights Barbuda's peculiar history, ecology, proprietorship, and slave community. From 1680 to 1870 the island was a private fief of the Codrington family, who owned Antiguan sugar plantations and lived in England. Barbuda never had plantations, and its slaves were proto-peasants who established customary land tenures in the context of isolation and benign neglect.

In Barbuda the post-emancipation era saw much continuity with the proto-peasant past. Customary land tenures continued virtually undisturbed until the recent impact of tourism and independent statehood with Antigua. Post-emancipation tenures were based on the co-existence of common tenure of inalienable bush lands, comprising most of the island, with the parcelling of lands in Codrington. Although the house and yard could be individually owned and alienated through bequest or sale, even in the absence of legal title deeds, they were customarily transmitted on the basis of either cognatic descent or residence and participation in the household. By contrast, except for land immediately surrounding fruit trees, which is individually owned and bequeathed, 'bush lands may not be individually owned and may not be bequeathed. All people of socially recognized Barbudan birth, parentage, or ancestry may exercise their use rights, even if they have been absent from Barbuda for a long time' (Berleant-Schiller 1987:117). The commons, therefore, are also linked to the migration tradition established after emancipation (Berleant-Schiller 1978:25).

I have suggested that Barbudan common tenure may be an extreme variant of Caribbean family land (Besson 1984a:60, 78 n16; cf. Lambros Comitas, personal communication 1974, cited in Berleant-Schiller 1987:119). Berleant-Schiller questioned this interpretation arguing that, despite several similarities between Barbudan common tenure and family land, the differences outweigh the similarities and are 'qualitative and profound' (1987:122). However, a reconsideration of the Barbudan case led me to suggest an extension of the hypothesis linking Barbudan post-slavery tenures and Caribbean post-emancipation family land (Besson 1987a:38-40 n5; 1992a:204-8; Besson and Momsen 1987:3-5). For Barbuda was not entirely isolated but served as the backlands for the Codrington plantations in Antigua. In addition, although Barbudan bush land is held in common, village land is parcelled and bequeathed. After emancipation, this mix of tenures, reflecting community and kinship, provided the basis for the ex-slaves' resistance to external attempts to impose commercial agriculture. This situation parallels the cases of the Bahamas and Nevis, where a similar combination of customary tenures provided the basis for resisting imposed development (Craton 1987; Momsen 1987; see also Olwig 1993 and Nevis chapter in this volume). Family land and common land are therefore variations on the theme of Caribbean customary tenures. This reinterpretation of Barbudan post-emancipation land tenures as rooted in both kinship and community is reinforced by Lowenthal and Clarke (1977:515, 1979:147-48).

The reinterpretation of customary tenures in post-emancipation Barbuda is further complemented by data in this chapter on Guyana, the Para region of Suriname, and Jamaica's Accompong maroon community. For in these three places customary land tenures reflecting the concepts of both community and kinship developed after emancipation. My research also reveals that a cognatic descent system functions in relation to the customary transmission of rights to provision grounds and groves of fruit trees within the wider context of the Barbudan commons, as well as in relation to village yards (Berleant-Schiller 1977:264), closely paralleling the situation in post-emancipation Accompong.

The contention that customary land tenures, reflecting kinship and community, in the post-emancipation Leewards were microcosmic variations on Caribbean regional themes is perhaps most clearly illustrated by the former Danish West Indian island of St. John, with an area of less than 20 square miles the smallest Leeward Island considered here. This island manifests the post-emancipation regional themes of persisting plantations, peasants reconstituted from slavery, free villages, and family land originating in proto-peasant customary landholding and linked with migration on a significant though attenuated and microcosmic scale. This becomes clear when Olwig's rich analysis of ego-focused bilateral kinship networks (1981a, 198lb, 1985) is complemented by regional perspectives on the ancestor-focused unrestricted cognatic descent systems at the heart of Caribbean family land.[9]

Olwig's (1985) study of St. John highlights the significance of ego-focused bilateral kinship networks of exchange, rooted in proto-peasant and post-emancipation free village communities and continuing as the basis of cultural identity in the contemporary tourism society. She shows that the Afro-Caribbean system of social reproduction and exchange, whereby the slave population, economy, and society were perpetuated, evolved as both cultural adaptation and resistance to the plantation system. The slaves developed a domestic economy based on plantation provision grounds and access to the sea. Kinship networks also emerged as a result of extra-residential conjugal relations among the slaves, with an individual's matrilateral kin resident on the same estate and affinal and patrilateral kin on other plantations. These networks provided the contexts for both autonomous communities and mutual aid.

This Afro-Caribbean system of exchange continued after emancipation among the post-slavery peasantry, established on small plots of family land inherited by all descendants and augmented by access to land on the estates. Family land developed especially in the free villages that evolved by the 1870s and 1880s from the proto-peasant communities based on the provision grounds at the margins of the plantations. After emancipation, the estates were devoted to cattle-grazing rather than sugar-cane or cotton and were controlled by a new immigrant plantocracy. Since the agrarian structure remained largely unchanged, the peasants combined farming, fishing, trading, and estate and migrant labour in an economy that was coherent but precarious. A flexible division of labour enabled household survival, and exchange networks provided a basis for the peasant community and a mode of cultural resistance against the new plantocracy. Most exchanges were among close kin on family land, and Olwig interprets family land use as 'part of the general system of sharing and exchange' (1985:136).

The establishment of the Virgin Islands National Park on St. John by an act of Congress in 1956 (the United States having purchased the Danish Virgin Islands in 1917) heralded the destruction of the post-emancipation peasantry and the development of tourism. The park annihilated the peasant economy by restricting access to beaches for fishing and to land for grazing and swidden cultivation, and by purchasing family land. However, within the tourism society, St. Johnians redefined their traditional networks of exchange as a basis of identity against the new American elite, pooling resources to express community solidarity in the face of an alien competitive society.

Olwig criticizes traditional analyses of the Afro-American family in the Caribbean, which focus on household structure and matrifocal family forms. 'With few exceptions', she argues, 'there has been little discussion of kinship structure as such, much less of the larger sociocultural systems'

(1985:xi). However, her emphasis on bilateral networks as the essence of Afro-Caribbean kinship overlooks the significance of the unrestricted cognatic descent system at the heart of family land as a major feature of Caribbean kinship systems. Moreover, the creation of family land was a significant mode of response and resistance among the post-emancipation peasantry to the persisting plantation system; family land was also more than a system of land use, being a central symbol of Afro-Caribbean autonomy and identity, which also enabled return migration. My reinterpretation of the St. Johnian data in terms of landholding cognatic descent groups or corporations complementing bilateral kinship networks, as outlined below, strengthens Olwig's argument that the Afro-Caribbean kinship system exhibits both adaptation and resistance (cf. Besson 1989).

First, the family-land system that emerged in post-emancipation St. John was clearly based on ancestor-focused cognatic descent lines. The land had been purchased by an ancestor, who left it as an estate for all the descendants, and such landholding corporations are symbolized by a common name and a family cemetery (Olwig 1985:138-39; 1987a:36). Second, such cognatic descent is unrestricted, since land rights are not lost by absentees and their children, thereby enabling migrants to return to their home community. The unrestricted nature of descent is also reflected in the overlapping descent groups, resulting from the retention of land rights by all descendants (Olwig 1985:95, 101-2, 135, 138-39; 1987a: 35-36). Third, the rationale for these dispersed unrestricted groups is economic and symbolic: 'the old people equated owning land with being free and felt that their ancestors had freed themselves from slavery or bondage to the plantations by acquiring land' (Olwig 1977:249). Fourth, Olwig's data implicitly suggest that the cognatic descent system in St. Johnian family land originated in the proto-peasant adaptation; for both male and female slaves had rights and a strong attachment to land, and a 'particular preference for living and being buried on their place of birth' (Olwig 1985:41).

Olwig's study also suggests that despite sales of family land resulting from the impact of tourism, some post-emancipation family land remains as a significant focus of the contemporary St. Johnian culture of resistance (1985:179-82; 1987a:40). This continuity parallels the situation in Negril, Jamaica, where after initial land sales, family land has been redefined as the basis of adaptation and resistance to the tourist industry (McKay 1987). St. John also shows similarities with Antigua, Barbuda, Tobago, and Accompong, where customary tenures continue to represent resistance in the face of encroachment from tourism (Berleant-Schiller 1987; Besson 1987a, 1992a, 1995).

CONCLUSION

Post-slavery peasantries and their customary land tenures typified the non-Hispanic Caribbean colonies. This reconstitution of peasant formations and customary tenures out of slave communities and economies occurred primarily in the context of the flight from plantations and the establishment of villages and continued a tradition of slave resistance. These developments were triggered by oppressive planter attitudes, policies, and legislation, factors that also constrained the development of post-emancipation peasantries.

Within such contexts customary land tenures became established as a basis of autonomy within the free communities and also enabled circulatory migration. Family land, based on unrestricted cognatic descent systems, evolved, for example, in Haiti, Jamaica, Barbados, Trinidad, the British Windwards, and French Martinique.[10] In Guyana, the Bahamas, Jamaica's Accompong maroon community, and the Para plantation region of Suriname, and among the Caribs of Dominica and St. Vincent and the Black Caribs of Belize, cognatic descent was linked more closely with the concept of community within the context of common land. Matrilineal landholding consolidated in the maroon communities of French Guiana and Suriname. Rather than being passive cultural survivals from Africa or Europe, such customary tenures represented dynamic Caribbean cultural creations in resistance to slavery, colonialism, the plantation system, and Eurocentric agrarian legal codes.

The Leeward Islands reflected these wider non-Hispanic Caribbean themes on a microcosmic scale. Antigua had a highly developed though small-scale plantation system with only a petty proto-peasant adaptation. But the ex-slaves established the region's first independent villages, and family land evolved in these communities. Montserrat had a small-scale proto-peasantry with customary land tenure and use, which evolved into a post-emancipation estate-based peasantry, since the establishment of villages was even more constrained. This constraint on peasant development also led to pronounced migration. Peasant communities with customary kin-based tenures only became established in the later post-emancipation period. In Nevis, where free villages were virtually stifled by the small-scale but highly developed plantation system, there was pronounced migration. The continuity of customary tenure from the proto-peasant past was primarily reflected within estate-based peasant communities and leasehold land settlements, though some family land also emerged. Barbuda, with its single peasant community linked to both the commons and the plantation society of Antigua, was a variation on wider Caribbean themes despite the absence of plantations. St. John, with its plantations, proto-peasants, free villages, and family land, perhaps most clearly reflected the regional scene.

From this regional perspective, it can be seen that family land systems were forged in Antillean peasant communities at the heart of the plantation-peasant interface: in post-revolutionary Haiti, the free villages of Jamaica, post-emancipation Barbados, Trinidad, the British Windwards, French Martinique, St. John, Antigua, Montserrat, and even tenuously in Nevis where the peasantry was almost entirely constrained. At the margins and frontiers of the plantation Caribbean, cognatic inheritance functioned within the wider context of common land, as in Jamaica's Accompong maroon reservation, the Bahamas, Guyana, the Para region of Suriname, among the Caribs of Dominica and St. Vincent, and the Black Caribs of Belize, and also in Barbuda. Only in the vast forest interiors of Suriname and French Guiana were former slaves sufficiently autonomous and unhampered by land scarcity to forge anew African-type restricted matrilineal systems.

The cases of Belize and the Bahamas show that the unavailability of land was not the only factor constraining the ex-slaves, who were also oppressed by labour control strategies. Moreover, land was not the only agrarian resource to be customarily transmitted among the slaves and their descendants as a basis and symbol of autonomy. Customary transmission also applied to trees among the proto-peasantry in Martinique, in the post-revolutionary Haitian lakou, in Jamaica's post-emancipation villages of Trelawny and the post-treaty Accompong maroon community, and in post-emancipation Barbuda. For the slaves and their descendants trees had a spiritual dimension and, like the eternal land, symbolized the continuity of kinship groups and communities (Besson 1988:44-45; Hennessy 1993:4). This is perhaps most clearly illustrated by Accompong's sacred Kindah Tree, which represents the continuity of the community and its family lines in this oldest surviving post-treaty corporate maroon polity. In the post-slavery era trees, like land, also symbolized the fruits of freedom.

ACKNOWLEDGEMENTS

My fieldwork in the free villages of Trelawny (1968–93) and in the maroon community of Accompong, St. Elizabeth (1979, 1989, 1991), Jamaica, was funded in part by the Social Science Research Council (UK), the Carnegie Trust for the Universities of Scotland, and the University of Aberdeen Travel Fund. Grants from the British Council, the University of the West Indies, St. Augustine Campus, and Goldsmiths' College, University of London, enabled research in Trinidad and Tobago (1992).

NOTES

1. For an analysis of how family land in the Trelawny villages relates to other tenures and the legal system see Besson 1974: chapters 4, 7, 8; 1984a:58, 76 n7; 1987b:110-11; 1988.
2. The possibility of African or colonial provenance of Caribbean family island is addressed more fully in my earlier articles (Besson 1979, 1984a, 1987a, 1992a; see also note 4 below). For responses to Carnegie's (1987) arguments on African survivals and folk tenures in Sturge Town, Jamaica, and a comment on Craton's (1987) Africanist argument for family

land in the Bahamas see Besson 1987b and 1992a:212 n6. Trouillot, who like Besson (1987b) and in contrast to R. T. Smith (1990) resolves the Carnegie-Besson controversy, notes that 'the only issue on which Carnegie and Besson really differ . . . is that of African retentions; my own position on this is closer to that of Besson' (Trouillot 1989:325 n2). Berleant-Schiller and Pulsipher (1986:16) also support my argument on family land as a customary tenure that has developed in the New World.

3. The treaty with the Leeward Maroons was signed in March 1739, a few months before the treaty with the Jamaican Windward Maroons in June 1739. In 1796, following the Second Maroon War (1795), the Leeward Maroon community of Trelawny Town was treacherously deported to Nova Scotia by the colonial government, which left Accompong as the sole surviving Leeward Maroon community (see e.g. Bilby 1984).

4. In response to this argument (Besson 1979, 1984a, 1987a, 1987b), R. T. Smith (1990) provides a spirited defence of the Roman-Dutch thesis for Afro-Guyanese children's property, which is not entirely successful but raises some intriguing issues. I allowed for the possibility of Roman-Dutch law (as well as other cultural influences) reinforcing Caribbean customary tenure in my original argument (Besson 1979:110, 1984a:75). The use of aspects of the law to reinforce customary tenures is also consistent with my analysis of the relationship between family land and the Jamaican legal code in Martha Brae (Besson 1974, 11:1-113; 1984a:76 n7; 1987b; 1988). I do not claim, as Smith assumes (1990:123), that family land is 'the sole form of tenure'; my analysis of the multiple tenurial complex of which family land is a part, is clearly spelled out (Besson 1974, Chs. 4, 7, 8; 1984a:58, 76 n7) and predates Carnegie's similar analysis (1987) for Sturge Town. Like Carnegie (1987:83), Smith (1990:123) uses the concept of Caribbean family land while denying its validity.

   There is clear evidence in the literature (e.g. Despres 1970:280; R. T. Smith 1971:253-55) of Guyanese customary tenure based on family lines as well as on communities (the latter stressed by R. T. Smith 1990). Smith's rebuttal of the family-land resistance thesis, while consistent with his underplay of capitalist class relations (R. T. Smith 1988; Besson 1990), is unconvincing for the Guyanese case in the light of his own data. For he notes the stranglehold of the plantation system and 'a working class that never escaped involvement in the plantation economy' and had a strong tradition of slave resistance (R. T. Smith 1990:125; cf. Farley 1964). Finally, much of the data that Smith (1990:122) calls for is available in regional sources (e.g. some 40 sources cited in Besson 1984a:77-78 n16; and 1974–1988).

   However, Smith is correct in highlighting the complexities of the Guyanese case, which can be more effectively dealt with by the regional perspectives of Besson 1987a, 1992a, and the present chapter. The Guyanese case, therefore, does not, as Smith (1990) argues, weaken the regional perspective on Caribbean customary tenures, but strengthens it. Moreover, Smith's strictures are not raised again in his 1992 essay, which explicitly supports my argument on family land (R. T. Smith 1992:269, 271-2, 276).

5. While Solien (1959) argues for a restricted non-unilineal system among the Black Caribs of the Caribbean coast of Central America, Gullick notes the dispersed and therefore unrestricted nature of descent among the Vincentian Caribs, which he identifies with the Black Carib system (Gullick 1976:252, 1985:18). For a fuller critical discussion of Solien's argument that non-unilineal descent must be restricted see Besson 1979, 1987a.

6. I have not included St. Kitts, the Leeward sugar island *par excellence*, for two reasons. First, St. Kitts has close similarities with Antigua; for example, in the stifling of a proto-peasantry and the constraints on post-emancipation villages (Goveia 1965:103; Hall 1971:2-3). Second, at the time of writing, I could not locate any information on post-emancipation customary land tenure in St. Kitts.

7. Antigua's area of 108 square miles contrasts with the areas of 10,597 and 4,244 square miles of the Greater Antillean territories of Haiti and Jamaica and is less than either Grenada or St. Vincent, with areas of 133 square miles, the smallest of the Windwards.

8. Antigua's first free village was Liberta.

9. These perspectives on cognatic descent in the Caribbean region derive from, and in turn advance, comparative kinship theory. Anthropologists traditionally thought that cognatic

systems, especially unrestricted cognatic descent (where all descendants are included and land rights are retained by absentees), could not function, and that societies without unilineal descent groups could only be typified by ego-focused bilateral kinship. However, a cognatic system, including unrestricted descent, can co-exist with bilateral kinship. Cognatic systems have, however, been mainly documented for the Pacific region and a few East African societies. See e.g. Goodenough 1955, Fox 1967:146-74, Caplan 1969, Hanson 1971, Hoben 1973.

10. The customary tenures based on kinship and community outlined in this chapter are not the only ones that emerged in Caribbean post-slavery peasant communities. As in Martha Brae, Jamaica, other tenures exist including purchased land, rented land, and squatting. However, family land and common tenure lay at the heart of post-slavery villages and provided more security than renting or squatting and perpetuated kinship lines and communities.

REFERENCES

Acosta, Yvonne, and Jean Casimir. 1985. 'Social Origins of the Counter-Plantation System in St. Lucia'. In *Rural Development in the Caribbean*, P. I. Gomes (ed.), 34-59. London: Hurst.

Barker, David, and Balfour Spence. 1988. 'Afro-Caribbean Agriculture: A Jamaican Maroon Community in Transition'. *Geographical Journal* 154:198-208.

Beckles, Hilary McD. 1991. 'An Economic Life of Their Own: Slaves as Commodity Producers and Distributors in Barbados'. In Berlin and Morgan, q.v., 31-47.

Berleant-Schiller, Riva. 1977. 'Production and Division of Labor in a West Indian Peasant Community'. *American Ethnologist* 4:253-72.

______. 1978. 'The Failure of Agricultural Development in Post-Emancipation Barbuda'. *Boletin de Estudios Latinoamericanos y del Caribe* 25:21-36.

______. 1987. 'Ecology and Politics in Barbudan Land Tenure'. In Besson and Momsen, q.v., 116-31.

______. 1991. 'Statehood, the Commons and the Landscape in Barbuda'. *Caribbean Geography* 3(1):43-52.

Berleant-Schiller, Riva, and Lydia M. Pulsipher. 1986. 'Subsistence Cultivation in the Caribbean'. *Nieuwe West-Indische Gids/ New West Indian Guide* 60:1-40.

Berlin, Ira, and Philip D. Morgan (eds.). 1991. *The Slaves' Economy: Independent Production by Slaves in the Americas*. Special Issue, *Slavery & Abolition* 12(1).

Besson, Jean. 1974. 'Land Tenure and Kinship in a Jamaican Village'. 2 vols. Ph.D. diss., University of Edinburgh.

______. 1979. 'Symbolic Aspects of Land in the Caribbean: The Tenure and Transmission of Land Rights among Caribbean Peasantries'. In *Peasants, Plantations and Rural Communities in the Caribbean*, Malcolm Cross and Arnaud Marks (eds.), 86-116. Guildford: University of Surrey, and Leiden: Royal Institute of Linguistics and Anthropology.

______. 1984a. 'Family Land and Caribbean Society: Toward an Ethnography of Afro-Caribbean Peasantries'. In *Perspectives on Caribbean Regional Identity*, Elizabeth M. Thomas-Hope (ed.), 57-83. Liverpool: Centre for Latin American Studies, Monograph Series No 11.

______. 1984b. 'Land Tenure in the Free Villages of Trelawny, Jamaica'. *Slavery & Abolition*, 5:3-23.

______. 1987a. 'A Paradox in Caribbean Attitudes to Land'. In Besson and Momsen, q.v., 13-45.

______. 1987b. 'Family Land as a Model for Martha Brae's New History'. In Carnegie (ed.), q.v., 100-32.

______. 1988. 'Agrarian Relations and Perceptions of Land in a Jamaican Peasant Village'. In *Small Farming and Peasant Resources in the Caribbean*, John S. Brierley and Hymie Rubenstein (eds.), 39-61. Winnipeg: University of Manitoba.

______. 1989. Review of Karen Fog Olwig, *Cultural Adaptation and Resistance on St. John*. In *Plantation Society in the Americas* 2:345-48.

______. 1990. Review of Raymond T. Smith, *Kinship and Class in the West Indies*. In *Man*, 25:371.

______. 1992a. 'Freedom and Community: The British West Indies'. In *The Meaning of Freedom: Economics, Politics, and Culture after Slavery*, Frank McGlynn and Seymour Drescher (eds.), 183-219. Pittsburgh: University of Pittsburgh Press.

______. 1992b. 'Oral Tradition in Caribbean Research: Case Studies from Jamaica, Trinidad and Guyana'. In *OPReP Newsletter*, Reginald Clarke (ed.), No. 18:3-6. Trinidad: University of the West Indies, St. Augustine.

______. 1995. 'Free Villagers, Rastafarians and Modern Maroons'. In *Born Out of Resistance: Caribbean Cultural Creativity as a Response to European Expansion*, Wim Hoogbergen (ed.). Utrecht: ISOR Press.

Besson, Jean, and Janet Momsen (eds). 1987. 'Introduction'. In *Land and Development in the Caribbean*, 1-9. London: Macmillan.

Bilby, Kenneth M. 1984. 'The Treacherous Feast: A Jamaican Maroon Historical Myth'. *Bijdragen tot de Taal, Land- en Volkenkunde* 140:1-31.

______. 1989. 'Divided Loyalties: Local Politics and the Play of States among the Aluku'. *Nieuwe West-Indische Gids/ New West Indian Guide* 63(3 & 4):143-73.

Bolland, O. Nigel. 1981. 'Systems of Domination after Slavery: The Control of Land and Labor in the British West Indies after 1838'. *Comparative Studies in Society and History* 23:591-619.

Brierley, John S. 1974. *Small Farming in Grenada, West Indies*. Winnipeg: University of Manitoba.

______. 1987. 'Land Fragmentation and Land-Use Patterns in Grenada'. In Besson and Momsen, q.v., 194-209.

Bush, Barbara. 1985. 'Towards Emancipation: Slave Women and Resistance to Coercive Labour Regimes in the British West Indian Colonies, 1790-1838'. In *Abolition and Its Aftermath: The Historical Context, 1790-1916*, David Richardson (ed.), 27-54. London: Frank Cass.

Caplan, Patricia. 1969. 'Cognatic Descent Groups on Mafia Island, Tanzania'. *Man*, 4:419-31.

Carnegie, Charles V. 1987. 'Is Family Land an Institution?' In *Afro-Caribbean Villages in Historical Perspective*, C. V. Carnegie (ed.), 83-99. Kingston: African-Caribbean Institute of Jamaica Research Review No. 2.

Clarke, Edith. 1953. 'Land Tenure and the Family in Four Selected Communities in Jamaica'. *Social and Economic Studies*, 1(4):81-118.

______. 1966. *My Mother Who Fathered Me: A Study of the Family in Three Selected Communities in Jamaica*. 2nd ed. London: Allen and Unwin.

Craton, Michael. 1985. 'Emancipation from Below? The Role of the British West Indian Slaves in the Emancipation Movement, 1816-34'. In *Out of Slavery: Abolition and After*, Jack Hayward (ed.), 110-31. London: Frank Cass.

______. 1987. 'White Law and Black Custom: The Evolution of Bahamian Land Tenures'. In Besson and Momsen, q.v., 88-114.

Dadzie, Stella. 1990. 'Searching for the Invisible Woman: Slavery and Resistance in Jamaica'. *Race and Class*, 32(2):21-38.

Davenport, William. 1961. 'Introduction'. *Social and Economic Studies*, 10:380-85.

Despres, Leo A. 1970. 'Differential Adaptations and Micro-Cultural Evolution in Guyana'. In *Afro-American Anthropology*, Norman E. Whitten and John F. Szwed (eds.), 263-287. New York: Free Press.

Edwards, Bryan. 1793. *The History, Civil and Commercial, of the British Colonies in the West Indies*. 2 vols. London: John Stockdale.

Farley, Rawle. 1954. 'The Rise of the Peasantry in British Guiana.' *Social and Economic Studies* 2:76-103.

______. 1964. 'The Rise of Village Settlements in British Guiana'. *Caribbean Quarterly* 10(1):52-61.

Fox, Robin. 1967. *Kinship and Marriage*. Harmondsworth: Penguin Books.

Gaspar, David Barry. 1992. 'Working the System: Antigua Slaves and Their Struggle to Live'. *Slavery & Abolition* 13:131-55.

Genovese, Eugene D. 1981. *From Rebellion to Revolution: Afro-American Slave Revolts in the Making of the New World*. New York: Vintage Books.

Goodenough, Ward H. 1955. 'A Problem in Malayo-Polynesian Social Organization'. *American Anthropologist* 57:71-83.

Goveia, Elsa V. 1965. *Slave Society in the British Leeward Islands at the End of the Eighteenth Century*. New Haven: Yale University Press.
Greenfield, Sidney M. 1960. 'Land Tenure and Transmission in Rural Barbados'. *Anthropological Quarterly* 33:165-76.
Gullick, C. J. M. R. 1976. 'Carib Ethnicity in a Semi-Plural Society'. *New Community*, 5:250-58.
______. 1985. *Myths of a Minority: The Changing Traditions of the Vincentian Caribs*. Assen: Van Gorcum.
Hall, Douglas. 1971. *Five of the Leewards 1834-1870*. Barbados: Caribbean Universities Press.
______. 1978. 'The Flight from the Estates Reconsidered: The British West Indies, 1838-42'. *Journal of Caribbean History* 10-11:7-24.
Hanson, F. Allan. 1971. 'Nonexclusive Cognatic Descent Systems: A Polynesian Example'. In *Polynesia: Readings on a Culture Area*. Alan Howard (ed.), 109-32. Scranton, Pa.: Chandler.
Hennessy, Alistair. 1993. 'Introduction'. In *The Autobiography of a Runaway Slave: Esteban Montejo*, Miguel Barnet (ed.), 1-12. London: Macmillan.
Henshall (Momsen), Janet D. 1976. 'Post-Emancipation Rural Settlement in the Lesser Antilles'. *Proceedings of the Association of American Geographers* 8:37-40.
Hoben, Alan. 1973. *Land Tenure among the Amhara of Ethiopia: The Dynamics of Cognatic Descent*. Chicago: University of Chicago Press.
Hoetink, Harry. 1985. '"Race" and Color in the Caribbean'. In Mintz and S. Price, q.v. 55-84.
Honychurch, Lennox. 1991. *Dominica: Isle of Adventure*. London: Macmillan.
Hoogbergen, Wim. 1989. 'Aluku'. *Nieuwe West-Indische Gids/New West Indian Guide*, 63(3 & 4):175-97.
Horowitz, Michael M. 1992. *Morne-Paysan: Peasant Village in Martinique*. 2nd ed. Illinois: Waveland Press.
Johnson, Howard. 1991. *The Bahamas in Slavery and Freedom*. London: James Currey.
Kopytoff, Barbara Klamon. 1979. 'Colonial Treaty as Sacred Charter of the Jamaican Maroons'. *Ethnohistory*, 26:45-64.
Larose, Serge. 1975. 'The Haitian *Lakou*: Land, Family and Ritual'. In *Family and Kinship in Middle America and the Caribbean*, Arnaud F. Marks and René A. Römer (eds.), 482-512. Curaçao: Institute of Higher Studies in Curaçao, and Leiden: Royal Institute of Linguistics and Anthropology.
Littlewood, Roland. 1993. *Pathology and Identity: The Work of Mother Earth in Trinidad*. Cambridge: Cambridge University Press.
Lowenthal, David. 1961. 'Caribbean Views of Caribbean Land'. *Canadian Geographer*, 5(2):1-9.
Lowenthal, David, and Colin G. Clarke. 1977. 'Slave-Breeding in Barbuda: The Past of a Negro Myth'. In *Comparative Perspectives on Slavery in New World Plantation Societies*, Vera Rubin and Arthur Tuden (eds). 510-35. Special issue, *Annals of the New York Academy of Sciences*, Vol. 292.
______. 1979. 'Common Lands, Common Aims: The Distinctive Barbudan Community'. In *Peasants, Plantations and Rural Communities in the Caribbean*, Malcolm Cross and Arnaud Marks (eds.), 142-59. Guildford: University of Surrey, and Leiden: Royal Institute of Linguistics and Anthropology.
______. 1980. 'Island Orphans: Barbuda and the Rest'. *Journal of Commonwealth & Comparative Politics*, 18:293-307.
McKay, Lesley. 1987. 'Tourism and Changing Attitudes to Land in Negril, Jamaica'. In Besson and Momsen, q.v., 132-52.
Marshall, Woodville K. 1968. 'Notes on Peasant Development in the West Indies since 1838'. *Social and Economic Studies* 17:252-63.
______. 1979. Commentary on Sidney W Mintz, 'Slavery and the Rise of Peasantries'. In *Roots and Branches: Current Directions in Slave Studies*, Michael Craton (ed.), 243-48. Toronto: Pergamon Press.
______. 1985. 'Apprenticeship and Labour Relations in Four Windward Islands'. In *Abolition and Its Aftermath: The Historical Context, 1790–1916*, David Richardson (ed.), 203-24. London: Frank Cass.
______. 1991. 'Provision Ground and Plantation Labour in Four Windward Islands'. In Berlin

and Morgan, q.v., 48-67.
Mathurin, Lucille. 1975. *The Rebel Woman in the British West Indies during Slavery*. Kingston, Jamaica: African-Caribbean Publications.
Mintz, Sidney W. 1959. 'Labor and Sugar in Puerto Rico and Jamaica, 1800–1850'. *Comparative Studies in Society and History* 1:273-81.
______. 1960. 'Peasant Markets'. *Scientific American* 203:112-22.
______. 1968. 'Caribbean Society'. *International Encyclopedia of the Social Sciences*, Vol. 2, 306-19. New York: Crowell Collier and Macmillan.
______. 1978. 'Was the Plantation Slave a Proletarian?' *Review*, 2(1):81-98.
______. 1979. 'Slavery and the Rise of Peasantries'. In *Roots and Branches: Current Directions in Slave Studies*, Michael Craton (ed.), 213-42. Toronto: Pergamon Press.
______. 1989 [1974]. *Caribbean Transformations*. New York: Columbia University Press Morningside Edition.
Mintz, Sidney W., and Richard Price. 1976. *An Anthropological Approach to the Afro-American Past: A Caribbean Perspective*. Philadelphia: Institute for the Study of Human Issues.
______. 1992. *The Birth of African-American Culture: An Anthropological Perspective*. Boston: Beacon Press.
Mintz, Sidney W., and Sally Price (eds.). 1985. 'Introduction'. In *Caribbean Contours*, 3-11. Baltimore: The Johns Hopkins University Press.
Momsen, Janet. 1987. 'Land Settlement as an Imposed Solution'. In Besson and Momsen, q.v., 46-69.
Olwig, Karen Fog. 1977. 'Households, Exchange and Social Reproduction: The Development of a Caribbean Society'. Ph.D. diss. University of Minnesota.
______. 1981a. 'Women, "Matrifocality", and Systems of Exchange: An Ethnohistorical Study of the Afro-American Family on St. John, Danish West Indies'. *Ethnohistory* 28:59-78.
______. 1981b. 'Finding a Place for the Slave Family'. *Folk* 23:345-58.
______. 1985. *Cultural Adaptation and Resistance on St. John*. Gainesville: University of Florida Press.
______. 1987a. 'Village, Culture and Identity on St. John, V.I.' In Carnegie (ed.), q.v., 20-44.
______. 1987b. 'Children's Attitudes to the Island Community: The Aftermath of Out-Migration on Nevis'. In Besson and Momsen, q.v., 153-70.
______. 1990a. 'The Struggle for Respectability: Methodism and Afro-Caribbean Culture on 19th Century Nevis'. *Nieuwe West-Indische Gids/New West Indian Guide*, 64(3 & 4):93-114.
______. 1990b. 'Cultural Identity and Material Culture'. *Folk*, 32:5-22.
______. 1993. *Global Culture, Island Identity: Continuity and Change in the Afro-Caribbean Community of Nevis*. Philadelphia: Harwood.
Otterbein, Keith F. 1964. 'A Comparison of Land Tenure Systems of the Bahamas, Jamaica and Barbados'. *International Archives of Ethnography*, 50:31-42.
Paget, Hugh. 1964. 'The Free Village System of Jamaica'. *Caribbean Quarterly*, 10(1):38-51.
Patterson, Orlando. 1967. *The Sociology of Slavery: An Analysis of the Origins, Development and Structure of Negro Slave Society in Jamaica*. London: MacGibbon and Kee.
Pemberton, Carlisle. 1985. 'Economic Behaviour of Peasants in Tobago'. In *Rural Development in the Caribbean*, P. I. Gomes (ed.), 76-102. London, Hurst.
Philpott, Stuart B. 1973. *West Indian Migration: The Montserrat Case*. London: Athlone Press.
Price, Richard. 1975. *Saramaka Social Structure: Analysis of a Maroon Society in Surinam*. Rio Piedras: University of Puerto Rico.
______. 1976. *The Guiana Maroons*. Baltimore: The Johns Hopkins University Press.
______. (ed.). 1979. *Maroon Societies: Rebel Slave Communities in the Americas*. 2nd ed. Baltimore: The Johns Hopkins University Press.
Richardson, Bonham C. 1992. *The Caribbean in the Wider World, 1492–1992*. Cambridge, Cambridge University Press.
Rodman, Hyman. 1971. *Lower-Class Families: The Culture of Poverty in Negro Trinidad*. London: Oxford University Press.
Rubenstein, Hymie. 1987a. 'Folk and Mainstream Systems of Land Tenure and Use in St. Vincent'. In Besson and Momsen, q.v., 70-87.
______. 1987b. *Coping with Poverty: Adaptive Strategies in a Caribbean Village*. London:

Westview Press.

Scott, Rebecca J. 1985. *Slave Emancipation in Cuba: The Transition to Free Labor, 1860–1899.* Princeton: Princeton University Press.

Smith, Raymond T. 1964. 'Ethnic Difference and Peasant Economy in British Guiana'. In *Capital, Saving and Credit in Peasant Societies*, Raymond Firth and B. S. Yamey (eds.), 305-29. London, Allen and Unwin.

______. 1971. 'Land Tenure in Three Negro Villages in British Guiana'. In *Peoples and Cultures of the Caribbean*, Michael M. Horowitz (ed.), 243-66. Garden City, Natural History Press.

______. 1988. *Kinship and Class in the West Indies: A Genealogical Study of Jamaica and Guyana*. Cambridge: Cambridge University Press.

______. 1990. Review of C. V. Carnegie (ed.), *Afro-Caribbean Villages in Historical Perspective.* In *Slavery & Abolition*, 11(1):121-25.

______. 1992. 'Race, Class, and Gender in the Transition to Freedom'. In *The Meaning of Freedom: Economics, Politics, and Culture after Slavery*, Frank McGlynn and Seymour Drescher (eds.), 257-290. Pittsburgh: University of Pittsburgh Press.

Smith, Keithlyn B., and Fernando C. Smith. 1988. *To Shoot Hard Labour: The Life and Times of Samuel Smith, an Antiguan Working Man, 1877-1982*. 2nd ed. Scarborough, Ontario: Edan.

Solien, Nancie L. 1959. 'The Nonunilineal Descent Group in the Caribbean and Central America'. *American Anthropologist* 61:578-83.

______. 1971. 'West Indian Characteristics of the Black Carib'. In *Peoples and Cultures of the Caribbean*. Michael M. Horowitz (ed.), 133-42. Garden City, Natural History Press.

Stewart, John. 1823. *A View of the Past and Present State of the Island of Jamaica*. Edinburgh: Oliver and Boyd.

Thoden van Velzen, H. U. E., and W. van Wetering. 1988. *The Great Father and the Danger: Religious Cults, Material Forces, and Collective Fantasies in the World of the Surinamese Maroons*. Dordrecht: Foris.

Thomas-Hope, Elizabeth M. 1978. 'The Establishment of a Migration Tradition: British West Indian Movements to the Hispanic Caribbean in the Century after Emancipation'. In *Caribbean Social Relations*. Colin G. Clarke (ed.), 66-81. Liverpool: Centre for Latin American Studies, Monograph Series No. 8.

______. 1986. 'Caribbean Diaspora, The Inheritance of Slavery'. In *The Caribbean in Europe: Aspects of the West Indian Experience in Britain, France and the Netherlands*. Colin Brock (ed.), 15-35. London: Frank Cass.

______. 1992. *Explanation in Caribbean Migration*. London: Macmillan.

Tomich, Dale. 1991. '*Une Petite Guinée*: Provision Ground and Plantation in Martinique, 1830-1848'. In Berlin and Morgan, q.v., 68-91.

Trouillot, Michel-Rolph. 1988. *Peasants and Capital: Dominica in the World Economy.* Baltimore: The Johns Hopkins University Press.

______. 1989. Review of C. V. Carnegie (ed.), *Afro-Caribbean Villages in Historical Perspective.* In *Social and Economic Studies*, 38:321-25.

Vernon, Diane. 1989. 'Some Prominent Features of Ndjuka Maroon Medicine. *Nieuwe West-Indische Gids/ New West Indian Guide*, 63(3-4):209-21.

Cultural Complexity after Freedom: Nevis and Beyond

KAREN FOG OLWIG

Much of the research on the post-emancipation Caribbean has been concerned with the strategies adopted by the freed as they sought to carve out a life of their own after the abolition of slavery. Two main avenues toward freedom are often delineated; both avenues involve a withdrawal from the plantations, but each applies radically different means toward this end. One route led to the establishment of free villages on the home island but outside the plantation sphere, whereas the other was oriented toward emigration to areas of greater economic and social opportunities, usually outside the island society. These two approaches have led some scholars to view African-Caribbean culture as rooted in peasant-like communities developing at the margins of the plantations, and others to emphasize the strong tradition for mobility and migration in African-Caribbean culture.

Inspired by some of the recent theories of cultural complexity, I shall suggest that the quest for freedom in post-emancipation Nevis was not unidirectional, in the sense that the emancipated put into social practice a specific set of shared cultural values developed during slavery. By the time of emancipation West Indian societies had long been characterized by several different 'cultural traditions', which influenced the way in which freedom was perceived and enacted in social life. Aspects of Caribbean cultural discourse and social practice which appear contradictory and hence difficult to interpret, if they are viewed within a conceptual framework of a single integrated, coherent cultural entity, can be subjected to analysis and interpretation, if they are examined in the light of the complex cultural processes that have characterized the island society through time. The patterns of rooting and mobility, which have been documented to be strategies of great significance during the post-emancipation period, reflect attempts to come to terms with the cultural complexity that has characterized Caribbean societies before and after emancipation.

In this article I shall analyse the cultural processes that characterized Nevis during the post-emancipation era. I shall thereby demonstrate that cultural complexity is not a recent phenomenon associated with the modern world of transnational relations but is part of the global systems of European expansion which have characterized the world for many centuries. The cultural complexity that is often thought to be the modern antithesis of tradition is a traditional, fundamental, dimension of life in the Caribbean.

APPROACHES TO THE POST-EMANCIPATION CARIBBEAN

The emancipated found it difficult to harvest the fruits of freedom within the plantocratic and patriarchal plantation systems (Hall 1971; Frucht 1975–76; Bolland 1981; Rodney 1981a; Olwig 1985, 1993), and many therefore opted to leave the plantations where they had been slaves. They adopted essentially two routes in pursuit of freedom. The first involved acquiring land and settling as small farmers in free villages outside the plantations (Marshall 1968; Mintz 1974, 1985; Besson 1984; Olwig 1985; Carnegie 1987; Trouillot 1989). The second concerned migration in order to take advantage of opportunities outside the sphere of influence of the plantation system, either by moving to urban areas or by leaving the local colonial society entirely (Patterson 1978; Thomas-Hope 1978; Richardson 1983). Only a small minority of the freed were able to aspire to upward mobility in the plantation society. They did this primarily by obtaining an education which qualified them for positions as school teachers or, more rarely, civil servants in the colonial administration (R.T. Smith 1982; Lowes 1987; Olwig 1990, 1993).

The delineation of several different patterns of social and economic development in the free Caribbean should not lead to the conclusion that the freed were thereby segmented into rigidly defined groupings. The identification of the former slaves either as plantation labourers, small farmers, and urban workers or as emigrants who opted out does not reflect actual social and economic life among the freed. Few small farmers were independent economically, and they frequently sought wage employment on plantations. Likewise, most plantation labourers carried on some sort of small farming, at least on a subsistence level (Frucht 1967; Rodney 1981b; R. T. Smith 1982). The acquisition of small plots of land by the freed, which occurred in many post-emancipation Caribbean societies, therefore, did not signify the rise of a population of independent farmers. Rather, it indicated a desire on the part of the freed to acquire land where they might settle in houses of their own and maintain some form of subsistence agriculture and thereby establish some autonomy within the colonial societies.

The widespread migration after emancipation displayed a similarly complex pattern. Few expected the move from their home community to involve a permanent resettlement elsewhere. Migration was viewed as a means of exploring opportunities which were supplementary, not alternative, to economic activities within the local community. In fact, many emigrated in order to acquire sufficient funds with which to purchase property and to afford better education for children at home – important avenues to achieve middle-class status. As noted by Elizabeth Thomas-Hope, 'lower class reference groups (as compared with those of the upper classes) remained predominantly local, so that the linkages of migrants with the home society were in most cases retained, and their eventual return constantly envisaged as a way of realizing their success' (1978:76; cf. Thomas-Hope this volume). While the lower-class segment of the population sought upward mobility in the home community through temporary migration, members of the established local middle classes emigrated in order to pursue professions abroad (Lowes this volume).

The picture of the free Caribbean that emerges from these studies is one of networks of interrelationships between people exploring a variety of social and economic opportunities on and off their island of birth. These relations cross-cut standard social, economic, and geographic categorization. The complex and fluid character of Caribbean social and economic relations in the post-emancipation era seems to have become a traditional pattern of some persistence. Thus important themes in studies of the contemporary Caribbean have been such features as occupational multiplicity (Comitas 1973), overlapping kin networks (Philpott 1968; Dirks 1972; Gussler 1980; Olwig 1985), and transnational societies (Sutton and Chaney 1987; Georges 1990; Glick-Schiller *et al.* 1991, Olwig 1993).

So far little attention has been devoted to the cultural implications of the whole complex of relations. On the contrary, in keeping with scholarly traditions within anthropology, studies of Caribbean culture have tended to delineate and analyse distinct, integrated, and bounded cultural units which are believed to provide natural frameworks of existence for different groups of people. Much of the anthropological discussion has been concerned with ascertaining the proper level of analysis of these unitary wholes. Thus cultural wholes have been equated with such entities as colonial societies integrated by shared British colonial values and practices (R. T. Smith 1967); various ethnic groups who maintain and further develop their particular cultural heritage (M. G. Smith 1965); occupational groups such as peasantries or plantation labourers who have developed distinct ways of life through time (Mintz 1974), and classes whose cultural orientation is informed by the 'struggle between labor and capital' (Rodney 1981b).

The various aspects of Caribbean culture have been analysed and subjected to widely different forms of interpretation depending on which perspective has been adopted as a framework of analysis. In the work of R. T. Smith, for example, middle-class norms and values have been an important subject of investigation because they represent a significant force, even though he acknowledged that the cultural orientation of the lower classes is somewhat different (1982). In the work inspired by Sidney Mintz, on the other hand, great emphasis has been placed on those cultural aspects that are unique to peasant culture (Mintz 1974; Besson 1984; Olwig 1985). The question arises, however, whether cultural distinction, integration, and wholeness are useful concepts in the study of Caribbean culture.

In a critical reappraisal of the concept of culture (Handler 1985; see also Malkki 1992), the anthropologists' preoccupation with distinct, integrated, and spatially bounded cultures has been seen as revealing a European form of thinking that is tied to the ideology of nationalism. In nationalist thought cultures are viewed as natural entities consisting of people who share a unique cultural heritage by virtue of being born and raised in particular areas. Nationalism rose to prominence in Europe during the nineteenth century and provided an important ideological basis for the establishment and consolidation of distinct and clearly bounded nation states. A nationalist way of thinking so closely tied to a European concept of culture is a questionable analytical tool in cross-cultural research. This critique of the close relation between cultural entities and the nationalistic enterprise has also been fuelled by historical and anthropological studies of the invention of tradition, which occurred as part of the establishment of national cultures in Europe and European colonies in the third world (Hobsbawm and Ranger 1983).

During the last few years attempts have been made to develop a more complex concept of culture, where movement, positioning, and interpretation are seen to be key features. An important point of view is presented by Appadurai (1990, 1991) and Hannerz (1992), whose work on cultural complexity is inspired by a realization that most human beings today are situated in a global ecumene characterized by world-wide movements of people, things, images, and knowledge. For them, the reinterpretation of global processes and impacts within local contexts is of primary importance. According to Appadurai these global flows (or scapes, as he chooses to term them) will be experienced as disparate and characterized by disjunction, and meaningful cultural contexts of life can only be created through the construction of 'imagined worlds', characterized by a coherence and order which bear little resemblance to the fragmentary and ruptured global landscape encountered in actual social life. In Appadurai's view anthropologists should pay particular attention to the role of the 'imaginative resources of lived, local experience' (1991:196).

In the work of Barth, global flows do not necessarily present a disorderly landscape in that he envisions the flows in the form of '"streams" of cultural traditions' which exhibit 'an empirical clustering of certain elements in syndromes that tend to persist over time' or, in other words, a 'degree of coherence over time' (Barth 1989:130, 131). These traditions are not invariable or permanent, however, in that their elements are modified when persons interact with one another and reinterpret the streams. The 'cultural construction of reality' that occurs at the local and regional level results from individuals engaged in 'multiple, more or less discrepant, universes of discourse' constructing 'different, partial and simultaneous worlds in which they move' (ibid.: 130). For Barth, these worlds are not just imagined but are grounded in social interaction where cultural meaning is constantly being reinterpreted. In what follows, I have drawn particularly on Barth's analysis.

So far most of the work on cultural complexity has been of a theoretical nature, largely because this conceptualization of culture is new, and because it is most relevant in the context of phenomena which either have tended to be overlooked in the past or have become apparent only recently. Global cultural flows, and the related cultural complexity, do not figure as new phenomena in the Caribbean but rather are something which has characterized much of the history of the area. Complex cultural processes have not yet been highlighted in Caribbean anthropological research but have tended to be downplayed as a crosscurrent disturbing the documentation and analysis of Caribbean culture. I would suggest that important insights into the nature of Caribbean culture can be gained if Caribbean life is seen to be informed by several different cultural traditions of some persistence and internal coherence. These traditions present the local population with various cultural elements which people can combine and interpret in different ways. This, in turn, leads to different social practices as individuals position themselves in relation to these traditions and engage in a cultural construction of reality as they see it.

THREE CULTURAL TRADITIONS IN NEVIS

By the time of emancipation, three cultural traditions, which can be seen to be related to the arrival of three groups of people on the island, can be delineated for Nevis. Since these groups had rather different social and economic roles in island society, various aspects of the cultural traditions came be to elaborated upon and emphasized in the island society.

The first cultural tradition to be established on the island is that connected with the development during the 1600s of a colonial society based on plantations. It is associated with the British settlers who came from the hierarchical rural society of early modern England, where inferiors found their place in an occupational, hierarchical family under the headship of a patriarch. In the West Indies, the patriarch evolved into a slave master, who personally or through a manager headed a large workforce of slaves, most of whom occupied such a lowly position in the hierarchy that they had no social identity except as their owner's property. This patriarchal system was not merely economic, however; for it was associated with familial traditions and institutions that, in various permutations, presented the under class – first white servants and then black slaves – with possibilities for expressing a cultural identity of their own making within an otherwise oppressive plantation system. Among these opportunities were local festivities in connection with the church year, such as Christmas mummings, and institutions associated with the agricultural cycle, such as markets. As the patriarchal family system evolved into the mature plantation system, the hierarchical order became expressed in ostentatious displays of a lavish life style on the part of the masters through the construction of spacious great houses, the consumption of luxurious material goods, and the use of numerous slaves as domestic servants for the planter family and as sexual objects for the master.

The second cultural factor was not a tradition in the strict sense of the word, in that it did not consist of one coherent organization of cultural beliefs and social practices but was a mixture of socio-cultural relations and values associated with the African slaves who were brought to the island from the early period of colonization. The slaves shared certain African cultural principles (Mintz and Price 1976), however, which became reconstituted in a subaltern African-Caribbean cultural tradition within the plantation society. An important cultural principle was found in the notion of kinship as based on relations of rights and obligations operating between elders and minors who were biological or adopted kinsmen. Kin groups, therefore, expanded or contracted depending on the elders' ability to attract and sustain a following. The kin groups, which provided a basic form of social organization, were cross-cut by religious cults – often connected with music, dance, and the use of masks – focused on local spirits, which drew participants from different kin groups. Another important principle was found in the common situation of belonging to several different, sometimes even opposed, partly overlapping socio-cultural groupings.

Subsistence farming which the slaves were allowed to perform in the marginal areas of the plantations was one of the most important loci for the emergence of an African-Caribbean cultural tradition. It led to the development of economic and social relations among the slaves, both on the provision grounds themselves and at the island's markets where slaves could sell their produce. Kin (fictive or bilateral) and affinal relations provided an important organizational framework for these activities. The relations which slaves developed among themselves were celebrated at wakes, in connection with births or burials, when they gathered to recognize a new member of their community or to show the dead their last respects. Other informal ties were created when slaves met during Sunday afternoons and on holidays recognized by the British planters to dance, drink, and play music together.

The plantation structure demarcated a hierarchical, bounded unit where each person was accorded a particular place. The slave community, in contrast, consisted of networks of overlapping ties developed within the confines of the plantation among people who were co-workers in the agricultural production, or across different plantations among people who were kinsmen or spouses, economic partners in the subsistence or market economy, co-performers in music and dance, or drinking buddies. Furthermore, whereas the plantation units were controlled by masters of European cultural background who admitted only a limited number into their cultural universe, the slave community's relations were diffuse and oriented toward African-Caribbean cultural values and practices.

By the end of the eighteenth century, a third cultural tradition developed on Nevis, when British missionaries, in particular the Methodists, became an influential force on the island. This tradition was closely connected with an ideology of respectability which had arisen among the European middle class during the course of the eighteenth century as part of the process leading to the modern nation state. The ideology of respectability with its emphasis on '"decent and correct" manners and morals and a proper attitude toward sexuality', had become a means whereby the growing middling classes in Great Britain displayed their moral superiority and hence their claim to respect in society (Mosse 1985:1-2). Respect was a central element in the attempts on the part of those in the middling class to legitimate their special position *vis-à-vis* the lower and upper classes, since they believed that respectability alone, not status or rank, should constitute the measuring scale of social standing. The ideology of respectability was also based on notions of equality and self-improvement through hard work and industriousness, with male-headed nuclear families as the main social units. From the 1780s, when Methodist missionaries began to work on Nevis, respectability became an increasingly influential cultural force. Missionaries preached among the slaves, who were attracted by their promises of equality to all 'in the sight of God' (Blackman 1988:2) and respectability in society to those who led a decent life.

During slavery the main importance of Methodism was the introduction of a socially recognized institution positioned outside the plantation regime, where slaves were allowed to meet and gain some respect in society. Since the proponents of respectability idealized an egalitarian society of hard-working and pious families, they were in ideological opposition to the plantocratic system with its feudal roots. As the plantocracy lost its power during the last part of the nineteenth century, the ideology of respectability and its associated social institutions gradually attained a dominant position in colonial society. Unlike the planters, who regarded African-Caribbeans as inferior beings naturally relegated to the lower levels of society, the missionaries saw African-Caribbeans as potentially equal in humanity, provided they abandoned their savage ways and adopted the faith of the missionaries and the life style related to it. Most of the freed and their descendants were not willing (or able) to undergo such a complete conversion, however.

By emancipation the three different cultural traditions had become a fact of life on Nevis. During slavery, the cultural traditions were associated with different population groups: planters of British background oriented toward the upper classes, labourers of African background associated with slave status, and missionaries and teachers affiliated with the rising middle class. After emancipation most of those of British background returned to Europe, leaving Nevis to the African-Caribbean ex-slaves, along with a few missionaries and representatives of the imperial government. The cultural traditions associated with the planters and the missionaries continued to be of central importance, however, largely because a small group of planters continued to own land on Nevis, and the educational system remained closely affiliated with the Methodist and Anglican churches.

The African-Caribbeans had to position themselves in relation to these traditions, as they created new lives after emancipation. How they did this depended on their personal background and access to social and economic resources. The cultural values and social expectations inherent in the different cultural traditions were reinterpreted by the enslaved, later freed, Nevisians. They did this primarily in rituals associated with the cultural traditions of the planters and missionaries. As the emancipated began to assert themselves as free citizens, however, they developed their own social institutions, where various elements of these traditions could be accommodated.

POST-EMANCIPATION SOCIETY ON NEVIS

The Plantation System

The early period of freedom on Nevis was to a great extent characterized by the attempt of the dominant plantocracy to maintain the old plantation hierarchy and all its privileges. Its aim was to secure the availability of inexpensive labour, and throughout the nineteenth century, the planters sought to keep labourers on the estates by various kinds of bondage. The apprenticeship system, a temporary form of bondage instituted in connection with emancipation, was exploited by the planters who, in the words of a Methodist minister, did not miss any 'nook in the law' that permitted them to impose 'hardship' on the labourers.[1] It was clear to the minister, however, that if the planters wished to 'retain the services of their former Negroes, they must bind them to the soil by a more enlightened and liberal policy . . .' Such enlightenment did not occur; on the contrary, planters persisted in their old ways. When apprenticeship expired in 1838, they offered wages described as 'very near to the door of subsistence' (Hall 1971:58) and instituted legislation to prevent 'the clandestine and fraudulent departure of Debtors and Persons under Contract of Service'.[2] With no Crown land on Nevis, squatting on public lands was not possible, and laws prohibiting trespass on private lands were so strictly enforced that there was virtually no squatting on the island.[3]

When subsistence-level wages proved too difficult for the planters to pay, they introduced a crop-sharing, or *métayer*, system, whereby workers received one half to one third of the crops instead of wages, and by the 1860s, all of the functioning estates were 'wholly or partially using métairie system'.[4] This was described by one visitor to the island as a 'conservative measure' reflecting 'submission to adverse circumstances' rather than 'enterprising struggle to overcome them'. Cane cultivation continued to be carried out in the old way, 'the hoe and the hand being the chief implement and power employed' (Davy 1854:485).

By maintaining the old plantation system, the planters succeeded in retaining their position of dominance in relation to the workers. T. Erskine Archibald, a planter on Nevis, testified on 24 May 1883 to the Royal Commission appointed to inquire into the state of the West Indian islands that there was no legislation concerning the métayer system, for which reason many workers had been victims of disagreements between planters and workers, where the former had 'allowed the crop of the latter to perish on the ground by a persistent refusal to grind the canes, or turned the estate stock into the field of young sprouts to feed them down' (House of Commons 1884:116). Another witness, Abraham Swanston, a mason, saw the whole system as a way of making the labourers dependent on the planters: 'Some people give out land "on share system" to bind the labourers to the estate; if they go to another estate, the original employers take land away' (ibid.:100). Mounting dissatisfaction with the continuance of the harsh plantocratic system on the island led workers to burn cane fields on several occasions during the latter part of the nineteenth century.[5]

Such workers' resistance towards the planter regime should not, however, be interpreted to mean that plantation work was regarded as undesirable. It was generally accepted that wage labour on plantations constituted a welcome supplementary income, and those planters who offered decent wages or who rented out their land on a long-term basis experienced much less difficulty in finding a sufficient labour supply (House of Commons 1884:110-11). Many planters were not willing – or able – to comply with these demands, and during the latter part of the nineteenth century the estates underwent a general period of decline. By the turn of the century, the old planter class had almost disappeared from the island, and their estates were falling into ruin. Many of the estates seen by Antonia Williams, who visited the island from England during the Christmas season of 1908, were described as in decay, which made it difficult to imagine the planter life on them 'in the old days'.[6] Estate land remained in the hands of a few private owners until the 1930s; after that virtually all the old planter families returned to Europe, and most of the land was acquired by the colonial administration.

The Mission of Respectability

As the planters lost their dominant position in colonial society, the ideology of respectability advocated by the missionaries grew in importance. According to the Methodists the only secure foundation for the colony was 'a steady, settled, pious peasantry'.[7] The establishment of such a peasantry depended on the freed being able to acquire their own land to cultivate and to establish family life based on church-blessed marriage and faithful worship of God, preferably in the Methodist chapel. The land issue was difficult, since virtually all land was owned by a plantocracy who viewed the land not just as an important economic resource but also as a means of controlling the labour force and, hence, of maintaining their position of privilege in society. A few days after the Emancipation Act was promulgated, a missionary heard that some of the freed had expressed a desire to 'procure a piece of land, erect a house, collect their family around them'. He immediately envisioned the plantation fields being divided into smaller lots each containing 'the house & of a free, pious, happy family', and he saw the 'liberate Negro' becoming 'as fond of industry, good order, and domestic comforts, as the peasantry of Britain'.[8] The missionaries were sorely disappointed when only the most well-to-do among the freed were able to obtain sufficient land of their own to become small farmers.

A few years later the missionaries saw a glimmer of hope when share-cropping was instituted, and land was allotted for individual workers and their families.

> In Nevis it really appears as though the working people are in a transition state between labourers & respectable tenants. There are a great Number of Acres of Cane land under cultivation by the Labourers for half the produce . . . Such an arrangement gives our people the greater ability to help themselves – If the Land Owners were only generally willing, I believe this could now easily raise up a class of Middle Men who would be what the Farmer is in England.[9]

It soon became apparent, however, that share cropping was not profitable for most people and did not lead to a settled peasant population but rather encouraged, or even necessitated, emigration in order to procure the cash needed to make ends meet.[10] The missionary reports throughout the nineteenth century, therefore, reflect disappointment about the continued landlessness of the vast majority and about the persistent emigration from Nevis that resulted. Regret was caused not only by a concern with the well being of the local society but also by an interest in the well-being of the local congregations, not the least their financial basis.

A persistent theme in the missionaries' reports concerned the importance of family life based on holy matrimony. They had no doubt that when the freed had an opportunity to 'collect their family around them' on the plot of land they hoped to acquire, this family would consist of husband and wife joined in holy matrimony and their children. They would form the farm unit with the father and sons cultivating the ground, the mother doing her housework assisted by the daughters, who also sold the family's produce at the market.[11] The Methodists did not, however, see the general establishment of the family unions they had visualized. Throughout the nineteenth century, they fought against extra-marital relations, and they were shocked to find that many respectable members of the Methodist Society allowed their daughters to live at home with 'bastard children'.[12] They consistently expelled members who themselves engaged in what the church perceived as immoral conduct. Among the excluded were a 'Chapel keeper by whom two young women are with child', a woman who 'openly received into her house a young man who was keeping company with one of her daughters', living with her in the mother's house,[13] and a female leader in the Methodist Society who had in her house and out-rooms 'no less than three couples living in fornication'.[14]

For the Methodists, therefore, it was a constant struggle to maintain an adequate number of God-fearing and moral members. As one missionary noted:

> I am satisfied that one principal cause [of decline in W.I. churches] is the defective social relationships, which our people sustain one to another. We no sooner admit a number of young people into Society, than we have to put them out or an equal quantity, because of this falling into the common sins of the country . . . there is a great want among our people of the possession and enjoyment of vital godliness . . . They seem to fancy that all is right if only their names are recorded on the Class-papers.[15]

The missionaries appear to have had no difficulty in recruiting new members, who saw the inclusion of their names in the membership lists of the Methodist Society as a significant act in and of itself. It was, however, much more difficult to recruit the sort of members that the Methodists desired, largely because the missionaries failed to convince their congregations of the desirability of adopting a life of British respectability that excluded the values and practices associated with the other cultural traditions on Nevis. The only people who made a conscious effort to lead the respectable lives expected by the missionaries were those who had 'a house to live in – a horse to ride and other property',[16] and who therefore could lay claim to middle-class status. For them, respectability became an important means to validate the privileged position in colonial society which they had managed to acquire. One of the most important institutions for the middle class became the private Excelsior School, founded in 1895 to provide secondary education for children of respectable parents. The school came to function as a gate keeper controlling who was admitted to the local educated elite and was thus able to gain access to civil-service posts vacated by the British.

The African-Caribbean Ccommunity

In their quest for freedom the emancipated had to deal with two cultural traditions which were not compatible with that within the African-Caribbean community. While the cultural traditions connected with the planters and missionaries are relatively well documented, that of the African-Caribbean community was rarely expressed directly but rather was revealed through responses to the other more dominant ones. Without doubt the freed wished to acquire their own plots of land where they might gather their families and settle on their own, as described in the Methodist records. Among those who succeeded were the 39 persons who in 1848 purchased approximately 150 acres in small lots from plantation-owner George Pollard. Virtually all the new owners built houses on their land and moved there from the plantations.[17] In 1863 some 800 persons were listed as freeholders on Nevis, and by 1876, 2,135 freeholders were reported. Their lots were quite small; thus in 1876 only 129 freeholders possessed two acres or more.[18]

While the freed did not own enough land to settle as full-time farmers, they nevertheless had enough to establish a certain amount of independence in relation to the planters. This was quite apparent to the proprietor, MrBlake, who complained to the Royal Commission in 1884 that labourers did not work 'as many days as they might' owing to the 'selling out [of] estates to labourers, and making them independent' (House of Commons 1884:99). Although the freed did not become proper farmers or peasants, they were able to experience a degree of independence from the planters by living on own land and thus having the option of working for the planters when they wished, not when they were forced to do so. Furthermore, the possession of tiny lots gave the freed social standing in the community (Great Britain, West India Royal Commission 1884:113).

Another important aspect of the purchase of land was the opportunity to provide a place where the family might live. The African-Caribbean concept of the family, however, departed significantly from that of the missionaries. The most basic divergence was found in the greater importance which the freed attached to kin relations rather than to marriage and the nuclear family. Parents did not ban daughters from their homes because they had sexual relations without being married, nor did they reject grandchildren born out of wedlock.

The central importance of kin in relation to land is perhaps most clearly revealed in the concept of family land, which evolved on Nevis as in so many other Caribbean societies during the post-emancipation period. Most family land was passed on informally, outside the colonial legal system, although the terms of ownership are specified in a few wills recorded at the Court House. In one will various portions of land were divided among children of the deceased, but the 'House and acre of land attached to it' were set aside for the four children and were 'never to be sold or divided but kept as a home for them all'.[19]

In another will the land was bequeathed to the owner's nine children 'as tenants in common, for their sole use and benefit each child to have equal right with each other to the full employment of all . . . as long as they live and remain unmarried'. Widowed children were to have the right to return to the land at any time should they 'be in need of a residence'. The will specified, however, that 'no one of the nine children herein included shall take to the family residence herein bequeathed any friends, Husband, wife, or any other relation to the discomfort or annoyance of any of the other portion of the family or without the consent of all . . .'[20] This egalitarian, kin-based family home on a small plot of land held in common for ever by all descendants of the original owner, whether or not they actually used the land or resided on it, was quite different from the industrious father-headed peasant family unit busily working the land which was visualized by the missionaries.

It would be wrong, however, to give the impression that the Methodist mission was perceived primarily as a cumbersome body imposing various restrictions on life. The mission continued to be as highly valued and frequented by the African-Caribbean population as it had been during slavery. Services in the Methodist chapels were well attended, in particular the love feasts, where people were encouraged to bear witness to their faith through testimony in the church. When a love feast was held in Charlestown during the apprenticeship period, the chapel which could hold 1,100 was described as 'crowded to excess' and the missionary experienced no difficulty 'in filling up the time' and had to ask people to wait with their testimony as 'two and three rose together' to speak.[21] During the 1840s, when money was needed for a new chapel in Charlestown, missionaries began to hold tea meetings, fund-raising events organized by the minister, where tea and cake were served and religious testimony was encouraged.[22] These tea meetings became popular because they provided 'a sort of safety-valve to the social feelings of our young people' and presented occasions where people could display their oratorical talents. This latter aspect was a source of worry to the missionaries who feared that the performance aspect of the meetings was taking the upper hand.[23]

Cultural Discourses and Social Practices

The plantation system, the African-Caribbean community, and the Methodist mission of respectability each represented widely different, even contradictory, cultural traditions associated with vital contexts of life on the island. The plantations controlled virtually all the land, and the local population remained dependent on wage employment on the estates. The institutions of respectability established by missionaries offered means of gaining recognition and upward social mobility in the colonial society, but they also were places of congregation and religious fellowship outside the control of the planters. The African-Caribbean community embodied social and economic relations imbued with cultural values that constituted a basic context of life for people of African descent.

All three cultural traditions were of fundamental importance to the local population, yet they were contradictory and seemingly incompatible. Before and after freedom, individuals moved in and out of the socio-economic contexts connected with these cultural traditions, being dependent field labourers at one moment, self-reliant provision cultivators and traders at the market at other times, honourable leaders and Sunday school teachers at the Methodist Chapel on yet other occasions. They were sometimes dehumanized units of labour, sometimes responsible kinsmen helping a network of relatives, and respectable couples joined in holy matrimony and working to improve the social standing of themselves and their children. The African-Caribbean population reinterpreted these constant changes – and the widely different and largely irreconcilable roles which they involved – in rituals where elements associated with the three traditions were brought together and combined in various ways.

Christmas celebrations, which dated back to the early period of slavery, represent such a cultural discourse. These celebrations were patterned on British Christmas mumming traditions dating back to medieval times, with peasants dressed up in costumes (often in caricature of their masters), allowed to sing, dance, drink, and perform in the homes of their fellow workers as well as their masters. As a reward for this entertainment, treats were given to the performers. The West Indian Christmas festivities followed this pattern, and from a formal point of view mumming was seen as part of the cultural tradition of the planters – an important point if the mummings were to be allowed and recognized by the masters. This European form, however, combined a multitude of cultural elements. European-like costumes might be adorned with fantastic masks and head gear that reflected the dancers' African background; recognizably European dances such as the quadrille might be performed to African-Caribbean rhythms (Dirks 1987; Bettelheim 1988).

In the cultural tradition of the Christmas mummings, masters had to recognize the lowliest persons as human beings with performing traditions and talents of their own, and even had to endure their critical commentary. The masters tolerated the Christmas mummings, partly because the mummings belonged to their own cultural background and recognized their position of superiority, and partly because the mummings were confined to the brief Christmas season and therefore constituted no threat to the daily routine of life.

The missionaries were not so benign in their attitude to the Christmas celebrations, however. To them the drinking, dancing, and music associated with the festivities represented evils which played havoc with the real meaning of Christmas, namely the celebration of the birth of Christ. From an early date they preached against the 'gluttony, drunkenness, quarrelling, fighting, dancing, and carousing' which were associated with these celebrations (Watson 1817:502). But condemnation did not lead to disappearance. On the contrary, in the course of the nineteenth century, the emancipated incorporated aspects of the Methodist culture of respectability which by then had attained a central position in the island society.

Antonia Williams' account of her visit to Nevis during the Christmas season of 1908 provides a fine description of the way in which elements from the three different cultural traditions were brought together in the Christmas festivities held by the African-Caribbean population. The mummers who performed for planters as well as for fellow villagers included three groups. Men 'in white masks and head dresses of peacocks' feathers about three feet high, and their clothes sewn all over with penny glasses and postcards, and any other tinsel', danced 'a mixture of quadrille, lancer and war dance', did 'discordant' singing, and played a drum and various home made instruments. A group was dressed in 'an odd mixture of European skirt and apron, and sort of war dress' decorated with postcards, and wore 'fringe and paper frills on their head' and 'white muslin masks with funny smug expressions'; they 'brought a Maypole and danced around it very slowly'. Several groups did 'representations' of David and Goliath, 'repeating long passages of scripture and a few quotations from Shakespeare' followed by dancing to drums.[24]

At the beginning of the twentieth century the Christmas mummings clearly incorporated elements from the cultural tradition connected with the planters, for example, the upper-class dances of quadrille and lancer, as well as English folk traditions such as the Maypole dance and war dance. Elements of the cultural tradition of respectability were most visible in the quotations from the Bible, and an assortment of European material culture included postcards, white muslin masks believed to have originated in Tyrol (Bettelheim 1988:59), and penny glasses. At the same time the mode of singing, dancing, and playing music remained very much within the African-Caribbean cultural tradition. Within the old English Christmas mummings, a cultural form had been found which allowed the values and practices of the subaltern African-Caribbean cultural tradition to be brought to the forefront.

A similar transformation can be detected in the African-Caribbean version of the tea meetings, which also evolved during the nineteenth century. As in the case of the Christmas mummings, the cultural framework was British, in this case, the fund-raising events which the Methodists began to organize at the time of emancipation. Within the formal structure of the tea meeting, however, the participants engaged in a hidden discourse on the nature and worth of the different cultural traditions in the island society. The minister was replaced by a toastmaster, church leaders by a court of king and queen and their attendants, pious testimonials by daring and virtuosic verbal performances, and God-praising congregations by an often raucous audience who had to be kept in check by the toastmaster. By employing the cultural form of the tea meetings the African-Caribbean people brought together different and contradictory strands of the cultural traditions which had an important impact on their lives. By giving elements of the other cultural traditions prominence in the ritual, they challenged the dominance of the tradition associated with English respectability.[25]

Toward the end of the nineteenth century, such discursive practices within the framework of ritual found a parallel in social institutions. One such institution was family land, where the private ownership of land was transformed to collective possession of land held in common by descendants of the original, legally registered owner. By thus transforming the terms of land ownership, a number of attitudes toward land, associated with the different cultural traditions on the island, were taken into account. Family land allowed Nevisians to become landowners, a position of great social importance within the cultural traditions associated with the missionaries and planters. Yet at the same time family land vested ownership in larger groups, which recognized the kin ties and obligations emphasized within the African-Caribbean cultural tradition.

The importance of family land as an institution where significant but divergent cultural expectations might be combined is borne out by the great symbolic value that is attached to family land. As Jean Besson has noted, family land is acknowledged to be an extremely scarce resource from an economic point of view, since an increasing number of people have a share in a small piece of land, yet it is a valuable and unlimited resource from a symbolic vantage point (1987; see also Besson's chapter in this volume). Family land can be regarded as a valuable resource only if it is not, in fact, used as an economic resource on which people have to rely for their daily subsistence. The institution of family land, therefore, is dependent on migration, which means that many do not take advantage of their claim to family land. By having a claim, however, migrants are assured a place to which they can return should they wish to do so, and in this way family land can be seen to have facilitated the act of emigrating.

Migration itself can also be viewed as a means of dealing with the three cultural traditions and the different conditions of life which they presented to the local population. Migration was desirable for those who rejected a servile life on estates and the subsistence-level wages offered by planters. Migration was also attractive to those who did not succeed in becoming respectable small farmers living on their own land, and it offered a way out for the many kinsmen who realized that a small lot of family land could only accommodated a few people. Migration was regarded as a temporary move which would enable the migrants to return to Nevis with the capital to resolve the cultural contradictions in island society; for their acquired resources would enable them to purchase land and thus gain prestige. Their desire was to become small farmers with sufficient economic means to give their children a good education. In this way they would consolidate their positions as respectable members of the rising local middle class. At the same time, they also wanted to help kinsmen and neighbours and thus receive recognition within the African-Caribbean community. While some succeeded in achieving their goal, at least in part, for most it remained an unfulfilled dream, and they either stayed away permanently or returned with little or no gain.

CONCLUSION

The co-existence of contradictory cultural traditions associated with essential aspects of life in Caribbean societies has constituted a problem for anthropologists who view culture as consisting of bounded, integrated, and autonomous entities. Analysis suggests that cultural development in the Caribbean – particularly during the post-emancipation era when the emancipated were granted greater freedom of movement – should not be sought in distinct cultures corresponding to local communities of peasants or plantation labourers, to different colonial societies, or to various ethnic groups. The three cultural traditions delineated for Nevis might, at one level, appear to be similar to the cultural entities that anthropologists seek to delineate in their studies. The Nevisian traditions did not, however, constitute bounded, autonomous, and independent cultural units but were associated with limited spheres of life, each of central importance to the

African-Caribbean population. Few, if any, people were able to confine their lives within a single cultural tradition and moved among the others as the need arose. The cultural tradition associated with settled farmers, as advocated by the missionaries, perhaps most resembles the time-honoured anthropological cultural units. It is natural therefore that peasant communities have been regarded as basic socio-cultural units in European nationalist thinking.

This case study in Nevis points to the importance of not reifying culture as a number of concrete and bounded entities. It suggests that a fruitful approach may be found in examining the different cultural traditions which developed in the Caribbean and in the way the local populations interpreted and acted upon these traditions. On Nevis interpretation took place within the framework of street festivals and tea meetings, both of which incorporated 'elements and energies from many traditions and rituals' (Bettelheim 1988:46). Social practices related to the three cultural traditions were combined within institutions such as family land which allowed people to fulfil the various social expectations associated with these cultural traditions. Festivals, tea meetings, and family land were not unique to Nevis but flourished in much of the Caribbean. Street festivals existed during slavery, whereas the tea meeting has been described as a 'major form of entertainment' during the last part of the nineteenth century (Abrahams and Szwed 1983:41, 46). Family land has likewise been documented for many Caribbean societies (Besson 1987, and in this volume). The prevalence of such Caribbean institutions where elements of several different, even contradictory, cultural traditions are combined in creative ways, clearly demonstrates the deep roots and profound significance of a culturally complex way of life in the area.

ACKNOWLEDGEMENTS

This analysis is based on my book *Global Culture, Island Identity* (1993). I would like to thank Birgitte Refslund Sørensen, Kenneth Olwig, and John Liep for their helpful comments on this chapter.

NOTES

1. Methodist Missionary Society Archives, Wesleyan Methodist Missionary Society Archives (London), Archive West Indies, School of Oriental and African Studies, London, Correspondence West Indies General, 1807-57, microfiches 1-727 (hereafter C): 512: 31 October 1834.
2. Nevis Blue Book (hereafter N), Nevis Archives at Alexander Hamilton Museum, Charlestown, Nevis, 1842:56.
3. N 1862:280-82; 1876:246; 1880.
4. N 1866:274.
5. N 1864:60; John Jones' Diaries, 1887, 1893-97, in Nevis Archives at Alexander Hamilton Museum, Charlestown, Nevis, 1895: 20 February.

6. Antonia Williams, 'A Tour through the West Indies', 1908-9:43-48. Manuscript in the library, The University of the West Indies, Mona, Jamaica. I wish to thank Barry Higman for having transcribed Antonia Williams' travel journal.
7. Methodist Missionary Society Archives, Wesleyan Methodist Missionary Society Archives (London), Archive West Indies, School of Oriental and African Studies, London. Correspondence, Antigua, 1833-90, microfiches 989-1296 (hereafter CA): 1029:10 August 1843.
8. C 506:22 August 1834.
9. CA 1032:16 January 1844.
10. CA 1068:13 March 1852.
11. C 506:22 August 1834.
12. CA 1068:13 March 1852.
13. CA 1130:8 June 1861.
14. CA 1132:10 September 1861.
15. CA 1174:26 November 1866.
16. CA 1013: September 1840.
17. Pollard Manuscripts, Title Deeds, Plantations in Nevis, 1739-1863, Dorset Record Office, County Hall, Dorchester, England.
18. N 1863, 1876.
19. Record of Nevis wills, Registrar's Office, Court House, Charlestown, Nevis. Probate Register B.2., Vol. 1-B, 1880, 15 November 1893.
20. Record of Nevis wills: 30 December 1904.
21. C 575:26 January 1837.
22. CA 1013:26 October 1840.
23. CA 1130:10 September 1861.
24. Williams, 'A Tour through the West Indies', 52, 54, 58.
25. This account of the Nevisian tea meeting is based largely on Roger Abrahams' work (Abrahams 1983; Abrahams and Szwed 1983).

REFERENCES

Abrahams, Roger D. 1983. *The Man-of-Words in the West Indies*. Baltimore: The Johns Hopkins University Press.

Abrahams, Roger D., and John F. Szwed (eds.). 1983. 'Introduction'. In *After Africa*. New Haven: Yale University Press.

Appadurai, Arjun. 1990. 'Disjuncture and Difference in the Global Cultural Economy'. *Theory, Culture & Society* 7 (2/3):295-310.

______. 1991. 'Global Ethnoscapes: Notes and Queries for a Transnational Anthropology'. In *Recapturing Anthropology*, R. G. Fox (ed.), 191-210. Santa Fe: School of American Research Press.

Barth, Fredrik. 1989. 'The Analysis of Culture in Complex Societies'. *Ethnos* 54 (3/4):120-42.

Besson, Jean. 1984. 'Land Tenure in the Free Villages of Trelawny, Jamaica'. *Slavery & Abolition* 5:3-23.

______. 1987. 'A Paradox in Caribbean Attitudes to Land'. In *Land and Development in the Caribbean*, Jean Besson and Janet Momsen (eds.), 13-45. London: Macmillan.

Bettelheim, Judith. 1988. 'Jonkonny and Other Christmas Masquerades. In *Caribbean Festical Arts*, J. W. Nunley and J. Bettelheim (eds.), 39-83. Seattle: The Saint Louis Art Museum in association with the University of Washington Press.

Blackman, Francis (Woodie). 1988. *Methodism 200 Years in Barbados*. Bridgetown, Barbados.

Bolland, O. Nigel. 1981. 'Systems of Domination after Slavery: The Control of Land and Labor in the British West Indies after 1838'. *Comparative Studies in Society and History* 23:591-619.

Carnegie, Charles V. (ed.). 1987. *Afro-Caribbean Villages in Historical Perspective*. V. Carnegie

(ed.), 83-99. Kingston: African-Caribbean Institute of Jamaica Research Review, No. 2.
Comitas, Lambros. 1973. 'Occupational Multiplicity in Rural Jamaica' [1964]. In *Work and Family Life*, L. Comitas and D. Lowenthal (eds.), 157-73. Garden City, NY: Anchor Books.
Davy, John. 1854. *The West Indies, before and since Slave Emancipation*. London. Reprinted 1971, London: Frank Cass.
Dirks, Robert. 1972. 'Networks, Groups, and Adaptation in an Afro-Caribbean Community'. *Man* 7:565-85.
______. 1987. *The Black Saturnalia. Conflict and Its Ritual Expression on British West Indian Slave Plantations*. Gainsville: University of Florida Press.
Frucht, Richard. 1967. 'A Caribbean Social Type: Neither "Peasant" nor "Proletarian"'. *Social and Economic Studies* 13:295-300.
______. 1975-76. 'Emancipation and Revolt in the West Indies: St. Kitts, 1834'. *Science and Society* 39:199-214.
Georges, Eugenia. 1990. *The Making of a Transnational Community*. New York: New York Academy of Sciences.
Glick-Schiller, Nina, *et al.* (eds.). 1991. *Towards a Transnational Perspective on Migration*. New York: New York Academy of Sciences.
Great Britain. West India Royal Commission 1884. *Report of the West India Royal Commission. Part III: The Leeward Islands*. House of Commons, Sessional Papers, vol. 46.
Gussler, Judith D. 1980. 'Adaptive Strategies and Social Networks of Women in St. Kitts'. In *A World of Women*, Erika Bourguignon (ed.), 185-209. New York: Praeger.
Hall, Douglas. 1971. *Five of the Leewards 1834-1870*. Barbados: Caribbean Universities Press.
Handler, Richard. 1985. 'On Dialogue and Destructive Analysis: Problems in Narrating Nationalism and Ethnicity'. *Journal of Anthropological Research* 41:171-82.
Hannerz, Ulf. 1992. *Cultural Complexity*. New York: Columbia University Press.
Hobsbawm, Eric, and Terence Ranger (eds.). 1983. *The Invention of Tradition*. Cambridge: Cambridge University Press.
Lowes, Susan. 1987. 'Time and Motion in the Formation of the Middle Class in Antigua, 1834–1940'. Paper presented at the annual meeting of the American Anthropological Association, Chicago.
Malkki, Liisa. 1992. 'National Geographic: The Rooting of Peoples and the Territorialization of National Identity among Scholars and Refugees'. *Cultural Anthropology* 7 (2):24-44.
Marshall, Woodville K. 1968. 'Notes on Peasant Development in the West Indies since 1838'. *Social and Economic Studies* 17:252-63.
Mintz, Sidney W. 1974. *Caribbean Transformations*. Chicago: Aldine.
______. 1985. 'From Plantations to Peasantries in the Caribbean'. In *Caribbean Contours*, S. W. Mintz and Sally Price (eds.), 127-53. Baltimore: The Johns Hopkins University Press.
Mintz, Sidney W., and Richard Price. 1976. *An Anthropological Approach to the Afro-American Past: A Caribbean Perspective*. Philadelphia: Institute for the Study of Human Issues.
Mosse, George L. 1985. *Nationalism and Sexuality*. New York: Howard Fertig.
Olwig, Karen Fog. 1985. *Cultural Adaptation and Resistance on St. John*. Gainesville: University of Florida Press.
______. 1990. 'The Struggle for Respectability: Methodism and Afro-Caribbean Culture on 19th Century Nevis'. *Nieuwe West-Indische Gids/ New West Indian Guide* 64(3 & 4): 93-114.
______. 1993. *Global Culture, Island Identity: Continuity and Change in the Afro-Caribbean Community of Nevis*. Philadelphia: Harwood.
Patterson, Orlando. 1978. 'Migration in Caribbean Societies: Socioeconomic and Symbolic Resource'. In *Human Migration. Patterns and Policies*, W. H. McNeill and R. S. Adams (eds.), 106-45. Bloomington: Indiana University Press.
Philpott, Stuart B. 1968. 'Remittance Obligations: Social Networks and Choice among Montserratian Migrants in Britain'. *Man* 3:465-76.
Richardson, Bonham C. 1983. *Caribbean Migrants: Environmental and Human Survival on St.*

Kitts and Nevis. Knoxville: University of Tennessee Press.

Rodney, Walter. 1981a. 'Guyana: The Making of the Labour Force'. *Race & Class* 22:331-52.

______. 1981b. 'Plantation Society in Guyana'. *Review* 4:643-66.

Smith, M. G. 1965. *The Plural Society in the British West Indies*. Berkeley: University of California Press.

Smith, R. T. 1967. 'Social Stratification, Cultural Pluralism and Integration in West Indian Societies'. In *Caribbean Integration*, S. Lewis and T. Mathews (eds.), 226-58. Río Piedras: Institute of Caribbean Studies.

______. 1982. 'Race and Class in thePost-Emancipation Caribbean'. In *Racism and Colonialism*, R. Ross (ed.), 93-119. The Hague: Martinus Nijhoff.

Sutton, Constance R., and Elsa M. Chaney. 1987. 'The Caribbeanization of New York City and the Emergence of a Transnational Socio-Cultural System'. In *Caribbean Life in New York City*, C .R. Sutton and E. M. Chaney (eds.), 15-30. New York: Center for Migration Studies.

Thomas-Hope, Elizabeth M. 1978. 'The Establishment of a Migration Tradition: British West Indian Movements to the Hispanic Caribbean in the Century after Emancipation'. In *Caribbean Social Relations*, Colin G. Clarke (ed.), 66-81. Liverpool: Centre for Latin American Studies, Monograph Series No. 8.

Truillot, Michel-Rolph. 1989. 'Discourses of Rule and the Acknowledgement of the Peasantry in Dominica, W. I., 1838-1928'. *American Ethnologist* 16:704-18.

Watson, Richard. 1817. *A Defence of the Wesleyan-Methodist Mission in the West Indies*. In *Works*, vol 6. London: John Mason, 1835.

Part III
Migration and Resistance

Post-Emancipation Resistance in the Caribbean: An Overview

GAD HEUMAN

The post-emancipation Caribbean experienced a large number of riots and disturbances. Often violent, these outbreaks occurred across the region and often recurred in individual colonies. This essay seeks to describe some of the major outbreaks, beginning with the most important of them, the Morant Bay Rebellion in Jamaica. It also discusses riots elsewhere in the Caribbean: in Tobago, Barbados, Dominica, St. Croix, and St. Vincent. The study then attempts to analyse the disturbances and to seek common explanations for them. It concludes by examining briefly how the riots were perceived by the ruling authorities and how they were suppressed.

REBELLIONS AND RIOTS

On 11 October 1865 several hundred blacks marched into Morant Bay, the principal town in the parish of St. Thomas in the East. Led by Paul Bogle, the crowd's first objective was the police station where they attacked the police and took all the swords, guns, and pistols from the station before marching to the court house to confront the militia. A member of the vestry, the political body that administered the parish of St. Thomas in the East, saw people in the crowd brandishing the police arms and heard them cry 'Colour for colour!' and 'War, war!' As the mob surged forward, the custos and head of the parish, Baron von Ketelhodt, cried out, 'Peace!' and other officials called out 'Peace in Her Majesty's Name!' But the people responded 'No Peace! Hell today!'[1] In the end, the crowd burned down the court house and killed eighteen of the officials and militia. In the days which followed, the people killed two planters and attacked many outlying plantations in the parish.

The government's response was swift and brutal. Governor Edward Eyre declared martial law in the eastern part of Jamaica; he also despatched British troops to the parish and organized the Maroons to deal with the outbreak. They rampaged through the parish, often killing people without trial and burning homes as they went. Although the rebellion was quickly suppressed, the month-long period of martial law resulted in the deaths of more than four hundred blacks. The severity of the repression led to demands in England for Eyre's resignation and trial; the subsequent controversy surrounding the governor meant that the rebellion and the nature of its suppression became a *cause célèbre* in England. Eyre was recalled, but not before the House of Assembly had abolished itself and instituted direct rule from London.

The Morant Bay Rebellion was the most serious post-emancipation outbreak in Jamaica but not the only one. In 1848 the *Falmouth Post* reported a conspiracy among the ex-slaves in western Jamaica and regarded it as a basis for a possible insurrection. Although there was no general outbreak, localized protests occurred in various parts of the island. Later in the year, a riot took place in Brown's Town, St. Ann, in which two people were killed and several others badly wounded. Another riot followed on an estate in St. Thomas-in-the-Vale, when more than 150 estate workers resisted police seeking to execute warrants (Simmonds 1982:77, 84, 88).

A serious riot also broke out in August 1848 on an estate in the parish of St. Mary, where a collecting constable and two policemen were attacked and severely wounded by a crowd of at least two hundred people armed with sticks. When the police returned a week later to issue warrants against twenty-four people involved in the assault, they were confronted by five hundred men armed with sticks and some weapons. In the mêlée some policemen were badly hurt and all fled. Another detachment of police met the same fate the following week, and it took the 2nd West India Regiment to restore order (Simmonds 1982:85-86).

Two riots occurred in 1859. The first, in February, was directed against the toll-gates in several parts of Westmoreland. Residents tore down the toll-gates in at least four different places in the parish, suggesting a concerted campaign against them. Public feeling against the tolls had been vented in a petition sent to the governor six months earlier, but he had ignored it. When some of the offenders were tried for their part in the toll-gate assault, people attacked the police station. Peace was ultimately restored when troops arrived from Port Royal (Hall 1959:248; Simmonds 1982:123).

The second major riot in 1859 originated in a property dispute at Florence Hall Estate near the town of Falmouth. The controversy was between Theodore Buie, a coloured man, and his Scottish aunt who sought to evict him from the property. Buie and about sixty others were arrested, but before they could be brought to trial, a large crowd attacked the police station and freed them. As the crowd stoned the police station, the police fired on them. They killed two women and severely wounded eight or nine others, one of whom died a few days later. In the process, the crowd set fire to the police station and prevented anyone from extinguishing it. They also sought to burn down other parts of the town and succeeded in destroying the Falmouth wharf (Anon [1859]:10-13; Simmonds 1982:128; Holt 1992:267-68). Jamaica thus experienced a significant number of outbreaks in the post-emancipation period. But its experience was not unique in the Caribbean.

In Tobago, toward the end of April 1876, there were distinct signs of unrest on Roxborough estate in the Windward district. Roxborough was owned by a Barbadian who employed many Barbadian workers, some of whom were apparently involved in arson attacks on the estate. When a party of policemen were sent to arrest the alleged arsonists, a crowd resisted the police. One of the policemen, Corporal Belmanna, fired into the crowd, killing a Barbadian woman and injuring a Barbadian man. The incident triggered a major riot; the police retreated to the estate's court house which the crowd surrounded and attacked. They demanded that Belmanna be handed over to them; instead, he eventually agreed to leave the court house as a prisoner and to be tried later in court for murder. However, the crowd managed to pry him away from his escort and beat him severely. Belmanna subsequently died from his injuries (Brereton 1984:112-13).

In the same year, Barbados experienced serious riots over the issue of confederation. The question was whether Barbados would be joined politically in a federation with the Windward colonies; however, the Barbadian planter class was strongly opposed to this plan. Confederation would have resulted in Barbados becoming a Crown Colony and losing its House of Assembly and representative form of government. For the planters, this would have meant a loss of power. Blacks, on the other hand, saw distinct advantages in such a change: for example, they believed that wages would be raised under the proposed scheme. Initially, there was a riot in which blacks sought to break up a meeting of those opposed to federation, which led to stone throwing and some pistol shots. Subsequently, more threatening riots developed in which freed people plundered estates and, especially, the estates' provision grounds. The riots were suppressed, but eight of the rioters were killed (Levy 1980:148-54; Craton 1988:158-60).

Two years later, an agricultural labourers' revolt broke out in St. Croix on 1 October, the day that yearly contracts for the workers began. Because of the nature of the annual contract, workers could be forced to work for an estate against their wishes. The 1st of October was therefore an emotive day for labourers in St. Croix, made worse by rumours that emigration for work elsewhere was being blocked. A serious riot developed in Frederiksted, in which shops were ransacked, and the customs house and homes were set alight. The rioters then attacked the plantations, causing enormous damage to the sugar mills, the great houses, and the crops. During the outbreak, the loss of life was high; official figures put the number of blacks killed at 84 while the unofficial total was closer to 250. By contrast three whites lost their lives (Dookhan 1974: 227-31; Tyson, in this volume).

In Dominica, freed people protested violently against the taking of a census in 1844, which they saw as a first step toward their re-enslavement. Initially enumerators were assaulted, but then the protest developed into attacks on estate property and managers. In restoring order, the militia killed four people and arrested three hundred. In St. Vincent, a labour strike in 1862 became a riot; freed people assaulted estate managers and plundered planters' houses and shops over a considerable area. The authorities killed four people and wounded at least seven others in putting down the riot; many people were sentenced to prison terms and flogged for their part in the outbreak (Chace 1989:121-23; Marshall 1983:88-102).

These outbreaks in Jamaica, Tobago, Barbados, St. Croix, Dominica, and St. Vincent are not a complete list of the riots and disturbances during the post-emancipation period in the Caribbean. For example, they do not include the riots which grew out of attempts to preserve cultural and religious practices, such as the John Canoe riots in Jamaica in the early 1840s and the Carnival riots in Trinidad in 1881 and 1884 (Wilmot 1990; Brereton 1979:171-73). But the riots discussed here do provide a basis on which to examine the underlying causes of these protests and to suggest features which some of them had in common.

UNDERLYING CAUSES

Bridget Brereton, writing about the Belmanna riots in Tobago, has identified low wages as central to understanding the outbreak. She goes further: 'the complex of grievances that centred on wages, stoppages, and estate shops' were 'the common sources of friction behind many post-emancipation disturbances in the Caribbean' (Brereton 1984:115). There was little doubt that these elements were important in explaining the outbreak of the Tobago riots.

For Tobago, Brereton described a situation in which many planters were short of ready cash as well as capital. Disputes over wages were therefore likely. Rates of pay after emancipation were low, averaging 10d. a day for resident labourers and 1s. for strangers (those not living on the estate). As Brereton notes, efforts to reduce these rates of pay in 1847–48 had led to strikes and emigration to Trinidad. An additional irritant for workers was a pattern of irregular payment and arbitrary stoppages of pay. When linked to the truck system, in which estates had their own shops, a type of debt peonage was created among the workers (Brereton 1984:111-12). There is considerable evidence, then, that the system of deducting wages to pay for debts contracted at estate shops was a significant grievance among estate labourers in Tobago.

These issues were also prominent in the St. Vincent riots of 1862. Labourers were particularly incensed at the withdrawal of sugar and rum allowances, which formed part of their remuneration. Although these allowances were not protected by law, the workers considered them sanctified by custom. The 'vox populi' statement of the labourers on Mt.

Bentinck estate made their grievances quite clear:

> We, the inhabitants of Mount Bentinck estate, have been monthly employed to work on the above estate, some at $4, others at $3, etc., along with our privileges (viz) our sugar, rum and provision grounds, *and we never received any notice that these were to be stopped, until when we came to receive them we found that the sugar and rum were stopped; we were all annoyed about it . . . We then said that at the expiration of the month, we must make other arrangements, during which time they went to the mountains and took away our provision grounds that we have worked in our time, without giving us notice to take out our provision; they have taken it out; and both manager and overseer are feeding upon labour; the month is up, and they will not pay us our money, and we will not work.*

As Woodville Marshall has pointed out, the labourers on Mt. Bentinck estate considered their allowances as a right. This was not only because of tradition; the molasses allowance formed part of the workers' wages and was important in itself or could be exchanged for cash or provisions. When the allowance was withheld, the labourers considered it a hardship. Marshall has concluded that the workers faced wage reductions of at least 25 per cent during 1862 (Marshall 1983:94-96).

As in Tobago, planters in St. Vincent ran estate shops. Again, this created a form of debt peonage, since the amount owed to the shop was deducted from the workers' wages. Disputes could easily arise, but 'labourers were ever on the losing end because the shopkeeper was often the pay-master' (Marshall 1983:97). Late payment of wages did not make these problems any easier.

Low wages were an important element in several other outbreaks as well. In St. Croix, wages actually fell below what was stipulated in the labour ordinance and were significantly lower than wages at the central factory which was opened in early 1878. Moreover, workers in St. Croix were unhappy about the power of managers to levy monetary fines for particular offences. As Isaac Dookhan has demonstrated, it did not help matters that the fines formed part of the managers' income (Dookhan 1974:229). Rioters in Barbados shared some of the same concerns about wages. Although the confederation issue had sparked the riots, traditional concerns about low and irregular wages were crucial. In addition, workers believed that federation would generate higher wages; moreover, their attack on the estates' provision grounds suggested that they were lacking food and were ultimately seeking a living wage (Tyson, in this volume; Levy 1980:154; Craton 1988:160).

In Jamaica, low wages were also a concern. Workers at Amity Hall estate in St. Thomas in the East, a plantation which was attacked during the Morant Bay Rebellion, complained bitterly about their wages. Moreover, there was a report a month before the rebellion that workers on several estates in the parish had gone on strike for higher wages.[2] Elsewhere, workers in the parish of Metcalfe expected an increase in wages in the autumn of 1865. When asked why they were staying away from work at the end of August and during the first half of September, the labourers responded that they were waiting for the new law which would compel employers to pay them 4s. per day. The law was to originate in St. Thomas in the East.[3] The issue of wages, then, was clearly an important element in the post-emancipation disturbances.

But the ex-slaves' hunger for land after emancipation was a further factor in the outbreaks. Many ex-slaves believed that the provision grounds away from the estates – the land which they used to grow their own crops – belonged to the people and not to the estates. They felt they should have this land without paying rent. It is likely that Augustus Hire, one of the planters killed in the days following the outbreak at Morant Bay, was a target of the crowd because of his stance on this issue.

Hire was the planting attorney for Amity Hall estate. Acting for the owners of Amity Hall, Hire had authorized a survey on land near the estate known as Rowland's Field. Hire had been unable to collect rent from people he believed were squatting on this land. When the surveyor and Hire began work in July 1865, they were surrounded by an armed crowd of more than a hundred blacks. The crowd seized the surveyor's chain, broke it, and became 'very violent'. Despite having the ringleaders arrested, Hire and his surveyor met considerable resistance when they returned again the following day. Hire recalled the precise words of one man, Henry Doyley, who grabbed the surveyor's chain. When Hire asked him what right he had to the land, Doyley responded, 'What God Almighty make land for? You have plenty; we have none.' The surveyor also reported that the crowd told him that 'if we wanted war, we should have war'. Hire's response was to bring the people involved in the scuffle before the Circuit Court; the case was scheduled to take place the week after Hire's murder.[4]

The difficulty in obtaining land was also a factor in the Belmanna riots in Tobago. There, Lieutenant-Governor Harley found that the labourers' difficulties in obtaining land may have been one of the precipitating causes of the outbreak. Some labourers told the Lieutenant-Governor that they wanted to buy or rent a few acres of Crown land (Brereton 1984:115). Even more fundamental was the connection between freedom and land. Dominicans believed that freedom implied more than a change in legal status; it also meant a grant of land. The editor of *The Dominican*, George Charles Falconer, maintained in 1844 that this belief in land ownership was a significant element in the 'Guerre Negre'.

> We must believe that the rebels consider themselves to have been first wronged. It is a fact that many have always regarded their freedom to be only a part of the restitution due to them for their former bondage and that between their Queen and their former Owners some thing more ought to have been given them – and that *something* many have not scrupled in times past to say – should have been a small piece of land!!! (Chace 1989: 125-26).

While land remained an emotive issue in the post-emancipation period, the judicial system was also regarded as a problem. Many freed people believed it was impossible to obtain justice in the local courts, since the magistracy was dominated by planters. Too often, the employers were judging the cases of their employees. High court fees also made it difficult for labourers and small settlers to pursue cases in court. One of the grievances of the crowd at Morant Bay and in the rebellion generally was the lack of justice in the parish. For example, when asked the reason for the rebellion the day after the events at Morant Bay, one of the rioters at Bath claimed it had broken out 'because the poor black had no justice in St. Thomas in the East . . . there was no other way to get satisfaction in St. Thomas in the East, only what they had done'.[5]

For the blacks in Jamaica, there was at least another alternative that some of them had tried. In several parts of St. Thomas in the East, blacks had organized their own courts. These people's courts were held in districts not far from Morant Bay, and offences were punished by fines and flogging. Such alternative courts seem to have existed in other parts of Jamaica as well and are further evidence of the people's dissatisfaction with the administration of justice. Although no evidence of people's courts has emerged in the other colonies under review, further research may well uncover them.

One of the recurring fears of the freed people was the prospect of re-enslavement. This was the motivating force behind the Guerre Negre in Dominica. As Russell Chace has noted, 'almost every affidavit and piece of testimony taken after the protest . . . points to the same conclusion, that the freedpersons firmly believed that they were to be re-enslaved, and that many of them were prepared to resist to the point of death' (Chace 1989:129). To some Dominicans, the fear of re-enslavement sounded implausible; however, a freedman named Saint Louis presented the case for this possibility.

> I think that our freedom can be taken away from us, because it was once done in another country near to us; it was the French who gave

> their people freedom, and afterwards made them slaves again; my parents told me so when I was quite a child, and I have remembered it ever since; what is done once can be done again, and we all know that liberty is good; I don't know but what the English will do like the French one of these days; it is only for the Queen to send a Gazette, and say 'make them slaves again,' and they will be all made slaves; if a man pays money, and does not get a receipt, he can be made to pay the money again; so it is with freedom; if we have been made free and have not paper to show for it, we can be made slaves again (Chace 1989:130).

Freed people in Jamaica shared these concerns. Rumours of re-enslavement helped to spark the conspiracies and disturbances of 1848 as well as Morant Bay itself. The threat of re-enslavement was often associated with the possibility of Jamaica joining the United States as a slave state. During the riots in 1848, the ex-slaves regarded 1 August as the day on which the whites would choose to re-enslave the blacks. The date was particularly significant, as the tenth anniversary of full freedom. In addition, the planters were experiencing a severe economic crisis; as a consequence, they sought to reduce wages on the estates, often by as much as 25 per cent. However, many ex-slaves regarded this loss of wages as a first step toward the reintroduction of slavery (Simmonds 1982:77, 80-81).

Women played a prominent role in many of these disturbances. At Morant Bay, the officials and the militia confronted a stone-throwing crowd in front of the court house. As the custos of the parish attempted to read the Riot Act, a member of the militia observed a woman he knew named Geoghegan throwing the first stone, which was followed by a hail of stones from other women in the crowd (Heuman forthcoming). The militia and the parish officials retreated into the court house, and eventually the crowd decided that the best method of attack was to burn the building down and force the volunteers and vestrymen to come out. It is likely that women were responsible for this plan. One witness claimed that a woman named Rosanna Finlayson 'said they must go and get a fire stick and trash, and set the school-room on fire. She said the white people were locked up in the court house, and if they set fire to the school room the whole people would be burnt up alive'. Five minutes later, the school house was on fire. It was adjacent to the court house, and it was not long before that building began to burn as well.[6]

The women in the crowd also encouraged the men to continue their attack on the court house. After the volunteers had fired at the crowd, some of the men had withdrawn. But women on one of the roads leading into the town reportedly told the men: 'Now, you men, this is not what you said in the mountain. You said you would come to the Bay and do so and so, and now you leave all this work to the women; go to the Parade and see what the Volunteers do to the men there.'[7]

Women also helped to determine the fate of Charles Price, a prominent black builder who was caught by the crowd after the burning of the school house. The crowd debated what to do with him, largely because of his colour. The women made their point of view very clear: 'We work for him on the road and he not pay us, and we burn bricks for the church at Morant Bay, and he not pay us. You need not keep him till before day.' Price was then beaten to death, despite offering £200 for his life.[8]

Women were involved in some of the other post-emancipation disturbances as well. In the labourers' revolt in St. Croix, women were among the leaders of the outbreak. Mary Thomas was known as 'Queen Mary' and called herself Captain; Axelline Salomon was referred to as 'the black Amazon'. In the Guerre Negre, a crowd of women abused one of the local enumerators seeking to carry out the census. Elsewhere on the outskirts of the principal town, Roseau, women harassed enumerators. In the Tobago riots, women were among the most prominent of those brutally attacking Corporal Belmanna (Dookhan 1974:230-31; Chace 1989:121-22; Brereton 1984:114).

WHITE PERCEPTIONS

Once the rebellion had broken out at Morant Bay, whites in Jamaica became convinced that they were dealing with a massive conspiracy. In their view, blacks were intent on killing the whites and coloureds and taking over the island, and therefore the outbreak had to be suppressed as quickly as possible. This line was adopted by Governor Eyre in his first despatch to the Colonial Office after the rebellion. Writing nine days after the events at Morant Bay, Eyre maintained that the rebellion had to be put down immediately; otherwise 'the insurrection would have been universal throughout the entire Island, and that either the Colony would have been lost to the Mother Country, or an almost interminable war and an unknown expense would have had to be incurred in suppressing it'.[9]

Eyre was certain that an island-wide conspiracy existed. He had no doubts that 'there had been an intercommunication between the negroes of the different parishes and an intention to act in concert for the destruction of the white and coloured inhabitants'. He believed some blacks outside of St. Thomas in the East had advance warning of the outbreak, while others were waiting to see the outcome of the rebellion before taking action. Although there was no evidence of 'any actually organized combination to act simultaneously', Eyre was convinced that the whole island was in great danger.[10]

The authorities in Tobago took a similar view of the Belmanna riots. Lieutenant-Governor Harley believed the riots 'disclosed that a latent feeling of discontent had existed in the district for some time, and there was sufficient evidence to show that there was a plot to effect a rising and get rid of the whites and seize the estates'. Although Brereton discounts his perspective on the riots, she notes that the lieutenant-governor's opinion was shared by many members of Tobago's small white community. One planter claimed that his labourers were threatening that 'as soon as the *warship* left they will rise and kill every white man on the Island. I am to go *first* . . .' In St. Vincent, the attorney-general made similar comments about the disturbances there: he believed that 'rioters intended to dispossess the whites of the land, and that a mass uprising would have occurred if the rioters had gained any success'. As in the case of Jamaica and Tobago, however, there is no evidence of an island-wide plot (Brereton 1984:119; Marshall 1983:101).

Yet freed people throughout the Caribbean shared common grievances in the wake of emancipation. Labourers in Tobago and St. Vincent were reacting to the withdrawal of privileges that had become customary, and they were not prepared to countenance the reduction of their wages or the abolition of their allowances. As Marshall has argued, rioters in St. Vincent were intent on defending their rights. They were seeking to administer 'a rough sort of natural justice on those who seemed to be oppressing them' (Marshall 1983: 101). The same was true in Tobago.

In Dominica and Jamaica, ex-slaves reacted violently in response to a different threat: the possibility of re-enslavement. Ex-slaves also equated freedom with land and wanted an impartial judicial system. Instead, they were faced with an often oppressive system of labour control. Across the region, in smaller and in larger territories, freedmen confronted similar problems and reacted in similar ways. Their ideas of freedom clashed with those of the ruling elite.

For freedom to become meaningful, freedmen wanted access to land as well as work at reasonable wages on the estates. Planters, on the other hand, generally sought to restrict wages on the estates and to limit the movement of freedmen off the plantations. The ruling class also attempted to maintain control of the formal political process. Whether in St. Croix or Tobago, these contradictory expectations of freedom led to political and economic frustration and, ultimately, to outbreaks across the region (for a general discussion of these issues, see Bolland 1981).

The freedmen's problems were made worse by the loss of representative institutions as a result of the post-emancipation riots and disturbances. In the face of pressure from below, planters and administrators generally sought to abolish the system of representative government and replace it with direct rule from London. This was an inadequate response to the problems faced by ex-slaves in the post-emancipation period and helped to create the conditions for the serious riots which would erupt a century after emancipation.

ACKNOWLEDGEMENTS

I am grateful to Bridget Brereton and Arnold Sio for their helpful comments on this essay.

NOTES

1. *British Parliamentary Papers*, 1866, [3683-1], XXXI, Report of the Jamaica Royal Commission, Part II, Minutes of Evidence and Appendix (hereafter JRC): Evidence of Arthur Warmington, p. 58; Evidence of James Britt, p. 178.
2. JRC, Evidence of John Anderson, p. 959; *British Parliamentary Papers*, 1866, [3682], XXX, Papers Laid before the Royal Commission of Inquiry by Governor Eyre (hereafter Papers), Shaw to Westmoreland, 2 January 1866, p. 501, subenclosure 4; *The Falmouth Post*, 1 September 1865.
3. JRC, Evidence of James Stewart, pp. 543, 545.
4. JRC: Evidence of Edward Eyre, Hire to Myers, July, 1865, p. 988; Evidence of Roger Swire, p. 951; Evidence of The Hon. Alexander Heslop, pp. 330-31.
5. JRC, Evidence of Henry Silvera, p. 484.
6. Papers, In the Special Commission, 7 March 1866: The Queen v. Bogle, Henry Theophilus and others for Felonious Riot, Evidence of Charlotte Carter, p. 360.
7. JRC, Evidence of Cecilia Gordon, p. 180.
8. JRC, Evidence of Henry Good, p. 30.
9. Colonial Office 137/393, Eyre to Cardwell, 20 October 1865, no. 251.
10. JRC, Evidence of Edward Eyre, p. 1006.

REFERENCES

Anon. [1859]. *The Florence Hall Controversy and the Falmouth Riots*. Falmouth, Jamaica: James Mockler.

Bolland, O. Nigel. 1981. 'Systems of Domination after Slavery: The Control of Land and Labor in the British West Indies after 1838'. *Comparative Studies in Society and History* 23:591-619.

Brereton, Bridget. 1979. *Race Relations in Colonial Trinidad, 1870–1900*. Cambridge: Cambridge University Press.

______. 1984. 'Post-Emancipation Protest in the Caribbean: The "Belmanna Riots" in Tobago, 1876'. *Caribbean Quarterly* 30:110-23.

Chace, Jr., Russell E. 1989. 'Protest in Post-Emancipation Dominica: The "Guerre Negre" of 1844'. *Journal of Caribbean History* 23:118-41.

Chutkin, Noelle. 1975. 'The Administration of Justice in Jamaica as a Contributing Factor in the Morant Bay Rebellion of 1865'. *Savacou* 11/12:78-85.

Craton, Michael. 1988. 'Continuity Not Change: The Incidence of Unrest among Ex-Slaves in the British West Indies, 1838–1876'. *Slavery & Abolition* 9:144-70.

Dookhan, Isaac. 1974. *A History of the Virgin Islands of the United States*. Epping, Essex: Caribbean Universities Press in association with Bowker, Publishing Company for the College of the Virgin Islands.

Hall, Douglas. 1959. *Free Jamaica, 1838–1865: An Economic History*. New Haven: Yale University Press.

Heuman, Gad. Forthcoming. 'Post-Emancipation Protest in Jamaica: The Morant Bay Rebellion'.

In *From Chattel to Wage Slavery*, Mary Turner (ed.). London: James Currey.

Holt, Thomas C. 1992. *The Problem of Freedom: Race, Labor, and Politics in Jamaica and Britain, 1832-1938*. Baltimore: The Johns Hopkins University Press.

Levy, Claude. 1980. *Emancipation, Sugar, and Federalism: Barbados and the West Indies, 1833–1876*. Gainesville: University Presses of Florida.

Marshall, Woodville K. 1983. '"Vox Populi": The St. Vincent Riots and Disturbances of 1862'. In *Trade, Government and Society in Caribbean History, 1700–1920*, B. W. Higman (ed.), 85-115. Kingston, Jamaica: Heinemann Educational Books.

Simmonds, Lorna Elaine. 1982. *'The Spirit of Disaffection': Civil Disturbances in Jamaica, 1838-1865*. M.A. thesis, University of Waterloo.

Wilmot, Swithin. 1990. 'The Politics of Protest in Free Jamaica: The Kingston John Canoe Christmas Riots, 1840 and 1841'. *Caribbean Quarterly* 36:65-75.

'Our Side': Caribbean Immigrant Labourers and the Transition to Free Labour on St. Croix, 1849–79

GEORGE F. TYSON

On 1 October 1878, Sarah Scott, a 32-year-old native of Barbados, who had been working as a plantation field labourer in the Danish West Indian colony of St. Croix for the past fifteen years, took her two children to the port of Christiansted, where she applied for passports to return to her native island. The Danish policemaster refused her application, which was perfectly legal and correct, offering no explanation for his action. Unwilling to resume work in the cane fields, Sarah and her children secured lodging in town, only to be evicted a few days later. Destitute, she threw herself on the mercy of the British Vice-Consul, who took the unfortunate family into his home.[1]

Sarah was one of several thousand contract labourers from the Caribbean region working on Crucian plantations at the time. Many of them shared her desire to quit the island, either to return home or to seek employment in more remunerative and less oppressive labour fields. On the same day that Sarah was acquiescing to a passport system that kept her captive on St. Croix, hundreds of other immigrants in the town of Frederiksted, 18 miles west of Christiansted, became so enraged with the obstructionism and provocations of the Danish constabulary that they attacked the police headquarters. This eruption triggered one of the most serious of all post-emancipation insurrections in the Caribbean.

Known locally as the 'Fireburn' because arson was the primary weapon employed by the insurgents, the uprising was directed not so much at the police as at an anachronistic labour law that immigrant and native labourers considered 'a species of slavery'. Although the uprising was ruthlessly suppressed with the loss of several hundred lives, the Fireburn compelled colonial authorities to enact new labour regulations embodying free-labour principles. This working-class victory had to be consolidated by a subsequent general strike which forced a reluctant plantocracy to relinquish the last vestiges of their coerced labour system.

'A SPECIES OF SLAVERY': THE LABOUR ACT OF 1849

The slaves of St. Croix gained their freedom by staging an island-wide rebellion in July 1848. But, even as they celebrated their emancipation, a group of planters was hurriedly devising a set of regulations intended, as one of them put it, to give the ex-slave 'a different view of the freedom [than] which he expects'.[2] These regulations became the basis of a new labour law issued by the Danish Governor on 26 January 1849 (Jensen 1979:68-69). Intended to be provisional, this law remained in effect with only minor modifications for thirty years.

The essential provisions of the Labour Act of 1849 were a mandatory annual contract for each plantation labourer and fixed wages for fixed hours of work. Thus, wages, hours, and the term of work were established by law rather than by free and open negotiations between employer and worker. The provisions relating to the annual contract required that on 1 October of each year labourers had to sign a contract that bound them to work on a plantation of their choice for a term of one year. Termination notice by either party could only be given during the month of August.

Field labourers were subdivided into three classes of wage earners in accordance with their strength and abilities: first-class workers received 15 cents per day; second-class workers 10 cents; and third-class workers 5 cents. All field labourers had to work 9 hours a day Monday through Friday. They received slightly higher wages for extra work on weekdays and on Saturdays. Bargaining for extra pay was prohibited.

Mandated benefits to be provided by the planters were minimal: free housing and use of a small provision ground. Workers could purchase fixed rations of salt fish and corn meal ('fungi') from the planter for 5 cents a day. Medical attention, which under slavery had been provided by the planter, now became the responsibility of the workers themselves, though persons judged seriously ill by management received free care if they stayed in the estate sick house. The planter had to provide shelter for the infirm, but family members had to feed and care for them. Workers had to obtain permission from management to collect wood, fruit, grass, and charcoal, and to keep livestock. Management was accorded considerable latitude in exacting fines for absenteeism, tardiness, negligence, and poor or lazy work. Buttressing the Labour Law were strict vagrancy regulations stipulating, among other things, that estate workers who had terminated their employment had to show the district policemaster evidence of new employment on another plantation or in the towns. If unconvinced, the policemaster could order the person to find work under threat of arrest and enforced labour. The planters who formulated these labour regulations pronounced them 'judicious and suitable'.[3] The ex-slaves, recognizing them as a new form of servitude, recorded their protest by a strike shortly after their issuance. The Danish colonial authorities sent police to force the strikers back to the cane fields (Dookhan 1974:225). Thus began the post-emancipation era in the Danish West Indies.

POST-EMANCIPATION LABOUR PROBLEMS

Above all else, the Labour Act of 1849 was intended to provide Crucian sugar plantations with a supply of cheap and regular labour sufficient to achieve production levels that could sustain the profit expectations of the heavily indebted plantocracy and its creditors. The law failed to accomplish the desired results, mainly because the supply of reliable labour proved inadequate to demand.

Ex-slaves were quick to take advantage of the provision in the Labour Law which allowed them to leave their plantations, with proper notice, on 1 October. Between 1850 and 1859 the number of plantation field labourers declined by 20 per cent, from 9,173 to 7,304.[4] At first, most freedmen sought to better their conditions or to join other family members by moving to another plantation. But once they realized that plantation life was much the same everywhere, increasing numbers of them, particularly young people, expressed their objections to the restraints of the Labour Law by moving into Christiansted and Frederiksted. This trend is reflected in the growth of the total urban population from 7,452 in 1846 to 8,719 in 1860. Then, as the towns filled up and employment opportunities there diminished, Crucians began emigrating to the neighbouring islands of St. Thomas, Tortola, Puerto Rico, and Vieques in search of land and/or better wages and working conditions.[5] Thus rather than keeping workers on the plantations, the Labour Law actually encouraged them to leave.

The growing labour shortage, coupled with the repressive nature of the Labour Law, reduced the reliability and productivity of the workers who choose to remain on the plantations. Throughout the 1850s, the planters complained about the poor work habits of their work force, which had to be tolerated because workers could not be easily replaced even with machinery. One estate manager lamented, 'The increasing use of implements in our cultivation makes up in some measure for our deficiencies in manual labour, but it does not make us independent of our people, who do much less than they would if we could discharge them and get others.'[6] Local critics were quick to point out that since the Labour Law did not reward industry and initiative, none could be expected. The provisions of the Labour Act, observed the United States Consul, 'render the condition of the laborers little above that of absolute bondage. The consequence is that the laborer feels no interest in the work which he is to perform, and has to be constantly watched and directed by a driver.'[7]

The planters intensified their efforts to compensate for decreasing labour inputs through agricultural and technological innovations, but new labour-saving machinery and steam mills failed to maintain sugar production levels. Whereas between 1840 and 1847 Crucian planters had exported an annual average of 20 million pounds of sugar, between 1849 and 1859 they averaged just 14 million pounds per annum, despite relatively good weather (Hatchett 1859). Plantation revenue shrunk correspondingly, since prices remained relatively stable.

One mechanism for offsetting losses caused by falling productivity was to reduce the rate of labour compensation. But by fixing wages the Labour Law placed legal limits on the cost benefits that could be extracted by this response. Moreover, labour shortages drove up labour costs. In order to induce workers to stay in their fields, planters began offering sign-up bonuses and increased privileges, such as larger provision grounds, variable working hours, sugar juice and rum in crop time, and extravagant allowances at Christmas and crop-over. Many planters began secretly paying higher wages than the law allowed.[8] These concessions had become so widespread and entrenched by the late 1850s that workers had began to consider them as rights. A planter memorial of 1861 complained,

> . . . the fact that the amount of labour disposable for agriculture being so inadequate and constantly decreasing has necessarily led labourers gradually vindicating a right to an extremely liberal interpretation of all enactments relating to their duties and rights and an access to many privileges on the estates (cited in Sircar 1971:136).

Thus owing to the labour scarcities which it generated, the Labour Act worked to make the workers richer and the planters poorer. One anxious planter warned that if the bribery, illegal wage payments, and other concessions were allowed to continue 'nearly all of the landed property in the colony [will be] in the hands of those who were formerly labourers'.[9]

With their labour costs rising and output falling, most Crucian planters faced financial ruin during the 1850s. Clearly, they had to do something to alter the unfavourable equation that had come to exist between labour and capital. One possibility was to revoke the Labour Law in favour of a truly free labour system. But such a solution implied unbridled competition for scarce labour resources, with attendant short-term wage increases and elimination of many marginal producers. Few of the heavily indebted Crucian planters took this proposition seriously. More to their liking was the solution hit upon in the British and French colonies: government subsidized immigration.

IMMIGRATION

Even before enactment of the Labour Law, Crucian planters familiar with post-emancipation labour developments in the British West Indian colonies had come to believe that immigration represented a solution to their problems. Between 1849 and 1851 a few planters experimented with Portuguese immigrants (Jensen 1979:127). But because of the high costs and the propensity of the Portuguese to leave field work at the earliest opportunity, most Crucian planters viewed these private initiatives with scepticism.[10] As their labour problems intensified, however, they became convinced that government-sponsored mass immigration from India, China, and Africa (as practised in Trinidad, British Guiana, and the French West Indies), could be their salvation.

In 1855 the Burgher Council enacted the 'Ordinance of September 13, 1855, Concerning the Raising of Funds for St. Croix Land-Treasury to Defray the Expenses of the Importation of Labourers from Foreign Places', which authorized the St. Croix Land-Treasury to raise a loan of $60,000 to finance the expenses associated with recruitment of foreign workers. Interest and principal of the debt were to be paid from a 10-cent tax assessed on all cultivated land and also by charges levied on the employers of the labourers. Thus the programme was supported by a mixture of public and private funding.[11] Individual planters remained free to import workers at their own expense.

The immigration program began slowly, much to the dismay of its plantocratic sponsors, who blamed the delays on bungling Danish authorities. Between 1855 and 1861, efforts to arrange large consignments of indentured workers from the Cape Verde Islands, Africa, Madeira, Venezuela, and China came to nothing. Nor did the Danish Government succeed in cutting a deal with President Lincoln to send to St. Croix refugee slaves from the Confederacy and liberated Africans from captured slave ships.[12]

In 1862 the Danish Government finally managed to conclude a convention with the British Government that allowed East Indians from Calcutta to be shipped to St. Croix. In order to facilitate this negotiation, the St. Croix Colonial Council enacted two new immigration ordinances. The Ordinance of 6 June 1862 raised the Immigration Fund loan to $65,000 to cover the costs of transporting the coolies to and from St. Croix. It also increased the financial contribution levied on planters receiving immigrants. Contractual details and terms of labour relating to the coolies were specified in the 'Ordinance Concerning the Immigration of Labourers from Foreign Places to the Island of St. Croix, and Their Treatment', which went into effect in October 1862. This Ordinance transferred administration of the immigration program from the Land-Treasury to a newly established Immigration Committee appointed by the governor and headed by a salaried Superintendent of Immigration (Jensen 1978:25-28).

The first shipment of 318 East Indians arrived in June 1863. Contracted to serve five years, they were distributed among fourteen sugar plantations. However, this experiment proved a dismal failure (Sircar 1971). The coolies found the working conditions so unbearable that when their term expired in

1868, all but 37 elected to return home rather than renew their contracts. The British Government, dismayed by reports from the resident British Consul, Henry Rainals, describing the poor treatment and misery of the coolies, refused to sanction any further East Indian immigration to St. Croix until effective protective measures had been implemented.[13] For their part, the Crucian planters maintained that the work of the coolies did not equate with the political and financial costs involved and decided to discontinue further recruitment from India. They could afford this posture because their labour needs were being satisfied by an unexpected source, West Indian immigrants.

Systematic recruitment of West Indian contract labourers had commenced in late 1859, when at least 88 workers from the Eastern Caribbean were sent to St. Croix by immigration agents commissioned by the Danish colonial government.[14] During the next three years 600 more Caribbean immigrants, mostly from Barbados, arrived.[15] These new workers did not suffice to cover annual losses from emigration and an excess of deaths over births, much less make up for the net labour losses since 1848. However, the situation changed dramatically in 1863, when hundreds of labourers from Barbados suddenly flooded into St. Croix.

Beset by unemployment and hunger in their over-populated homeland, the Barbadians (a.k.a. Bajans) were lured to St. Croix by recruiting agents promising cash bounties of $8.00, free outward passage on inter-island schooners, and full-time employment under paternalistic labour regulations and benevolent English-speaking planters. Knowing nothing about St. Croix, the Barbadians took their bounties, their free passage, and their chances on the rest of it. At the end of 1863, nearly 2,000 had reached 'the garden of the West Indies', much to the delight of the Crucian planters, who divided them up (not without their customary bickering) and set them to work in the cane fields under one or two year contracts.[16]

Mass immigration from Barbados ended as abruptly as it began. In 1864, concerned with the loss of surplus labour, the plantocrats controlling the Barbados Assembly enacted a law severely restricting the activities of recruiting agents (Roberts 1955:254). Consequently, only 7 immigrants came from Barbados to St. Croix that year. The numbers increased slightly in subsequent years; but after 1863 most Bajan immigrants came via other islands where they had previously gone to work.[17] As the Barbados connection contracted, Crucian recruiting agents turned their attention to other islands. Between 1864 and 1870, no fewer than 2,200 additional immigrants reached St. Croix, most of whom came from Antigua, St. Kitts, and the Dutch Antilles.[18]

Overall, some 5,000 immigrant labourers entered St. Croix between 1859 and 1870. About half of these newcomers elected not to stay. While several factors contributed to this substantial out-migration, most observers attributed it to the Labour Law, which many immigrants found too restrictive compared to the free labour conditions and higher wages prevailing elsewhere in the Caribbean.[19]

Dissatisfied immigrants not only withdrew their labour from St. Croix, they also actively discouraged their countrymen from going there. Recruiting agents blamed the dearth of immigrants from Barbados after 1863 on the negative reports spread by correspondents on St. Croix and by returning immigrants, which were picked up and widely circulated by local newspapers.[20] After dispatching a large contingent of Antiguans to St. Croix in 1865, the recruiting agent in St. John's found a year later that he could only entice Bajans to go to 'the dreaded St. Croix; . . . no Antiguans being willing to leave from what those in St. Croix have written to say about the place'.[21] The *St. Kitts Agricultural Report* for 1869 stated that 'the emigration to St. Croix, once prevalent here, as lately in Antigua, has for some time ceased, the labourers having learnt by degrees that a change from this to the Danish Islands is only a transition from freedom to demi-slavery'.[22]

On the other hand, by 1870 a total of 2,870 immigrants had settled more or less permanently on St. Croix.[23] These newcomers adapted to their new environment and to the Labour Act, which, despite its low wages and confining provisions, nevertheless guaranteed them employment, living conditions, and privileges comparable if not superior to those found in their homelands. Consul Rainals, hardly a friend of the Crucian plantocracy, had to admit that the immigrants 'are, as a general rule, pretty well treated here; if they choose to work they need never be without it, and their rate of wages, the same as that of the native labourers, may be considered fair and reasonable'.[24] Their adjustment was made easier by the fact that they shared a common language and many cultural traditions, not only with native workers of African descent, who spoke an English-based Creole, but also with plantation managers, who were mostly Scots-Irish. Three-quarters of the sugar plantations where they lived and worked were owned by Britons.[25] Indeed, the immigrants found that in most respects St. Croix was a British colony under Danish rule.

According to the 1870 Census, the immigrants were distributed as follows: 56 in Frederiksted, 88 in Christiansted, 4 at the Friedensfeld Moravian Mission, 6 in the hospital, 31 in prison, and 2,685 in the rural districts. All of the 2,685 rural immigrants, who represented 19 per cent of the total rural population, lived on plantations. Of these plantation inhabitants, 2,570 persons, or 96 per cent, had been born in the Caribbean region.

Contract workers born in the British colonies comprised 88 per cent of the Caribbean immigrants living on the plantations; 11 per cent were born in the Dutch islands (including St. Martin), and the remaining 1 per cent were from the French West Indies, Puerto Rico, Venezuela, and Colombia. Barbadians predominated nationally, comprising 65 per cent of all Caribbean immigrants and 73 per cent of British West Indians. Antiguans ran a distant second in both categories.

The Caribbean immigrants were distributed among 128 sugar and stock plantations throughout St. Croix. More than 95 per cent of them resided on the sugar plantations. Even though the immigrants totalled just under 20 per cent of the rural population, they comprised 30 to 40 per cent of the work force on many plantations. On four plantations (Retreat, Orange Grove, Clifton Hill, and Mount Pleasant), immigrants outnumbered natives.

Occupationally, 94 per cent of rural immigrants worked in the fields. Only seven were classified as artisans and 17 as domestics. The 2,408 field hands represented 27 per cent of all field workers on St. Croix; 76 per cent of them (1,354 males and 480 females), were classified as first-class labourers. These men and women were widely considered to be the best workers on the island. Collectively they made up 36 per cent of all first-class labourers, while the males constituted 43 per cent of all first-class male labourers.

Male immigrants outnumbered females by slightly more than two to one. Sixty-eight per cent of all immigrants, and 70 per cent of the males, were between 16 and 35 years of age. The great influx of virile West Indian men during the 1860s had the effect of shifting the rural sex ratio on St. Croix in favour of males for the first time in fifty years.

TABLE 1
NUMBER OF TYPE OF IMMIGRANT DOMESTIC UNITS IN THE RURAL DISTRICTS OF ST. CROIX, 1870

Household Type	Number of Households
Immigrant male and female	126*
Immigrant male with children	22
Immigrant female with children	187
Immigrant with native female	62
Immigrant female with native male	32
Immigrant siblings	04

Source: Rigsarkivet, St. Croix Census, 1870.
* Includes 2 females married to immigrants from St. John.

The relatively stable character of this population is indicated by the fact that more than 40 per cent of rural immigrants lived in household arrangements comprising at least one parent and a child. As shown by Table 1, the most common domestic unit was male-female cohabitation, and most of these couples were married. Two-thirds of the male-female units included children, a third of whom had been born on St. Croix. It is likely, moreover, that many of those living alone with their children had a partner on another plantation.

The census data demonstrate that by 1870 immigrants had become a major component of plantation communities on St. Croix and that natives had begun to accept and co-mingle with them. As shown by Table 1, 43 per cent of the cohabiting or married relationships recorded on the plantations involved a native and an immigrant. In 62 instances an immigrant male lived with a Crucian female, while 32 Crucian males shared a household with an immigrant female. Half of these couples had conceived Crucian children who were living with them. Overall, at least 361 Crucian children in 1870 had an acknowledged immigrant parent. In nine instances, under-age immigrant children were living with natives. Three Crucian households were caring for elderly immigrants.

By 1870, any resentment that may have existed between native and immigrant had begun to give way to working-class solidarity. The two groups stood as one before the Labour Law and within the exploitative plantation economy. Shared lives in field and village and common cultural traditions drew these workers into a fellowship. But the legal and economic parity that helped each group tolerate their constricted circumstances was about to be shattered along with the coerced labour regime that had brought Crucians and West Indians together.

BUILDING THE TINDERBOX

The importation of several thousand immigrant workers in the 1860s had the desired effect of stabilizing the size of the plantation field-labour force, which mushroomed from 7,304 in 1859 to 8,543 in 1863 and then levelled off at about 8,000 workers over the next decade.[26] This increase was not as great as the planters desired, but it sufficed to check the trend toward higher levels of worker compensation and other relaxations of the Labour Law, which had characterized the 1850s. Indeed, the planters quickly took advantage of the massive influx of immigrants in 1863 to revoke or reduce the wage and benefit concessions previously made to native labourers. Native workers responded by threats of violence and incendiarism.[27] By the end of 1863, more than 500 of them had left the island in quest of freedom and a better livelihood.[28]

A regular supply of labour during the 1860s enabled planters in the prime sugar growing districts to increase production and revenue by bringing more land under cultivation. Thus annual sugar exports between 1862 and 1871 averaged 15.7 million pounds compared to 14.0 million pounds in the 1850s, an increase of 12 per cent (Quin 1892:10-11). But after a decade of relative prosperity, Crucian sugar planters fell on disastrously hard times in the 1870s. A succession of dry seasons starting in 1872 resulted in a sharp drop in sugar production. Annual sugar exports for the years 1872 to 1878 averaged less than a third of their level in the 1860s (Quin 1892:10-11).

Concurrently, intensifying competition from European-grown beet sugar drove down sugar prices from $72.66 per hogshead in 1870 to $56.43 per hogshead in 1878. The aggregate value of exports fell from $865,000 per annum in 1862-1871 to $539,000 per annum in 1872-1878 (Quin 1892:10-11). The hard-pressed planters borrowed heavily from mercantile houses, most particularly the Danish firm of Moses Melchoir and Son, and also from the Colonial Government, which advanced a total of $596,000 in the period 1872–79. None the less, numerous failures and bankruptcies occurred, with the result that sugar production ceased on several marginal properties.[29]

Plantation workers also suffered hardship during these years. The drought destroyed their provision crops, fruit trees, and livestock,[30] depriving them of critical sources of supplemental income and severing one of the main ties that bound them to the plantations. Many lost their jobs owing to estate closures or lay-offs by cost-conscious planters. Thus natives and immigrants learned that in times of distress the Labour Law afforded them no job security. By choice or necessity labourers began leaving the plantations. Between 1870 and 1878 the field force shrunk by more than 2,000 workers, a net loss of 26 per cent.[31] A few ex-plantation workers ended up in the towns, but since urban jobs were also scarce, most were drawn off the island by employment opportunities elsewhere. 'During the last few years', observed the British Vice-Consul the Reverend John C. Dubois in 1877, 'many of the labourers and mechanics [have] been induced to remove to the neighbouring Spanish islands by the higher wages offered there'.[32]

The planters did not possess the financial resources or, in time of drought, the need to replace lost labourers with new immigrant recruits. Moreover, few regional migrants considered St. Croix a land of opportunity, particularly since better wages and working conditions could be found in Trinidad, British Guiana, and Puerto Rico. Consequently, fewer than 600 immigrants came to St. Croix between 1871 and 1876. Only two arrived in 1877 and two more in 1878.[33] Unable to obtain a sufficient supply of new labour, the planters tried to slow down the rate of out-migration by making it more difficult for labourers to emigrate. In the early 1870s, after planters on the Colonial Council complained that not enough was being done by colonial authorities to prevent labourers from leaving the Island,[34] the Danish police began demanding health certificates, monetary sureties, and higher than usual fees from workers applying for passports. Police on St.

Thomas co-operated by sending back to St. Croix as vagrants those emigrants who, in their opinion, lacked sufficient funds or employment prospects.[35]

To prevent labourers from earning enough to buy their way out of the Danish West Indies, plantation owners or their surrogates began fining the workers for the least infraction. They also prevented workers from terminating their contracts on the grounds that notice had been improperly given. Here too, they seem to have had the co-operation of the police, who ignored labourers' complaints that the Labour Law was being violated and abused. The increased use of fines and the difficulties of getting passes to quit the plantations figured prominently among the grievances of those involved in the Fireburn Insurrection.[36]

The planters also dealt with the problem of a shrinking work force by hiring day labourers (called porters) from the towns. This practice, which stimulated a movement of enterprising plantation workers to the towns in the mid-1870s, embittered residential plantation labourers, because porters received higher wages and could work whenever they pleased. The porter system was particularly galling to the immigrants, who found it far more difficult than natives to establish town residency in order to become porters. Employment of porters and the discontent associated with it became widespread during the crop of 1877–78, which, owing to heavy rainfall, was the largest in six years. To maximize their output from the fortuitous weather, many planters even began allowing the porters to reside temporarily on the plantations, thus further provoking the ire of contracted workers.[37]

Discontent over wage inequalities, differential employment opportunities, and the break-down of the social compact prescribed by the Labour Law was exacerbated by the opening of the first central factory in early 1878. Seen by many as the initial step in modernizing and revitalizing the slumping sugar economy, the central factory aggravated deteriorating labour relations on the plantations in several ways. First, the law establishing the factory stipulated that the Labour Act must be repealed within three years of its opening, thereby creating expectations of imminent labour reform among rural workers. More significantly, the Government-operated factory hired some 400 workers, nearly all of them natives, at wages twice as high as those legally allowed to plantation workers. Like the porters, factory hands were free to work whenever they pleased.

Such blatant government disregard for the Labour Law undermined respect for both the Law and the colonial authorities who enforced it.[38] Plantation workers were upset not only over violated principles, but because factory workers with money and time on their hands began gallivanting about with their women. One immigrant who participated in the Fireburn told the British Consul,

> My cousin, sir, works at the central factory and comes and goes as he pleases. I work a fortnight, and have 60 to 80 cents to show for it; he works a fortnight, and comes out with a handful of silver; he comes to the estate and with his money entices away our wives and women; he goes on the spree with them for a week, sends them back to the estate with money to pay the fine for absence, and the day is coming, sir, when we shall have to father the factory children. Is this justice? Is this bearable?[39]

A BLOW FOR FREEDOM: THE FIREBURN INSURRECTION[40]

For many fieldhands the injustice had indeed become unbearable. During the late summer of 1878, some plantation labourers in the Frederiksted District held secret meetings at which they resolved that on Contract Day, 1 October, they would demand the same wages as paid at the central factory, and, if unsuccessful, they would leave the island. The planters had forewarning of their intentions because, during September, many workers, after trying unsuccessfully to negotiate higher wages, ceased cultivating their provision grounds and gave their termination notice.

On 1 October the discontented labourers went to Frederiksted, where their efforts to obtain higher wages failed. When some of them applied for passports to leave St. Croix, the police demanded payment of $4.80, rather than the prescribed fee of 32 cents. It was also discovered that all of the inter-island sloops and schooners which had been anchored in Frederiksted Road had mysteriously sailed away during the night, so even those who could pay for their passports were unable to leave.

Incensed over what they considered a conspiracy to keep them on St. Croix to work for low wages against their will, and uncertain as to their next course of action, labourers gathered during the late afternoon into an agitated crowd of several hundred persons. Some began drinking and engaged in heated verbal exchanges with the constabulary. According to one knowledgeable source, they 'were bitter in the denunciations of the officials, planters, owners of vessels, and the law. They accused the officials of charging them ten [US] dollars for a passport, while a white man could get one for thirty-three cents, and the planters and owners of vessels with having entered into an agreement to keep vessels away from the port'.[41] When a policeman attempted to arrest one of their most vituperative leaders, Joseph LaGrange, the crowd boldly rescued him and chased the police into Fort Frederik, which served as police headquarters.

As the workers debated attacking the fort they were approached by Reverend John C. Dubois, a man who had earned their respect as the British Vice-Consul and Rector of the Anglican Church. Dubois listened to their complaints and managed to persuade them to leave town. But, as they were departing, two policemen on horseback suddenly rode into their ranks with drawn sabres in an effort to disperse them. The infuriated crowd drove off the police and pursued them back to the fort.

Again Dubois intervened. After he volunteered to help the workers prepare a memorial of grievances for submission to the governor, they agreed to return to their plantations. Dubois accompanied them to the outskirts of town, where, as he addressed them about the need for peaceful behaviour, a woman suddenly ran up shouting that a black policeman had beaten a worker to death. The crowd rushed to the town hospital. Learning that the man had not died but had been badly beaten, they marched on the police holed up in Fort Frederik. As they entered the fort's inner courtyard, the undermanned police fired on them, killing and wounding several persons. The unarmed crowd responded by hurling stones, conch shells, and abuse. At this point a notoriously unpopular, arrogant, and (we must conclude) excessively foolish planter, George Fontaine, brazenly rode into the crowd with his pistol drawn, threatening to shoot anyone who would not let him pass. He was quickly knocked from his horse and beaten so severely that he later died.

In retaliation for the deaths of their comrades, the enraged protesters began to destroy property, starting first with two houses belonging to the police. Then, emboldened by heavy drink and the arrival of hundreds of newcomers from nearby estates, they commenced looting and burning the houses and businesses of the most prominent citizens. The destruction continued through the night. By early morning, when a military contingent sent from Christiansted arrived on the scene and forcibly dispersed the rioters, a third of Frederiksted had been reduced to ashes.

As word of these events spread into the countryside, individual groups of labourers began to loot and burn great houses and sugar works. This phase of the uprising started on 2 October and lasted for two or three days, during which time 53 sugar plantations and 15 stock estates suffered major damage, amounting to $603,800. The initial attacks on plantation property appear to have been spontaneous reactions against the symbols of oppression and exploitation, prompted, in the words of one immigrant ringleader from Antigua, by a desire to 'avenge the negro blood spilled before the fort'.[42] However, vandalism on subsequent days was often orchestrated or carried out by militant bands under radical leaders, who roamed the countryside intimidating less bellicose villagers into incriminating acts of violence, a pattern (and tactic), characteristic of many eighteenth- and nineteenth-century Caribbean uprisings, including the 1848 Emancipation Rebellion on St. Croix. To identify themselves to one another, the insurgents used the words 'our side'.

As random violence flickered throughout the countryside, the forces of repression began to mobilize in the towns. On the evening of 2 October, Governor James August Garde arrived from St. Thomas with military reinforcements. The following day Danish troops advanced along Centerline Road towards Frederiksted engaging and routing one or two groups of insurgents on their march. On 4 and 5 October French, British, and American warships arrived on the scene, allowing Danish troops and a group of plantation owners, managers, and overseers known as 'The Volunteers' to fan out into the countryside, where they engaged in indiscriminate killings, beatings, and arrests. By 9 October the insurgents had been pacified, and order had been restored throughout the island.

The loss of life during the conflagration was high, particularly among the plantation labourers. Three whites were killed by the insurgents – planter Fontaine and two Danish soldiers brutally murdered at Estate Carlton. By contrast, Governor Garde officially stated that 84 blacks had died, including twelve ringleaders executed between 7 and 12 October by sentence of a court martial.[43] Unofficially, he placed the death toll closer to 250, a figure independently confirmed by the American consul.[44] The disparity was striking. As the American and British Consuls noted in their dispatches, the insurgents had refrained from killing, even when men, women, and children were at their mercy. By contrast, there were numerous reported incidents of indiscriminate violence by 'The Volunteers', who took every opportunity to avenge old scores.

More than 400 labourers were arrested and imprisoned. About a third of the most serious offenders were held without trial for nearly two years, during which time several died from yellow fever and other diseases.[45] The lack of a speedy trial and the deplorable conditions of their captivity so outraged British Consul George A. Stevens that he urged the British Foreign Office to protest to the Danish Government on behalf of the imprisoned British subjects. An official protest lodged in 1880 led to improved conditions. The trials, which were eventually held in the late summer of 1880, resulted in death sentences being imposed on 40 men and women, 23 of whom were British immigrants. In 1881 the King of Denmark commuted all sentences to various terms of imprisonment.[46]

It is hardly surprising that immigrants, who comprised over 40 per cent of the field labourers in 1878, should have played a prominent, even decisive, role in the Fireburn. The reporter for the *New York Herald* wrote that 'the rioters are largely composed of English negroes',[47] while Governor Garde estimated that at least a third of the insurgents were foreign workers.[48]

More important than their number was the leadership they provided. The Royal Commission sent to investigate the causes of the disturbance found that immigrants used the wage inequalities introduced by the porter system and the central factory to arouse native resentment against the Labour Act and the ruling class.[49] British consular records demonstrate that immigrants helped conceive the plan to leave the island if higher wages could not be obtained on 1 October, and that they comprised most of the crowd that gathered outside the fort when this plan ran afoul of police obstructionism. Court records show that immigrants led the attacks on the Frederiksted police and on Frederiksted itself, although these acts of retribution were not part of their original plan. Referring to the looting and burning in Frederiksted, one of the immigrant leaders, a man styling himself a scholar, explained to Consul Stevens that 'we never meant it; we only wanted better terms or permission to go. The burning was the work of friends of the killed before the fort, an after thought.'[50] Another immigrant participant told Stevens: 'we meant no mischief, but when we asked to go away and the Police at Frederiksted asked us to pay four Dollars and eighty cents for each ones Passport, the devil got into our heads.'[51]

Among the Caribbean immigrants who seem possessed by the devil on 1 October and the days that followed were Mary Thomas, and James Emanual Benjamin, two Antiguans sentenced to death for their part in the burning of Frederiksted and various plantations. Mary Thomas, the notorious 'Queen Mary' immortalized in Crucian legend and song for her deeds during Fireburn, was a 30-year-old plantation worker residing at Sprat Hall plantation in 1878. Like most of her co-leaders, she was a long-time resident, having come to St. Croix in the mid-1860s. James Benjamin, aged 20, had been on the island for more than ten years.[52] Two other immigrants who figured prominently in the disturbances were Joseph Clark of Barbados, who led the attack on the two Danish soldiers killed at Estate Carlton, and Charles Max of Jamaica, a leader killed by the soldiers during a one-sided engagement at Anna's Hope plantation outside of Christiansted.[53]

As noted above, 23 of the 40 insurgent leaders sentenced to death in 1880 were foreign workers. Eight of the twelve ringleaders executed by summary court martial between 7 and 12 October were immigrants. They were Daniel Philip from St. Kitts, Henry Adams from St. Eustatius, James DeSilva and Samuel Henry from Antigua, Joseph Parris and Thomas Graydon from Barbados, John Adams from St. Thomas, and Joseph Harrison from Jamaica.[54] Thomas Graydon, alias 'Colonel Peter', who along with Samuel Henry, had been drummed out the British West Indian Regiment at Barbados, was declared to be the 'Captain General' of the insurgents during his trial. According to Consul Stevens, Mary Thomas, who Graydon had named 'Queen of the Antigonians', served as the principal witness against him at his trial. Graydon went to his death with dignity and defiance. Stevens described his execution as follows: 'On being tied up to a tree prior to being shot, the Judge having called out his name, he replied "All right Sir," and placing one leg before the other presented his chest to the soldiers, saying to the crowd, "Take warning from me".'[55]

A STRIKE FOR FREEDOM

Danish authorities did take warning from Thomas Graydon and his followers. They realized that if St. Croix were to avoid another social conflagration the Labour Law must be repealed and replaced with free labour regulations. Governor Garde began privately advocating new legislation immediately after the Fireburn. However, action was delayed until a Royal Commission had an opportunity to investigate the causes of the disturbances and propose remedial measures. After visiting the Danish West Indies in February and March 1879, the Commission issued a report in May that, among many other things, recommended repeal of the Labour Law and its replacement with a masters servants ordinance and vagrancy legislation based on Danish precedent.[56]

At this juncture, Danish colonial administrators were overcome by indecision and secrecy, perhaps because they were deeply involved in a bitter controversy with the British planters and the British Government over indemnification for Fireburn property losses. Thus the Commission's Report was not released in the islands nor was new labour legislation introduced in the local Colonial Councils, which had to debate and approve any such measure.

In July 1879, as the Danes dithered and procrastinated, the embittered workers, apprehensive that prolonged official silence indicated that no new legislation would be forthcoming, began issuing warnings that they would not peacefully remain in a state of semi-slavery after 1 October. They let it be known to the Reverend Dubois and several planters that another uprising was being contemplated because the Labour Law had not been changed.[57] The threat was duly reported to Governor Garde, who though considering it exaggerated, none the less sent night patrols around the island. A few days later, on 1 August, the Governor publicly proclaimed repeal of the Labour Law as of 1 October, when it would be replaced by new, as yet unspecified, regulations. Seventeen days later Garde submitted draft legislation to the St. Croix Colonial Council.[58]

On 13 September the new labour regulations, taking the form of a master-servants ordinance and a vagrancy act approved by the Colonial Councils of St. Croix and St. Thomas, were provisionally issued by Governor Garde. The master–servants act declared that planters and labourers were free to negotiate terms, hours, wages, and benefits, which had to be specified in a signed, written contract that could be renounced at any time by either party with due notice. Work for less than one month required no written contract.[59] While this ordinance was by itself reasonably fair and equitable, undue support for the planter interest was manifest in the vagrancy law, which specified that workers without permanent employment would be arrested and could be sentenced to work without payment on a plantation by the court. With the vagrancy law in force, the planters obviously had the upper hand in any wage negotiations, since the workers either had to find employment in the towns, or emigrate. But urban employment opportunities were limited, and as the workers well knew, emigration was next to impossible because of the obstructions and costs involved.[60]

As a new era of free bargaining opened before them, planters and labourers began organizing themselves into collective blocks. Even as the new regulations were debated in the Colonial Council, the plantation labourers let it be known that they would settle for nothing less than monthly contracts, a weekly wage of 25 cents, free housing and provision grounds, and optional medical care for 2 cents per week. Among themselves they agreed not to return to work until their terms were met. The labourers felt that because a large crop was under way, the planters would have little choice but to give in to their demands.[61]

Exactly how the workers organized themselves and arrived at this united front is unclear. In so far as is known, they formed no union or formal association. Presumably, leaders on each plantation persuaded their fellow workers that individual interests would be best served by collective bargaining and collective action. According to some reports, violence was threatened against anyone who broke ranks.[62] Foremost among the leadership and militant rank and file were British immigrant workers, whose resolve had been strengthened by a rumour that a British ship would be sent to St. Croix on 1 October to transport anyone wishing to return to their native islands.[63]

Concurrently, the planters met and formed a formal Association, which agreed that its members would offer the labourers yearly contracts, a weekly wage of 20 cents for first class labourers, free housing and provision grounds, and mandatory medical care for a fee of 2 cents per week. Association members agreed that they would not present their terms to the workers until a week after 1 October, hoping that during that time the workers would exhaust their meagre savings and be forced by threat of arrest under the vagrancy act to accept the planters' offer.[64]

October 1st came and went without incident or wage negotiations. Danish Prince Valdemar came into Frederiksted harbour aboard the Danish warship *Dagmar* and was warmly greeted by several thousand black Crucians peacefully assembled at the dock. A British warship already on the scene as a precautionary measure returned to St. Thomas the next day.[65]

On 4 October British Consul George Stevens arrived in Frederiksted roadstead on board the HMS *Blanche*, commanded by Captain Charles Knowles. Stevens and Knowles discovered 'that every soul on the island [had] struck work since October 1st'. While Stevens went to discuss matters with Vice-Consul Armstrong at Bülowsminde near Christiansted, Knowles made his way to the house of Vice-Consul Dubois, where he offered to repatriate any dissatisfied British subject. Dubois informed him that 2,000 to 3,000 persons stood ready to accept his offer. Startled and incredulous at this news, Knowles asked Dubois to start a registration of those wishing to leave.[66]

A few hours later Consul Stevens reached Dubois's house, where several hundred British immigrants had assembled. Inside, he spoke with four of the immigrant leaders, who told him that the immigrants wanted to leave the island because 'they had been kept down long enough under the former Labour Act and they saw no possibility of making terms under the new one', since the planters seemed to be insisting on a one-year contract and inadequate compensation.[67] The outlook of the labourers was summed up by a Barbadian representative, who told Stevens that the planters'

> terms have not been made known to us, they have only been hinted at, and we have been left in the dark and told that nothing will be done for a week, the object of the delay being that we should spend the little we have and when, as we must do, we help ourselves to everything off the Estates, we will be taken up as vagrants and made to work for nothing, hence our wish to get away at once; the duty of our employers was, on the 1st October, to hand us in their terms in writing and give us their views and leave us free to act. On our side, we said long ago, that we would have no more contracts but live and work on the estates, the same as in our native Islands, under a monthly engagement with a fortnight's notice on either side and twenty-five cents cash wages in lieu of ten, as formerly and all the former privileges which are worth about eight or nine cents more, and making a total of thirty-three to thirty-four cents per diem.[68]

On the afternoon of 6 October Dubois, who had already registered over 1,000 immigrants, told Captain Knowles that at least 3,000 persons wanted assistance to leave. Aware that he could only take a fraction of that number aboard his ship, Knowles announced to the crowd waiting outside Dubois's house that he had not come to take them away. The policemaster then told them that free passports would be issued to anyone seeking to leave at their own expense. As Knowles steamed out of Frederiksted roadstead, the disappointed immigrants milled about town. As a precaution, 100 men from the *Dagmar* were sent ashore, a show of force that persuaded the crowd to disperse.[69]

Their hopes of repatriation shattered, the British immigrants turned their attention to insuring the success of the island-wide general strike. When Consul Stevens returned to St. Croix on 11 October, he found the hungry workers willing to compromise on the question of wages but determined not to accept yearly contracts. As one British immigrant told him,

> Work, we wish to work, but the Masters don't want us to work, they will not pay us, they want us to remain slaves; they want us to contract for a year; the Judge told us there were to be no more contracts and that we were free from the 1st October and we mean to be free. God has sent all these fine canes, their profits can be seen with any eyes, but all is for the Planter . . . We asked twenty-five cents and all the former privileges, but today we are agreed to take twenty cents and the former privileges, so we could settle about the wages; we can work and are ready to turn to tomorrow, but we will make no contracts.[70]

When asked why the workers were so opposed to a yearly contract, he explained,

> . . . there are no contracts in our Islands, none in Porto Rico, none in Crab-Island, there, people are taken by the day, week or month; they give notice if they are not properly treated, and they get notice if they are not wanted and they quit. It brings Justice to both sides; when a man gets a good master, he will not leave; but the only way to get a good master is not to be signed . . . Not even if they chop and mash us up in pieces will we contract. In Barbados is job-work and a good man may gain seventy-five cents a day, while a bad workman can gain twenty-five, but there we are at home and if we are ill, our Governor has a hospital for us and if we die, we are buried; here we pay for a Doctor, but we see one once a year, and he never gives us more than two cents of salts and only God makes us well.

Another immigrant, Nathaniel Benjamin of Barbados, later told Stevens,

> I would sooner drown myself and my son than enter again into a yearly contract; it is worse than slavery, for a slave owner has an object in keeping his slaves fat the same as oxen and horses, but in Sainte Croix they work us for a year and get all they can out of us and if we lose condition and are not able to work, they send us adrift at the end of our Contract.[71]

On 15 October Knowles and Stevens, concerned that the workers were being unfairly starved into submission, informed the planters and Governor Garde that if a settlement was not reached within three days they would remove all the British immigrants wishing to leave. Three days later planter representatives replied by requesting more time, pointing out that recent settlements on a few estates seemed to indicate that the strike was ending.[72]

At this juncture, Knowles and Stevens began to disagree on what course of action to pursue. Knowles, fearful that any repatriation would be difficult, risky, and harmful to British planter interests on St. Croix, insisted that the strike be allowed to take its course without further interference by British representatives.[73] Stevens, on the other hand, remained determined to help the British workers escape a life of bondage in what he considered a tyrannical foreign land. 'As I see it', he wrote to Knowles,

> the British labourers who ask to be removed are at most three thousand; men [and women] who, after being much abused, are now confessedly the best hands in the country . . . They form, according to all calculations, one-fifth of the Labourers in the Island; the remaining four-fifths being 'Cruzians' or natives of St. Croix, and their removal can be only a temporary misfortune, while their retention in a state of semi-slavery, must ever be attended with dangerous and disastrous results, a condition which the autocratic ruler of these Islands will never remedy until compelled to turn his thoughts to the necessity of class legislation on terms more in accordance with the requirements of the age . . . To any honest and disinterested Englishman living out here, the manner in which the Negroes have been treated is simply revolting.[74]

While the two Englishmen bickered over their imperial responsibilities and sought further instructions from their respective masters in the Admiralty and the Foreign Office, some of the hard-pressed labourers began agreeing to yearly contracts in exchange for premiums of $8.00. Most, however, steadfastly stood their ground in the face of starvation and planter threats of eviction. During the last week of October, their resolve and unity began to pay off, as several planters broke ranks with the Association and made settlements for contract periods of less than one year. On 1 November the Association accepted the inevitable and allowed its members to negotiate whatever terms they pleased.[75]

Both sides gained and lost something in the resulting settlements. The planters prevailed in the case of wages and benefits, giving first class labourers 20 cents a day, providing free housing and provision grounds, and charging for medical care. The labourers dictated the term of employment, which varied according to the desires of the individual. A survey of 4,450 labourers on 78 estates taken in January 1880 showed that 950 worked by the day without any contract. Of the 3,200 labourers who had signed their contracts after the new regulations had gone into effect, 600 had contracts for one month, and the remainder for varying lengths of time under one year.[76] In subsequent years, more and more workers chose to work by the day or month, thus maintaining their precious and hard earned freedom of choice and movement.

CONCLUSION

Between 1859 and 1878 more than 5,000 Caribbean immigrants, half of them from Barbados, were brought into St. Croix to preserve the plantation system and a set of laws that guaranteed plantocratic hegemony. For more than a decade the contract labourers served that purpose well, largely because those who could not endure the working conditions were able to emigrate to more attractive labour markets. The two to three thousand foreign labourers who settled on St. Croix did so because they found job security, a tolerable standard of living, and a culture similar to their own. Most of the migrants, particularly the Barbadians, had been driven from their homeland by unemployment, starvation, and limited opportunity for self-improvement. For such people, the certainties provided by the Labour Act of 1849 could offset the loss of freedom it demanded.

Immigrants' willingness to accept legally mandated low wages and constraints on their time and movement derived, in part, from the knowledge that the safety valve of emigration was available to them. They could always go home, or so they believed. Their tolerance also stemmed from a reassuring awareness that their condition and their opportunities differed in no way from those of native workers. The inequalities in status that bred immigrant discontent and truculence elsewhere in the Caribbean (Johnson 1971) were absent in St. Croix during the first fifteen years of the immigration.

But deteriorating environmental and economic conditions in the 1870s forced the plantocracy to take measures that undermined immigrant tolerance of a legal system that held them in partial bondage. Foreign labourers found that in times of distress the Labour Law offered them no protection against unemployment, the revocation of privileges, and the imposition of fines that reduced their income. Immigrants seeking to leave found it increasingly difficult to do so. Long-standing wage and opportunity parities with natives were disrupted, first by the porter system and then by the central factory. With the opening of the central factory in 1878, the Labour Law and the social order it supported lost all meaning for most immigrants. On 1 October of that year they went to Frederiksted to demand wage equality or to exercise their freedom to move elsewhere. Obtaining neither, they exploded into violence against the police, the most palpable upholders of a law and a system that denied them the freedom and equality they sought. What followed in the next few days was the chaotic aftershock of that initial, unintended explosion.

Beyond the anger and violence, the beginnings of an incipient labour movement involving natives and immigrants can be discerned in the planning that took place before the events of 1 October 1878. That movement was nurtured by the heavy loss of life during Fireburn and by the subsequent reluctance of dithering Danish officials and a recalcitrant plantocracy to abandon their coerced labour regime. It grew toward maturity during the general strike of October 1879, which gained for labour full freedom of time and movement. But, ironically, it failed to mature precisely because of that success. In the years that followed, the architects of the general strike – immigrants and young natives – left St. Croix in increasing numbers for richer prospects elsewhere. The movement of people which helped to lubricate the transition from slavery to freedom in the Danish West Indies thus carried to other shores the talents best suited to labour mobilization and organization. Not until the early twentieth century and the general strike of 1916 did new native leaders emerge to bring a union of plantation labourers into existence on St. Croix.

ACKNOWLEDGEMENTS

This essay has benefited from comments by Karen Fog Olwig and Svend E. Holsoe.

NOTES

1. Public Record Office, Kew, Foreign Office Papers (hereafter FO), 425/127, George A. Stevens to Salisbury, 16 Oct. 1878, No. 23. p. 27.
2. Staffordshire County Record Office, Stafford, England, Dyott Family Papers (hereafter Dyott Papers), Henry Walker to Richard Dyott, Oct. 26, 1847, D3388/83/12.
3. Dyott Papers, Henry Walker to Richard Dyott, 26 Jan. 1849, D661/10/2/3/5.
4. The figure for 1850 comes from Rigsarkivet, Copenhagen, Denmark (hereafter RA), Koloniernes Centralbestyrelse, 'Folkemaengden 1850' #1016. The figure for 1858 is from RA, Vestindiske Reviderede Regnskaber, St. Croix Matriklerne 1758-1915. Somewhat different totals are recorded in the set of St. Croix Matriklerne in Record Group 55 (hereafter RG 55) at the United States National Archives and Record Service, Washington, DC (hereafter NARS). Throughout this essay, the number of field labourers is the total of all first, second, and third class workers. A portion of the decrease in the plantation work force can be attributed to an excess of deaths over births, a pre-emancipation trend that continued on St. Croix throughout the nineteenth century. A complete set of vital rate statistics for this period are wanting. However, the fragmentary data that are available for the period 1869–79 show between 25 and 50 more deaths than births per annum for the rural population. Thus, at most, excess mortality accounted for less than 25 per cent of the total population decrease.
5. See 'Letter to the Editor', *St. Croix Avis*, 2 Nov. 1852.
6. Guildhall Library, London, Baring Brothers Papers, Mss. 18321, HC 5.5.1, Part 1 (hereafter Baring Brothers Papers), Beech to Baring Brothers, 14 May 1852.
7. Consul James W. Siler, 'Danish Dependencies: Santa Cruz', in US Secretary of State, *Annual Report on the Commercial Relations between the United States and Foreign Nations, 1871* (Washington, DC: Government Printing Office, 1872), p. 277.
8. Dyott Papers, Frank Newton to Richard Dyott, 30 Oct. 1850; Baring Brothers Papers, Beech to Baring Brothers, 30 Sept. 1851, commenting 'it is awful to think how much we are at the mercy of these people'; letter of 'Custodia', *St. Croix Avis*, 29 Sept. 1857; letter of 'An Old

Subscriber', *St. Croix Avis*, 11 March 1859.

9. B. J., 'Bribing Labourers', *St. Croix Avis*, 23 Aug. 1855.
10. Baring Brothers Papers, Beech to Baring Brothers, 2 March 1851 and 14 May 1852.
11. A copy of this ordinance can be found in NARS, RG 55, Box 342. Between 1859 and July 1882, the Immigration Fund expenditures totalled of $184,660, to which planters receiving immigrants contributed $51,175, or 28 per cent (see NARS, RG 55, St. Croix Colonial Council Proceedings, 18 July 1882, Statement by Governor Arendrup, p. 178, Box 2105).
12. Documentation relevant to the various immigration schemes can be found in RA, Koloniernes Centralbestyrelse, #907-910. See also Jensen (1978) and Nielsen (1973).
13. See his letters in FO 22/320 and 22/321, and his summation of the scheme's failure in FO 22/338, Rainals to Earl of Clarendon, 19 Feb. 1866.
14. Nielsen 1973:33-35. In 1859, 133 Portuguese immigrants also entered St. Croix from Jamaica; see Baring Brothers Papers, Beech to Baring Brothers, 28 April and 27 July 1859; and 'Notice', *St. Croix Avis*, 8 March 1859.
15. Nielsen (1973); NARS, RG 55, 'List of Immigrants from Barbados during the Years 1859-1870', Box 338.
16. Nielsen (1973); NARS, RG 55, St. Croix Colonial Council Proceedings, 18 July 1882, Statement by Governor Arendrup, p. 177, Box 2105. Direct immigration from Barbados ceased in 1873, when the Barbados Emigration Office disallowed emigration to non-British territories (Roberts 1955:259).
17. NARS, RG 55, 'List of Immigrants from Barbados during the Years 1859–1870', Box 338.
18. NARS, RG 55, 'Statement of labourers introduced into the Island of St. Croix since the 23 Aug. 1864', Box 338; 'List of importation of immigrant labourers from 26th of March 1866 to 26th November 1870', Box 216.
19. See, for example, letter of 'N. N.', *St. Croix Avis*, 28 Oct. 1864; letter of 'Reformer', *St. Croix Avis*, 10 March 1865; letter of 'Plain Words', *St. Croix Avis*, 21 March 1865; letter of 'Free Discussion', *St. Croix Avis*, 31 March, 1865; 'Editorial', *St. Croix Avis*, 30 Jan. 1870. See also, NARS, RG 55, Charles Bryan, 'General remarks respecting the Immigrants introduced from Barbados to St. Croix, 22 Aug. 1866', Box 338.
20. NARS, RG 55, Immigration Committee Correspondence, Charles Bryan to F. B. Dubois, 26 July 1866, Box 338; T. Thompson to Dubois, 26 Sept. 1866, Box 2141.
21. NARS, RG 55, Immigration Committee Correspondence, T. Thompson to F. B. Dubois, 27 Aug. 1866, Box 2141.
22. Quoted in *St. Thomas Tidende*, 19 Jan. 1870.
23. RA, Koloniernes Centralbestyrelse, Det statistiske Departement, St. Croix Folketaelling [Census], 1870. This figure does not include migrants from the Danish colonies of St. Thomas and St. John.
24. FO 22/320, Henry Rainals to Earl Russell, 26 March 1864.
25. Great Britain, Foreign Office, *Diplomatic and Consular Reports on Trade and Finance* (London: Her Majesty's Stationary Office, 1876) (hereafter DCRTF:), 'Report by Consul Palgrave on the Agriculture and Industry of St. Croix for the Year 1875', pp. 813-14. According to Palgrave, Britons owned 93 of the 132 sugar estates and 18 of 74 stock estates; he also estimated that slightly less than half of the black population was British and that 'the white agricultural and commercial population, planters, managers, overseers and shopkeepers, is either by birthplace or descent, almost wholly British; and of this again, two-thirds at least are Irish, and half the remaining third Scotch'. For an assessment of the pronounced British character of St. Croix at the time see FO 425/127, Francis Armstrong and John C. Dubois, 'Report from the Vice-Consulates of St. Croix for the Year 1877', Confidential, pp. 12-14. The development of British influence in St. Croix is treated in Hall (1985).
26. RA, Vestindiske Reviderede Regnskaber, St. Croix Matriklerne 1758–1915.
27. Baring Brothers Papers, Richard Knight to Baring Brothers, 11 Aug. 1863.
28. NARS, RG 55, St. Croix Colonial Council Proceedings, 26 June 1871, p. 10, Box 2105; FO 22/331, Henry Rainals 'Report on the Navigation, Trade, Agriculture of the Island of St. Croix . . . in the Year 1864'; letter of 'N. N.', *St. Croix Avis*, 28 Oct. 1864. See also Jensen (1979:79).

29. DCRTF:1876, 'Report by Consul Palgrave on the Agriculture and Industry of St. Croix for the Year 1875', pp. 817-18.
30. DCRTF:1878, 'Report by Vice-Consul DuBois on the Trade and Commerce of Frederiksted for the Year 1877', p. 1493.
31. RA, Vestindiske Reviderede Regnskaber, St. Croix Matrikleme 1758–1915.
32. DCRTF:1878, 'Report by Vice-Consul DuBois on the Trade and Commerce of Frederiksted for the Year 1877', p. 1493.
33. Ibid.; Nielsen 1973:33-35.
34. NARS, RG 55, St. Croix Colonial Council Proceedings, 26 June 1871, p. 11; 26 May 1873, p. 259; 7 July 1873, p. 273; 1 Sept. 1873, p. 276.
35. FO 425/127, Stevens to Salisbury, Oct. 16, 1878, pp. 26-28; FO 22/423, Stevens to Salisbury, March 13, 1879, enclosing 'Extracts from Journal kept at the British Vice-Consulate, St. Croix, 1873–1877'.
36. FO 425/127, Stevens to Salisbury, 16 Oct. 1878, p. 28; 'Report of the Royal Commission of Inquiry into the Causes which led to the Disturbances in the Danish West Indies in October 1878' (hereafter 'Report'), p. 119.
37. FO 425/127, 'Report', p. 121. The porter system, which had been widespread in the 1850s, fell into disuse during the 1860s (see Jensen 1979). In the early 1870s most planters on the Colonial Council opposed government efforts to encourage the porter system on the grounds that it undermined the principle of wage equality and provoked unrest on those estates where it had been practised (see NARS, St. Croix Colonial Council Proceedings, 21 Oct. 1873, Box 2105).
38. NARS, U.S. Consular Despatches, St. Croix (Microfilm T233), Consul V. V. Smith to Seward, 22 Oct. 1878; FO 425/127, 'Report' (p. 122), which observed, 'the Sugar Factory . . . acted as a system of porters upon a greater scale'.
39. FO 425/127, Stevens to Salisbury, Oct 16, 1878, p. 26.
40. The account of the outbreak and course of the Fireburn Insurrection is based on the following sources: FO 425/127, Stevens to Salisbury, 2 Oct. 1878, pp. 2-3, 10 Oct. 1878, pp. 5-11, and 16 Oct. 1878, pp. 26-30; 'Account given by the Rev. J. C. Dubois, Her Majesty's Vice-Consul at Frederiksted, Santa Cruz, respecting the Rising among the Negro Plantation Labourers in that Island on the 1st October, 1878', pp. 19-20; 'Report of the Royal Commission of Inquiry into the Causes which led to the Disturbances in the Danish West Indies in October 1878', pp. 117-148; NARS, U.S. Consular Despatches, St. Croix (Microfilm T233), Consul V. V. Smith to Seward, 22 Oct. 1878. Except for the 'Report of the Royal Commission of Inquiry', these sources contradict much of the information found in the highly slanted and attenuated official version of events presented in Governor James A. Garde, 'Statement concerning the State of Siege declared in the Island of St. Croix from the 2nd to the 31st October 1878, and the events which caused said state of seige', *St. Croix Avis*, 23 Nov. 1878 and 'Report to the Governor . . . by Acting Policemaster in the Jurisdiction of Frederiksted, R. Petersen', *St. Croix Avis*, 30 Nov. 1878. Indeed, Reverend Dubois denounced Petersen's report as 'a misrepresentation from beginning to end' (FO 425/127, Dubois to Stevens, 2 Dec. 1878, p. 61). The account of events on 1 October found in Charles Edwin Taylor, *Leaflets from the Danish West Indies* (London: Wm. Dawson and Sons, 1888), pp. 151-166, closely parallels and amplifies my sources. Taylor relied heavily on Dubois, but he made no mention of the role of immigrants.
41. NARS, U.S. Consular Despatches, St. Croix (Microfilm T233), Consul V. V. Smith to Seward, Oct. 22, 1878.
42. FO 425/127, Stevens to Salisbury, Oct. 16, 1878, p. 28.
43. 'Statement concerning the State of Siege declared in the Island of St. Croix from the 2nd to the 31st October 1878, and the events which caused said state of seige', *St. Croix Avis*, 23 Nov. 1878.
44. FO 425/127, Stevens to Salisbury, 10 Oct., 1878, p. 10; NARS, U.S. Consular Despatches, St. Croix (Microfilm T233), Consul V. V. Smith to Seward, 22 Oct. 1878.
45. FO 22/435, Vice-Consul F. Armstrong to Stevens, 15 Oct. 1879; FO 22/431, Dubois to Stevens, 5 April 1880.
46. FO 22/435, Stevens to Salisbury, 20 Oct. 1879; FO 22/421, C. Wyke to Salisbury, 14 Jan

1880, No. 4; FO 22/431, Stevens to Salisbury, 17 April 1880, with enclosures, Stevens to Salisbury, 24 Sept. 1880; FO 22/439, Wyke to Granville, 6 Aug. 1881.

47. *New York Herald*, 22 Oct. 1878.
48. FO 425/127, Stevens to Salisbury, 10 Oct. 1878, p. 10;
49. FO 425/127, 'Report', pp. 121-22.
50. FO 425/127, Stevens to Salisbury, 16 Oct. 1878, p. 28.
51. FO 22/431, 'Consul Stevens Observations . . .', enclosed in Stevens to Salisbury, 31 Jan. 1880, No. 13.
52. FO 22/441, Stevens to Granville, 13 Sept. 1881; FO 22/439, 'British Negroes sentenced to penal servitude for life', enclosed in Wyke to Granville, 6 Aug. 1881, No. 14.
53. For Joseph Clark, who fled to Tortola with seventeen other immigrants, see FO 425/127, Stevens to President Hickson, 9 Oct. 1878; for Charles Max, see FO 425/127, Stevens to Salisbury, 16 Oct. 1878, p. 28.
54. *St. Croix Avis*, 9, 12, 16 Oct. 1878.
55. FO 425/127, Stevens to Salisbury, 10 Oct. 1878, p. 10.
56. FO 425/127, 'Report'.
57. FO 22/435, Dubois to Stevens, 21 July 1879, enclosed in Stevens to Salisbury, 23 July 1879; FO 22/431, Dubois to Stevens, 13 Jan. 1880.
58. Ibid.; FO 22/431, Stevens to Salisbury, 5 Aug. and 8 Sept. 1879.
59. NARS, RG 55, 'Ordinance for Regulating the Relations between Masters and Servants in the Danish West India Islands, 24 October 1878', Box 338.
60. FO 22/435, Stevens to Salisbury, 8 Sept. 1878, No. 43.
61. FO 22/431, Dubois to Stevens, 13 Jan. 1880.
62. FO 22/435, Knowles to Inglefield, 8 Oct. 1879, No. 38.
63. Ibid.; FO 22/431, Dubois to Stevens, 21 July 1880.
64. FO 22/435, Stevens to Salisbury, 1 Jan. 1880.
65. FO 22/435, Stevens to Salisbury, 15 Oct. 1879, No. 55.
66. FO 22/435, Knowles to Inglefield, 8 Oct. 1879, No. 38; Dubois to Stevens, 13 Oct. 1879; FO 22/431, Dubois to Stevens, 21 July 1880.
67. FO 22/431, Stevens to Salisbury, 15 Oct. 1879, No. 55.
68. Ibid.
69. Ibid.; FO 22/435, Knowles to Inglefield, 8 Oct. 1879, No. 38.
70. Ibid.
71. FO 22/431, Stevens to Salisbury, 28 Oct. 1879, No. 60.
72. Ibid.; Stevens to Salisbury, 15 Oct. 1879, No. 55.
73. FO 22/431, Knowles to Stevens, 23 Oct. 1879, enclosed in Stevens to Salisbury, Oct. 28, 1879, No. 60.
74. Ibid.
75. FO 22/431, Dubois to Stevens, 20 Nov. 1879, enclosed in Stevens to Salisbury, 22 Nov. 1879, No. 65.
76. 'Labour, Contracts in St. Croix', *St. Croix Avis*, 17 Jan. 1880.

REFERENCES

Dookhan, Isaac. 1974. *A History of the Virgin Islands of the United States*. Epping, Essex: Caribbean Universities Press in association with Bowker, Publishing Company for the College of the Virgin Islands.

Hall, N. A. T. 1985. *The Danish West Indies: Empire without Dominion 1671–1848*. St. Thomas: Division of Libraries, Museums and Archaeological Services, Occasional Paper No. 8.

Hatchett, P. B. 1859. *Statistics Regarding Landed Properties in the Island of St. Croix From 1816 to 1857* . . . St. Croix: *St. Croix Avis*.

Jensen, Peter Hoxcer. 1978. 'Indførsel af fri Arbejdskraft til St. Croix 1849–76, med særligt henblik på immigrations og arbejdslovgivningen'. M.A. thesis, Aarhus Universitet.

_____ 1979. 'Plantagearbejdernes vilkår i Dansk Vestindien fra Slaveemancipationen til Øernes

Salg'. Prize Essay, Aarhus Universitet. Johnson, Howard. 1973. 'Barbadian Immigrants in Trinidad 1870–1897. *Caribbean Studies* 13:5-30.

Nielsen, Aase R. 1973. 'Immigration af arbejdskraft til St. Croix 1860–1879'. M.A. thesis, University of Copenhagen.

Quin, John T. 1892. *Statistics concerning Sugar Production in St. Croix from 1862-1889*. St. Croix: John T. Quin, Printer.

Roberts, G. W. 1955. 'Emigration from the Island of Barbados'. *Social and Economic Studies*, 4:245-88.

Sircar, K. K. 1971. 'Emigration of Indian Indentured Labour to the Danish West Indian Island of St. Croix 1863–68'. *Scandinavian Economic History Review*, XIX, 2:133-48.

Island Systems and the Paradox of Freedom: Migration in the Post-Emancipation Leeward Islands

ELIZABETH M. THOMAS-HOPE

Emancipation in the Leeward Islands, as elsewhere in the Caribbean, was not the final attainment of freedom for the former slave populations. In order to achieve and experience liberty, an entirely new culture had to emerge, which would bear the hallmark of personhood and the re-articulation of self in society. It also necessitated the reorientation of self in place; for the plantation was not just a system, it was a specific locality. The emergent culture had to reflect the new society's sense of place; the island of bondage could no longer contain and constrain a people if that people were to be free either metaphorically or actually. Marronage, or withdrawal, became legitimized by the Act of Emancipation.

The sense of personhood that followed emancipation was manifested in numerous ways. A new relationship developed between the workers and those who needed their labour, but the freedom to sell or withdraw one's labour was limited by the structures and opportunities which existed at home and abroad. Control over land and economic resources, as well as over the avenues to status and power, meant that whatever the nature of the imagined world of liberty, the reality was island systems within which the culture of the slaves was transformed into a culture with new strategies for viability and upward mobility.

None of these processes led to the ex-slaves' control over their country's resources – they remained marginalized in an economic sense. Selling their labour at home and abroad led to new mechanisms of exploitation by the plantocracy. Migration took on special significance in the consolidation of freedom and in the culture of the free black population which developed after emancipation.

EMANCIPATION AND FREEDOM

The landscape of the Leeward Islands had been altered dramatically by the introduction of sugar cultivation in the seventeenth century. The islands were transformed from estates based on the co-existence of people, cultivated crops, and indigenous flora and fauna to plantations devoted to sugar monoculture worked by a large number of slaves, who were controlled by a small number of Europeans.

By the end of the eighteenth century the population of the Leeward Islands comprised well over 83,000 Negro slaves, fewer than 3,000 free people of colour, and about 8,400 whites (Goveia 1965). The islands had been severely denuded of their primary forest cover; the good land was heavily cropped with sugar cane interspersed with cattle grazing, while mountainous or waste land sustained slave provision grounds. The poor quality and limited size of the provision grounds, together with droughts and hurricanes from time to time, resulted in chronic malnutrition and associated disease. Periodic epidemics also occurred, and the death rate was generally high. The clearing of forests for crops invariably resulted in soil erosion and a decline in fertility. This led to more intensive working of the land under cane and to the importation of additional slaves to work the fields, which only exacerbated the food problem and caused greater erosion, pressure on provision grounds, and a degraded ecosystem.

In Nevis, for example, the lack of low-lying land led to cane cultivation on the high ground, causing widespread soil erosion and reducing the land available for slave provisions. The slaves felled the trees and worked the cane, while the planters ran commercial ventures in sugar and its by-products. The polarization of the economy was reflected in the divisions of society: profit-making and marginality or mere survival; land ownership and lack of ownership.

Each island was constrained physically by small size and sugar-plantation dominance and socially by rigid criteria of power, status, and opportunity. Slave societies had been dynamic, and resistance had formed an inherent part of that dynamic: marronage was an ongoing feature. Sometimes the withdrawal was covert and subtle, at other times overt and blatant. But while resisting the system, the slaves had also had to adapt in order to survive. After emancipation, migration became an important part of the process of withdrawal or resistance, yet at the same time, part of the process of adaptation.

The plantations of the Leeward Islands were peripheral to the mainstream of Caribbean sugar interests, and the white creoles guarded their position even more closely than in the major sugar-producing colonies. The eighteenth century's legacy was a rigid social system within each island and a marginal economic position within the region. At the same time, the Leeward Islands had no viable alternative except to adapt to the changing imperatives of the wider economic framework of metropolitan demands for sugar production.

Although marginal to British and later North American centres of economic activity, Leeward Islanders after emancipation were within the labour markets of both. Paradoxically, while migration served the interests of capital expansion (through participation in the inter-regional and international labour force), it also served the interests of the ex-slaves. Migration produced a new framework within which Leeward Islanders could participate in economic activity central to regional interests and, at the same time, could adapt to an official freedom within the limits of their island system.

MIGRATION IN THE ARTICULATION OF FREEDOM

Since the Act of Emancipation did not of itself create, let alone guarantee, a meaningful freedom for the slaves, the change in status from slave to free person would have been merely a legal statement had there been no opportunities for movement from the plantations. In the first place, freeing slaves did not mean freeing land. By controlling the land, planters maintained their control over labour, and especially in the smallest islands, little land was outside the plantation's sphere of ownership and control.

Throughout the British Caribbean (with the exception of Antigua), emancipation was followed by four years of apprenticeship. In Antigua the requirement to remain on the plantations was unnecessary, since the slaves had no practical option but to stay where they were. Frequent drought, the lack of forested mountains, and provision grounds on marginal estate land meant that whether slave or free, the workers could not sustain themselves independent of work on the plantation.

In St. Kitts reaction to the imposition of the apprenticeship regulations was violent. For weeks following the day of official emancipation (6 August 1834), there were major outbursts of rioting and people fled to the hills (Hall 1971). In retaliation the British troops burned the huts of the former slaves, pursued them, and pressed them back onto the estates. This action confirmed their worst fears that an Act of Emancipation did not bring the realities of freedom.

So determined were the planters to avoid ex-slaves leaving the estates in St. Kitts that they passed a series of laws which effectively favoured the plantations in the competition for land. The continued control of land meant that plantation owners had to be responsible for feeding the workers. But the fact that either access to provision grounds or the supply of food was a regulation of apprenticeship left the workers just as beholden to the paternalism of the plantation owners as they had always been (Hall 1971).

Two centuries of a plantation system based on slave labour and the concept of slavery had firmly entrenched the pattern of social relations. The plantation infrastructure had so consolidated the system of paternalism, subservience, and personal denigration of the black population that no act of Parliament alone could possibly overturn and undo its effects. Slavery had meant total dependence upon the plantation and lack of choice in work and residence. The obligations and lack of personhood continued virtually unchanged after emancipation, while land (and all that it implied) was controlled by the plantations. The requirements of the plantations demanded conditions of work that were fundamentally incompatible with personal freedom. Once people had the notion that freedom was attainable, it was inconceivable that they would re-orient their minds and re-align their work practices to meet such demands. In general, the only way the ex-slaves of the Leeward Islands could engage in and consolidate their freedom was to leave the islands altogether.

Planters had moved slaves between plantations and sometimes even to other islands. The only other reason that slaves had left the plantations was to escape. Not surprisingly, those who escaped could never return. If found and brought back to the plantation, they met certain punishment and possible death. Likewise, slaves who quit their island illegally by ship could not return. There was no means of accommodating or adapting to the system; one could only withdraw permanently. Therefore, anyone who ran away had to lead the life of a fugitive, which meant leaving not just the plantation but also one's kith and kin, the only people to provide any comfort in an alien land where little or nothing could be called one's own.

Marronage was a heroic but unattractive option for slaves in the Leeward Islands. Evidence suggests that deportation was regarded as a severe punishment (Eltis 1972). The chances of establishing viable clandestine settlements only occurred in large territories – notably Jamaica and Dutch Guiana (Suriname) – where Maroon communities were located in the virtually impenetrable terrain, and even there, they were secure only after a prolonged period of fighting.

Departure from plantation or island during slavery, unless arranged as part of a commercial transaction between plantation owners, was an implicit act of escape. After emancipation, the same removal for similar reasons – freedom – was known as migration. The tension in the dialectic of servitude and marronage was transformed as was the terminology. The freedom to return was new, and this new possibility transmitted an energy to migration which created its own momentum. To withdraw and then return became a major element of post-emancipation freedom; it did not imply the permanent severance of kinship ties. Migration, both within the islands and away from them, brought flexibility to the relationship between worker and estate rather than a total loss of labour. Thus migration did not become an alternative to island culture so much as a major agent in the transition to freedom and a part of the emerging culture of the post-emancipation generations of Caribbean people.

ISLANDS AND REGION

Before emancipation Leeward Islanders were already being shifted by official arrangement to the southern Caribbean as slave labourers. After emancipation the movements were voluntary, even spontaneous. By 1845 peasants from the Leewards regularly sold or bartered their food crops in the Windward Islands and Trinidad. Later, towards the end of the century, thousands of seasonal cane harvesters travelled annually to Cuba and the Dominican Republic. While Jamaicans and Barbadians competed for work in Cuba, the Leeward Islanders went to the sugar plantations of Trinidad and British Guiana (Guyana) and constituted the main foreign work force on the sugar plantations of the Dominican Republic between 1900 and 1940 (Bryan 1985).

The migration of Leeward Island labour, especially to Trinidad and British Guiana, increased greatly after emancipation and helped fill the requirements of their expanding sugar industries. By 1837 agents were known to be purchasing apprenticeship contracts for ex-slaves in Tortola, Montserrat, Nevis, and St. Kitts. In 1838, after the abolition of apprenticeship, Nevis and St. Kitts enacted laws to reduce the departure by requiring proof of financial responsibility towards the family. Laws passed in the other Leeward Islands prohibited recruitment and established various regulations to stem the departure of labourers.

Most of the emigration restrictions were not sanctioned by the colonial authorities but reflected the desperate efforts of Leeward Island planters to prevent the total erosion of their labour force. Wages in the southern Caribbean were higher than those in the Leeward Islands, and it was reported that the peasants were emigrating in considerable numbers because the uncertainty of the tenure of their houses and provision grounds was a threat to their independence.

Despite the efforts of Leeward Island planters, large numbers of labourers departed illegally. By July 1841 Trinidad's agent-general, Thomas Johnston, estimated that 8,000 people, twice the official number, had come from the smaller islands to Trinidad (Richardson 1983). In 1842 four sailing vessels were reportedly plying between Nevis and Trinidad, carrying a steady stream of migrants. Nevisian planters estimated that by that time, almost 3,000 workers had emigrated from the island, a third of them illegally. It is impossible to know the true numbers involved, however. Official figures would be underestimates because many left illegally, but people were also enumerated more than once owing to the considerable return flow and multiple departures. Most migrants returned home after earning some money and left again later.

At first the movement from the Leeward Islands to the Dominican Republic was spontaneous rather than organized. Steamships and schooners sailed from St. Martin, Anguilla, and the Virgin Islands to the Dominican Republic. Passage to the Dominican Republic was free, since the captains received six dollars for each worker landed at San Pedro de Macoris, the chief sugar port in the south-east of the country. However, the migrants, who were generally issued with six-month permits, had to pay for the return trip. Those who arrived in this way were mostly Kitticians, followed by Antiguans, Nevisians, and Montserratians. Other migrants included Virgin Islanders, Dominicans, Windward Islanders, and Turks Islanders (Hoetink 1988).

Approximately 2,000 to 2,500 workers arrived in the Dominican Republic each year for the sugar harvest, which lasted from December/January to June. The seasonal workers were almost all cane cutters, paid by piecework. In addition to the short-term migrants, a number of Leeward Islanders settled in the south-eastern districts of the Dominican Republic, in or around San Pedro de Macoris, and engaged in a range of plantation occupations, ranging from engine driving to cane cutting. At their peak in the 1920s they would have numbered around 4,000. Locally they were known as the 'British', referring to their English-speaking identity in contrast to the Hispanic character of the host society, and were also called 'Cocolos', denoting their black racial identity – an issue of major local concern among the predominantly white and mulatto population and the basis of discrimination against them. Seasonal movements continued until the Great Depression of the 1930s. Thereafter entry permits were no longer issued, and workers were deported (Del Castillo n.d.).

THE ESTABLISHMENT OF TRANS-ISLAND COMMUNITIES

The migration culture which developed after emancipation became an intrinsic part of Leeward Island life, even though the actual migration field changed. By the end of the century steamships were providing a regular mail service between the Leewards, Bermuda, and Canada, and between 1900 and 1906 the chief destination of Leeward Island migrants was Bermuda, where they provided a labour force for the dockyards and military installations.

Despite the substantial labour losses sustained by the plantations, the population of the Leeward Islands was not necessarily declining (Proudfoot 1950). The migrations represented withdrawal from the plantations rather than severance from the island community of kinship ties and friends. Contrary to expectations, census figures for St. Kitts and Nevis show population increases between 1838 and 1884, in St. Kitts from 21,578 to 28,177 and in Nevis from 7,470 to 9,570.

The high level of mobility among the Leeward Islanders confirmed their reputation for unreliability in Trinidad and British Guiana. Not only did workers tend to return home as soon as they had earned what they perceived to be enough money, but within Trinidad and Guiana they frequently moved among estates. Since their ultimate aim was to purchase land and a house in their home island, they seldom purchased land at their destinations and maintained their freedom to come and go. In addition, immigration to the Caribbean from the Indian subcontinent lowered wages, and in 1848 only 2,641 of the 11,339 Leeward Islanders who had entered Trinidad in the preceding decade remained (Richardson 1983).

The significance of migration for Leeward Island culture lay principally in the close contact migrants maintained with their families. They retained their place in the household and society, and a system of reciprocal obligations between migrants and their households in the home island was established. In some years, 90 per cent of the working male population of Anguilla migrated on a seasonal basis to the plantations of the Dominican Republic. The migrants (most of whom were men) brought back money which they used primarily to build houses or to buy land. Likewise, remittances were part of the migration process and helped maintain close contact with the home society and underscored the commitment to return. From the 1910s to 1930s thousands of pounds were remitted by postal orders.

By 1917 about 900, or approximately 10 per cent, of the inhabitants of the town of San Pedro de Macoris were Cocolos from the Leeward and Turks and Caicos Islands (Bryan 1985). In other centres in the south-east of the Dominican Republic migrant workers comprised a similar proportion of the population. By the early twentieth century significant numbers of migrants and their Dominican-born families were scattered throughout the principal commercial and agricultural centres, forming a small but visible minority.

Trinidad, British Guiana, and the Dominican Republic had become part of the Leeward Islanders' new world of work and opportunity for freedom. They were part of the known world of the migrants themselves and imagined world of the rest of Leeward Island society. Further, they were part of the image of opportunity and the means of earning money to purchase land and thereby achieve either the freedom or the sense of freedom from employers and the plantation system in their home islands (Thomas-Hope 1992).

Once home, most migrants settled only temporarily, before setting off again when the opportunity or the need arose. By the turn of the century, lives and livelihoods of the Leeward Islanders had been adapted to the recurrent departure and return of a large proportion of their population.

Not just the ex-slaves but the brown population and creole whites as well became trans-island in their social and economic networks (Lowenthal 1972). The creole whites also migrated between islands for marriage, thereby extending family estates and widening the choice of marriage partners. The island world had been extended to incorporate a wider environment of work and opportunity. The trans-island family and community had become the norm, and a culture of 'trans-islandness' had been established.

The planters continued to monopolize land ownership throughout the nineteenth century. The landless ex-slaves continued to be mobile, extending their activities further afield. In so doing, migration played a major role in people's adaptation to the island ecosystems. Migration extended work opportunities beyond the limitations of tiny island resources and severe ecological constraints by allowing participation in the wider regional system. In this context, migration and the image of migration became part of the behavioural patterns associated with livelihood strategies, social relationships, status, and social mobility. Not surprisingly, an entire culture evolved in which migration was an integral part.

MIGRATION AND ISLAND CULTURE

After emancipation and apprenticeship social developments took place reflecting African antecedent cultures, the legacies of slavery, the continuing presence of the plantation, and a spatially mobile population. Through the participation of the lower classes in external labour markets, opportunities were extended to incorporate the wider region and enlarge the area from which work and household financial support could be obtained. The post-emancipation culture of work and social relations developed in association with this mobility. Likewise, the societal system of the islands influenced the culture of migration, its pattern of circulation, reciprocal obligations with the household left behind, and the meaning and value placed on it.

The livelihood strategies of the former slaves depended on flexibility in the type of work the individual was able and willing to undertake. Multiple occupations enabled people to engage in whatever work opportunities existed locally and permitted them to combine various kinds of work abroad (Dirks 1972; Philpott 1973; Richardson 1975; Midgett 1977). Migration extended work opportunities beyond the limitations of the local and national economic environment, and became closely linked to the achievement of one or more of the objectives of work.

Multiple occupations permitted a combination of jobs, one of which usually provided subsistence (farming in the case of rural households), while one or more other activities on an *ad hoc* or regular basis supplied an income to finance small luxuries or investments of various kinds (for example, in livestock or land). A second or even a third job could be pursued despite the fact that the income brought in was negligible, simply because it was regarded as having some status. Migration of varying duration provided capital to support less remunerative but higher status work back home. The lack of commitment to a full-time occupation permitted absences abroad without the individuals being particularly disadvantaged. Experience gained abroad became a valuable asset in resuming a livelihood strategy on the return to the home island.

A further aspect of the practice of occupational multiplicity was the involvement of more than one family member in the overall occupational strategy of the household. In rural areas women usually participated in farming, took charge of the marketing of farm produce, and were essential to the management of farm production and finances. The fact that cultivation declined when the male household head migrated was probably more closely related to the fact that remittances obviated the necessity for continued exertion in farming rather than to the inability of the migrant's spouse to manage. Lack of people to assist with heavy work, chiefly owing to unwillingness on the part of younger household members, also contributed to the decline in cultivation, especially in the absence of a male farmer, but this occurred with or without migration.

Although it has been suggested that migration brought about the feminization of farming, this statement is strongly contradicted by the fact that ever since slavery women had been farmers and controlled the marketing of produce. Migration in the post-emancipation period would simply have helped to consolidate this pattern of female participation in small-scale farming, especially for household subsistence and cash cropping.

Land-tenure practices among the rural populations of most Caribbean countries accommodated the sequential or long-term absences of family members and gave a security of tenure to those who went as well as to those who stayed. Family tenure, as Besson has pointed out, illustrated 'the resistance of Afro-Caribbean peoples to plantation slavery and the persistence of plantation monopoly in the rural sector' (Besson 1984:70). What is more, this type of tenure accommodated another aspect of societal adjustment, namely migration. Land-tenure practices of this type provided the newly formed peasantries (the future small-farming populations) with a measure of security in the event of migration. Such security was hardly measurable in economic terms but was highly significant in symbolic and psychological terms.

The lower-class family and household evolved a number of mechanisms to cope with the absence of some of its members through migration. One such mechanism was a system of reciprocal obligations (Midgett 1977; Gussler 1980; Pessar 1982; Olwig 1984, 1993). Members of both the household and the wider kinship network traditionally helped to facilitate migration by offering financial assistance or by undertaking domestic responsibilities. In return, economic support or gifts, depending on the level of obligation deemed appropriate, were expected from the migrant. Children were absorbed into other households in an unofficial, but effective, arrangement of reciprocal support. Aged parents were also assisted by the wider family, based on the tacit agreement of financial obligations being assumed by the migrant whose responsibility was delegated.

Marriage patterns also adapted to migration (Smith, R.T. 1956; Smith, M.G. 1957, 1962; Frucht 1960; Otterbein 1966). Formal marriage, which generally occurred late in life, invariably came after the period of active migration when the couple had benefitted financially from the migration. Indeed, in some cases migration facilitated the marriage of men by making possible the purchase of land and a house, often deemed an essential basis for marriage.

The social acceptance of different types of union during the lifetime of an individual encouraged the delay in formal marriage and permitted freedom of movement. In the absence of the nuclear family as the norm, the household composition could alter to accommodate changes in union status of the household head and other adult members. This flexibility meant that members of a household could be dispersed through the complex kinship network, and at a later stage the household could be reconstituted, if that were still deemed desirable. This is not to say that these arrangements were trouble free. Nevertheless, an institutional structure developed which facilitated the migration of parents and operated to support such practices. The success of these institutions was in large part due to the fact that they provided safeguards and a measure of security both to migrants and to family members who remained at home.

Social mobility increased once the immediate uncertainties over freedom and emancipation had passed and here, too, migration played a critical role. The social system in the islands evolved within a context where power was based on land ownership, status on colour, and opportunity on the successful mimicry of British behaviour and customs. The ex-slaves had none of these attributes, and for them migration provided the opportunity for land ownership, status by a route other than colour, and the chance to acquire the speech and fashions of the metropolis.

Migrants and those who desired to migrate perceived that their activity or intended activity abroad would produce the finance needed to raise their standard of living in terms of material comforts and would provide the assets on which independence, security, and status were based. Land and a house were the principal items, and migration for work was known to make possible the accumulation of capital for their purchase.

By the early decades of the twentieth century, education was beginning to play a greater role in class mobility, compensating for and at the same time starting the process of breaking down – the rigid association of class and colour. Education became a critical factor in the acquisition of professional occupations and thus middle-class status. Opportunities for secondary education and vocational training – chiefly in the teaching profession – were limited for children of the black working class. Although with difficulty, hard work, and dedication, migration began to play a role in providing the capital from which to start the accumulation of sufficient money to assist in the education of children. This was the means whereby the inter-generational upward mobility of an increasing number of black working-class people was achieved.

Even where formal qualifications were not acquired, work experience and in-service skill training were important to the migrant's success and to perceived migration achievement. Furthermore, migrants commonly valued a wide variety of experiences as contributing to their general cultural improvement. Symbols such as standard grammatical speech, public behaviour deemed socially respectable, and evidence that the horizons of the mind had been extended beyond the confines of insular parochialism were all highly valued.

Migration acquired its own prestige, adding status to respectability. New ways of speaking, even new ways of walking and conducting oneself in public, a sense of having been out and seen something of the world, provided the education and rite of passage which were to give a positive focus to a movement which had occurred initially in such negative circumstances. A migrant's prestige was enhanced through the material assets acquired and by having lived and worked abroad. The nature of the actual work undertaken overseas was often not readily disclosed, since it was invariably of an equally low or even lower status than the work performed locally. Despite this, the perception was that work done in a foreign country was of intrinsically higher value by the very fact of its location. Since work commanded higher monetary returns elsewhere, its value – and thus its status – was enhanced. This view was of prime importance in the migration process, for it indicated that location rather than type of work determined its status.

Within Caribbean societies the avenues for upward mobility were based on the rigid association of occupation and race, which sustained a class structure with negligible opportunities for mobility without the combination of acquiring both a higher status occupation and a lightening of colour. The avenues of social mobility were limited and could only be achieved inter-generationally, but migration helped people acquire these material assets which defined a person's status in society.

PARADOXES OF FREEDOM

In the period following emancipation, migration was critical in the adjustment to the new constraints and opportunities of freedom and brought into focus many of the paradoxes which still characterize modern Leeward Island societies. These included the contradictions of island identities and regional linkages; the interests of metropolitan capital and the freedoms in society to be exploited or used to turn exploitation to personal advantage; lower-class resistance to the former plantation system by the withdrawal of labour yet the adaptation to the wider societal system which migration permitted – a system which has never changed fundamentally.

Freedom of movement took on a special meaning for Caribbean peoples, and island boundaries no longer fixed the parameters of opportunity. The island's opportunities now extended to incorporate a wider world. That world had its own limits based on the expansion of capital into the Caribbean region and the associated pattern of labour markets. At the regional level, migration brought different parts of the Caribbean together, whereas their colonial history had consistently fragmented them. At the same time, migration heightened the differences of race and culture which had developed in the region during the colonial period. The appellations 'British' and 'Cocolos' highlighted the cultural and racial terms by which migrants were identified. These terms underlined the significance of the different identities of separate colonial histories in the perception of 'the other', even when 'the other' was the nearest neighbour in a physical sense.

The insularity factor was also present in the separate British colonies and in their views of other islands of similar colonial tradition. The terms used to describe Leeward Islanders – 'Down Islanders' in the Virgin Islands and 'Old Islanders' in Trinidad and British Guiana – reflected in the first instance the 'differentness' of neighbouring islanders even though they shared a common language. Language also demonstrated the deep allegiances of the Caribbean colonies to their own metropolitan countries and cultural traditions – a characteristic which later presented problems in the attempts at regional integration and economic co-operation. Nevertheless, migration and especially the constant ebb and flow of cane cutters to other islands served to eliminate the actual and perceived isolation of very small islands.

The freedom which came from emancipation included the essential ingredient of human liberty in permitting freedom within the labour market, freedom to move away from the plantation, freedom to own land, and freedom to be recognized as a person in a legal sense. The liberty to sell one's labour led to new forms of exploitation at home and abroad; freedom to own land did not provide the financial means for doing so; and freedom to be a person in law did not provide the means for the expression of personal aspirations and goals.

At the level of the household and family, the trans-island culture allowed the economic viability of very small islands. As an integral part of the societal system, the migration culture ameliorated the structural inequalities and exploitation of the regional labour markets, transforming them into opportunities both at the societal and individual level.

While lower-class resistance to the plantation system might have provided one alternative, resistance alone was not enough, since the old system officially continued and the power still lay in the hands of the plantocracy and its agents. Thus adaptation was as important as resistance in order to survive within the system and without being totally dominated by it.

The paradox of migration was its characteristic of circulation: the withdrawal of one's labour – the resistance of ex-slaves to the plantation system – became part of the process of adaptation. Migration served less as a means of rejecting the home environment and more as a mechanism of incorporation, extending island environments and interacting with new real and imagined worlds. Migration provided a sense of freedom, which made the return to unchanged structural and labour conditions tolerable through the improved personal economic and social status that it allowed.

The constraints of the island systems were not solely of a physical nature but embraced the entire institutional structure, including the avenues to mobility within the society. Freedom alone could not sustain the emerging society, and either a totally new alternative system had to evolve or new forms and structures had to be incorporated into the old system. Certainly freedom from the plantation did not imply freedom from the economic and legal systems where the real power resided. Migration, therefore, was both a radical force that directly confronted the existing plantation system and at the same time a conservative force that enabled the individual to pursue freedom and mobility without altering the structural framework. Migration assisted a new culture of freedom to evolve without fundamentally changing the *status quo*, in particular the class structure and the distribution of power.

CONCLUSION

Each change in international and national circumstances brought with it constraints and opportunities for each sector of the highly stratified Leeward Island societies. For more than a century and a half after emancipation, these societies continued to evolve out of groups of often disparate peoples in foreign, sometimes alien, lands and out of the demands and expectations of freedom from a system rooted in bondage for some and absenteeism for others. These societies had to adjust to the ever-changing imperatives of an international economic system over which they had no control.

There is a dynamic interaction between the migration process and the forces of the wider international and national frameworks within which it occurs. However, an explanation of migration would be incomplete if it failed to go beyond these frameworks and take account of the human element. For whatever the imperatives of the global and national patterns of inequality and interaction, the migration process would not have been perpetuated if it had been devoid of significance and meaning to the people themselves.

Migration persisted as an expression of the pursuit of personal freedom and an acceptable identity, as well as of survival and material viability. As such it inevitably encompassed the dilemmas of absenteeism and belonging, of resisting the constraints to freedom and opportunity and accommodating to the post-emancipation plantation system that conditioned the political, economic, and social spheres of life. Migration expressed the dialectic of enslavement and marronage, of resistance and adaptation.

Migration as a way of life and a part of culture was not unique to the Caribbean. Yet the psychological impact of these international linkages was more powerful in the Caribbean than in many other regions for at least two reasons: West Indians were uprooted immigrants, and the culture – a reconstituted creole culture – was moulded by the psychological impact of the plantation and slavery. Migration was a component of the overall mobility to which Caribbean people aspired. The concept of mobility, and thus the value of migration, went deep into society's consciousness, extending beyond the single generation and forming part of an on-going process. The fact that so many people were perceived to do well from migration continued to endorse its value into and throughout the twentieth century.

REFERENCES

Besson, Jean. 1984. 'Family Land and Caribbean Society: Toward an Ethnography of Afro-Caribbean Peasantries'. In *Perspectives on Caribbean Regional Identity*, Elizabeth M. Thomas-Hope (ed.), 57-83. Liverpool: Centre for Latin American Studies, Monograph Series No 11.

Bryan, Patrick. 1985. 'The Question of Labour in the Sugar Industry of the Dominican Republic in the Late Nineteenth and Early Twentieth Centuries'. In *Between Slavery and Free Labour: The Spanish-Speaking Caribbean in the Nineteenth Century*, Manuel Moreno Fraginals, Frank Moya Pons, and Staley L. Engerman (eds.), 235-51. Baltimore, The John Hopkins Press.

Del Castillo, José. n.d. *La inmigración de braceros azucareros en la República Dominicana 1900-1930*. Santo Domingo, Cuadernos del Centro de Investigaciones Antropológicas, Vol. 262, No. 7.

Dirks, Robert. 1972. 'Network Groups and Adaptation in an Afro-Caribbean Community'. *Man* 7:565-85.

Eltis, David. 1972. 'The Traffic in Slaves betwen the British West Indian Colonies, 1807–1833'. *Economic History Review* 25:55-64.

Frucht, Richard. 1968. 'Emigration, Remittances and Social Change: Aspects of the Social Field in Nevis, West Indies'. *Anthropologica* 10:193-208.

Goveia, Elsa V. 1965. *Slave Society in the British Leeward Islands at the End of the Eighteenth Century.* New Haven: Yale University Press.

Gussler, Judith D. 1980. 'Adaptive Strategies and Social Networks of Women in St. Kitts'. In *A World of Women*, Erika Bourguignon (ed.), 185-209. New York: Praeger.

Hall, Douglas. 1971. *Five of the Leewards, 1834–1870.* Barbados: Caribbean University Press.

Hoetink, Harmannus. 1988. 'Labour "Scarcity" and Immigration in the Dominican Republic c.1875-c.1930'. In *Labour in the Caribbean*, Malcolm Cross and Gad Heuman (eds.), 160-175. London: Macmillan Caribbean.

Lowenthal, David. 1972. *West Indian Societies.* London, Oxford University Press.

Midgett, Douglas K. 1977. *West Indian Migration and Adaptation in St. Lucia and London.* Ph.D. diss., University of Illinois, Urbana.

Olwig, Karen Fog. 1984. 'Women's Networks and Wage Employment in the West Indies'. *Antropologiska Studier* 35-36:13-18.

______. 1993. *Global Culture, Island Identity: Continuity and Change in the Afro-Caribbean Community of Nevis.* New York: Harwood.

Otterbein, Keith F. 1966. 'A Comparison of the Land Tenure Systems of the Bahamas, Jamaica and Barbados'. *International Archives of Ethnography* 50:31-42.

Pessar, Patricia R. 1982. 'The Role of Households in International Migration and the Case of U.S.-Bound Migration from the Dominican Republic'. *International Migration Review* 16:342-64.

Philpott, Stuart B. 1973. *West Indian Migration: The Montserrat Case.* London: Athlone Press.

Proudfoot, Malcolm. 1950. *Population Movements in the Caribbean.* Port of Spain, Trinidad: Caribbean Commission.

Richardson, Bonham C. 1975. 'Plantation Infrastructure and Labour Mobility in Guyana and Trinidad'. In *Migration and Development: Implications for Ethnic Identity and Political Conflict*, H. I. Safa and B. DuToit (eds.), 205-224. The Hague and Paris: Mouton.

______. 1983. *Caribbean Migrants: Environment and Human Survival on St. Kitts and Nevis.* Knoxville: University of Tennessee Press.

Smith, M. G. 1962. *West Indian Family Structure.* Seattle: University of Washington Press.

Smith, R. T. 1956. *The Negro Family in British Guiana.* London: Routledge and Keegan Paul.

Thomas-Hope, Elizabeth M. 1992. *Explanation in Caribbean Migration.* London: Macmillan.

Part IV
Postscript

The Wayward Leewards

DAVID LOWENTHAL

This book explores the shifting fortunes of the Leeward islands in the context of general trends in the post-emancipation Caribbean. To survey each of the several dozen inhabited islands, or to include every significant trend, was beyond our capacity. Yet both our geographical and subject-matter range are substantial. And some important and provocative conclusions emerge.

To present a few of these is the aim of this essay. I begin with a cursory sketch of post-slavery trends throughout the Americas, notably those bearing on topics stressed herein – patterns of land tenure, employment, migration, social structure, race and class, and relations between local societies and overseas influences. Next I discuss how far the Leewards exemplify or depart from wider post-emancipation trends. Finally I address key issues about this period that remain unresolved and suggest the research approaches they might require.

AFTER EMANCIPATION – A HEMISPHERIC OVERVIEW

Throughout the plantation realm from the southern United States to Brazil, the post-slavery saga was one of early anxieties that failed to eventuate followed by great expectations that were never realized. Wherever slaves had been numerous, planters and the regimes they controlled predicted imminent social breakdown and economic ruin, chaos and violence. Nowhere did this happen; the harbinger of St. Domingue proved a false alarm, for no new Haitis emerged from the ashes of freedom. Instead, ruling social and economic institutions carried on with remarkable continuity, barring a brief hiatus in the American South.

Reformers' hopes of interracial harmony and social progress proved likewise chimerical. Abolitionists and former slaves shared dreams of a future in which freed men and women would become true citizens. The ending of forced servitude was expected to generate advances in all realms of life. But like the fear of anarchic dissolution, this anticipation everywhere came to nought. In the American South, virulent reaction followed a short interval of biracial reconstruction, leaving the freed slaves as maltreated as before. In Brazil and Cuba, slavery lingered on through the nineteenth century, by its end scarcely distinguishable from peonage in general. Earlier emancipation had great symbolic value in the Caribbean, but former slaves and generations of descendants remained largely landless, impoverished, unschooled, and disfranchised. In the phrase of a nineteenth-century colonial official, 'a race has been freed, but a society has not been formed' (Bell and Morrell 1928:432, citing Harris [1848]).

Growing expectations of equality and autonomy exacerbated these disappointments throughout plantation America. Each long-awaited advance – sovereignty, suffrage, racial equality under law – failed to dismantle structures of economic, political, and social control that left the majority impotent and impoverished.

Hopes were still-born in four realms of life. Most critical was the continued hegemony of the plantocracy. Pre-emancipation planters or those who bought them out monopolized land and other resources, including labour. They also kept or rapidly resumed control over local affairs. Ex-slave participation in government soon ended in the American South, with blacks disfranchised for another full century. In the British Caribbean property qualifications for voting and office-holding excluded all but a tiny proportion of ex-slaves; adult suffrage did not become the norm until the 1940s. The French and Dutch Caribbean effectively disfranchised slave descendants by reserving all significant powers to Paris and Amsterdam.

Emancipation did weaken the old plantocracy and often changed its make-up. But its hold did not actually end until after the Second World War. *The Fall of the Planter Class* famously chronicled by Lowell Ragatz (1928) required three further generations to become a reality, and in many ways, in many places, it is hardly yet the case that Massa Day Done (Williams 1961).

A second setback was relative if not absolute economic decline. Agricultural exports became less and less profitable throughout plantation America. Beleaguered by indebtedness, soil exhaustion and erosion, modernization costs, and labour forces no longer wholly coercible, producers were increasingly undercut by Indian cotton, European sugar beets, Asian spices and hardwoods. Specific setbacks – the devastation of American Civil War, the withdrawal of British tariff preferences for Caribbean sugar – augmented these misfortunes. From the mid-eighteenth century, when Guadeloupe seemed a pearl equal in value to Quebec, the Caribbean had sunk by the Second World War to seem scarcely worth fifty decrepit destroyers. In the islands, economic decline has been endemic whatever the regime. If nowhere else quite matches Haiti's despair, none the less Castro's Cuba, the Puerto Rican 'miracle', the Trinidad oil bonanza have all alike foundered.

Linked with this decline was the reduction of metropolitan interest. Economic malaise, the West India trade's reduced clout, the decay of imperial enterprise generally have crippled the Caribbean since emancipation. Strategically and otherwise the Caribbean is now far less consequential than it was through the eighteenth century. Few even recall

Eric Williams' 1950s federal *cause célèbre*, the American naval base at Chaguaramas; Guantánamo is just a Cold War memory; not even the rocket launcher at Kourou rouses Cayenne from torpor. The American South, too, suffered prolonged neglect within the Union from which it had sought to secede. European interest began to wane long before current political devolution. The fin-de-siècle imperial visions of Joseph Chamberlain were an aberrant hiccup in a chronicle of steady British divestiture.

The fourth trend was a hardening of racial exclusion, especially acute between 1850 and 1950. Disillusioning those who had banked on freedom to reduce rather than raise barriers, intensified racism stemmed partly from emancipation itself. Elites who had depended on divisions between free and slave to maintain social barriers now relied solely on racial distinctions. The coloured middle-class suffered a like predicament; with freedom extended to all, they themselves lost status when lumped with emancipated blacks.

Anti-black prejudice inherent in slavery became harsher still in its aftermath. Discrimination based on colour became a legalized norm. In the British Caribbean non-whites were expressly excluded from office or high rank, not only by local whites but by Whitehall. In the American South, Jim Crow legislation brought apartheid into every realm of life, and mob lynching evinced race hatred more apparent even than during slavery.

Non-white exclusion was justified by pseudo-scientific racism. Whites had always seen Africans as inferior – and hence suited for slavery – but only after the 1830s did this bias harden into genetic explanation. Enlightenment and post-Enlightenment thought conceived racial differences as ameliorable by example, by education, and by admixture. But towards the mid-nineteenth century, romantic nationalism increasingly emphasized blood purity and immutability. Such strictures applied not only to black and white but to all supposed races.

A 'Teutonic germ' theory ascribing all virtues to unmixed Germanic stock prevailed among Western savants for half a century or more. Above all, Mendelian genetics and Social Darwinism lent a scientific imprimatur to discrimination against non-whites (Horsman 1981). Racial prejudice based on genetic myth still afflicts slave descendants everywhere in the Americas, whether they form a majority or a minority, whether divided biracially or along a colour spectrum, whether under autonomous or colonial, democratic or autocratic rule.

Such in broad outline are the post-emancipation trends of the hemisphere. Looking at the Leewards, let us see how its component parts reflect these wider developments.

LEEWARD ISLANDS TRENDS

All islands are atypical even when they resemble one another more than the

Leewards do. They differ as entities; they differ in their highly important connections with the world outside; they differ in what is known about them. Comparative data on islands are extremely difficult to gather and to collate; administrative differences make most statistics non-comparable; few scholars ever examine more than one island in depth. The generalizations offered here are hedged with uncertainty and marred by many lacunae.

Rough contiguity aside, the Leewards are anything but cohesive; few physical or cultural generalizations fit them. Even their number varies; Dominica was administratively a British Leeward island from 1871 until 1940 when removed to the Windwards; Saba, Sint Maarten, and Sint Eustatius, indubitably Leeward in location, are known as the Netherlands Windwards. Physically the islands are highly diverse, embracing volcanic cones, limestone and sandstone pavements, and rugged metamorphic remnants.

Their cultural heritage is equally diverse. English, French, Dutch, Danish, and American institutions and linguistic traits have syncretized with African, Indian, and other; residual sugar and cotton plantations share the economic scene with fishing and lobstering, saltpans and subsistence farming, tourism, and a lively tradition of smuggling and salvaging wrecks. Racially the Leewards range from islands largely black (Barbuda), brown (Anguilla), and white (St Barthélemy) through various admixtures, with Syrian, Chinese, and other minorities.

All these differences might lead one to suspect that the Leewards had nothing in common beyond marginality and unimportance. Perhaps the French economist Havard Duclos (1956) had this in mind when setting up his now-forgotten mutual assistance grouping of the five small islands (whose problems and promises were equally neglected by their imperial overlords) known as MABES (Sint Maarten, Anguilla, St Barthélemy, Sint Eustatius, Saba): '"maybe" it will work'.

What is alike about the Leewards is, indeed, mainly their insignificance. None but Antigua contains more than 40,000 people; most of the hundred-odd inhabited islands have fewer than 10,000. All are small in area as well, though rugged terrain may belie it: none but Antigua exceed 60 square miles.

Leeward littleness is not only absolute but relative; larger islands border them to the west – Jamaica and Puerto Rico, Hispaniola and Cuba – and to the south – Martinique and the Windwards, Barbados and Trinidad. Smaller in size, resources, and numbers than other once-British, French, Dutch, and American territories, the Leewards have not come first with any imperial power since 1763, when St. Kitts was a rich focus of Anglo-French rivalry. The exception was the Danish Virgin Islands, Denmark's sole imperial possession until sold to the United States in 1917. Most of the Leewards count for so little as to be colonies of colonies. They have been seen and hence see themselves as second-class, second-rate, marginal even within a marginal colonial realm. If Puerto Rico is at stake who cares about St. Croix? With Jamaica at risk Anguilla becomes a joke – the mouse that roared. And the French and Dutch islets are too small to weigh in any balance.

Marginality is the key to my first distinction between the Leewards and the rest of Plantation-America, especially the rest of the Caribbean. I noted above that the whole realm declined once slavery ended – economies wound down, enterprises failed, estates mortgaged, moribund, abandoned. This happened sooner and more swiftly in the Leewards than anywhere else, save in some of the Windwards.

Most of the Leewards abandoned sugar. Montserrat, always marginal for sugar production, gave way to cotton under share-cropping. The decline of sugar in Antigua was slower but inexorable. Only in St. Croix and St. Kitts did sugar estates truly survive. In St. Croix this was a consequence of later emancipation and keen Danish support; in St. Kitts of fertile soils and unusual entrepreneurial stability.

Elsewhere the saga was one of remorseless decline, hastened by estate bankruptcy and by land degradation due to abandonment and squatting. In the end, the crops that replaced sugar – coconuts, cotton, bananas – failed for reasons of scale as much as for any other cause. Antigua's cotton industry could not afford a technology competitive with long-staple producers elsewhere, Montserrat growers could not produce enough bananas to make scheduled stops by container-ships worthwhile.

The Leewards became socially as well as economically marginalized. Some white elites pulled up stakes or were forced out, though not to the same extent as in the Windwards. But Windward whites were succeeded by coloured elites, many of them French former free-coloured folk long linked with local coffee, cacao, and commerce; the coloured middle class in the Leewards lacked this landed social strength. Moreover, white persistence in Antigua and St. Kitts, St. Croix and St. Thomas left intact habits of racial exclusion matched in the Windwards only by St. Vincent. Even the larger Leewards were too small and poor to sustain an economically viable, self-confident, middle-class coloured network. Hindered in Antigua and St. Kitts-Nevis by white monopolization of key estate and civil service posts, middle-class formation was virtually non-existent in Montserrat, where shopkeepers and traders, clerks and teachers instead came in from Antigua. In the British Virgins, St. Thomas, and Anguilla specialized and often illicit enterprise lent small entrepreneurs a degree of stability.

Meanwhile, migration opportunities for the skilled and the educated continually drained island communities of potential leaders. More than anywhere else in the Caribbean, the Leewards generally suffered erosion of existing social institutions and failed to develop those they lacked.

Aggravating more than stemming socio-economic decline was the persistence of imperial involvement in local affairs. The erosion of local institutions encouraged intrusion from London and Paris, Amsterdam and Copenhagen, and vice versa. However rudimentary were schooling and sanitation, however feeble the transport network, however ineffectual the development schemes, these interventions brought the Leewards a level of European and American connection belying their size and worth.

By contrast, the larger Caribbean territories were on the whole run by local elites. The Windwards were abandoned to their own inadequate devices, the Federation riots of the 1880s underscoring their impoverishment *vis-à-vis* neighbouring Barbados. The Leewards suffered no equivalent neglect, though marginal islands like Barbuda were at times wholly forgotten.

Thus while Leeward Island collective identities became less supportive, many inhabitants had access to a wider range of opportunities than other West Indians. Indeed, the decay of home communities made folk readier to seek employment elsewhere, for seasonal or longer terms, to sustain their families. The absentee mentality endemic with the planter class spread to all.

Migration and return became integral to the Leeward way of life. Many ventured to Dominica, Guadeloupe, Puerto Rico, others to farther-flung Trinidad, Curaçao, Guiana, the Dominican Republic. Diverse contacts abroad made Leewardites more sophisticated travellers than, say, rural Jamaicans or Haitians. Links with existing emigrant nuclei in the United States and elsewhere facilitated migration. Inter-Leeward shipping and seafaring skills suited Leeward Islanders to marine trades. Small numbers and easy proximity via the Virgin Islands after 1917 encouraged clandestine, but containable and hence condoned, movement to Puerto Rico and the United States mainland that still continues.

In these respects Leeward Islanders have more in common with small islanders elsewhere, from the Pacific and the Indian Ocean to the Mediterranean and the North Sea, than with the rest of plantation America, even the Caribbean (Lowenthal 1985). The culture of emigration, with supportive emigrant communities, is of long standing throughout the Leewards. Few other islands have connections abroad that matter as much as for most Leeward folk.

Small-island needs that promote such interchange also enhance traditions that bind islanders within an ongoing community. Anguillan kinship networks that stretched to New York and London buttressed the breakaway from St. Kitts that at length won Anguilla its enviable 'colonial' status.

Barbudan family linkages at home and abroad (Leicester; New York) came to the fore with the notorious auction sale of the Codrington Papers in London in 1981 (Chamberlin 1983:208-26). Warehoused prior to export, these papers were for years the focus of 'Roots' television programmes showing Barbudans perusing old documents and saying, 'Oh, here's a Beazer, he must have been my great-grandfather'. A rooted sense of ancestry here coalesces with the enduring unity of a community of whom three-fourths are now off the island (Lowenthal and Clarke 1979, 1980).

Perhaps the most startling Leewards anomaly is the relative economic health of many of its constituents. Contrary to conventional wisdom, the smaller, resource-poor places now often seem the most viable. The reversal of roles within the Caribbean Community (CARICOM) underscores the point:

> In the early days, the larger islands did not wish to federate with the smaller ones, which they regarded as problem cases and a threat to their own viability. Now it is the other way around. The MDCs [Major Developed Countries] are the problem cases within CARICOM, and the LDCs [Lesser Developed Countries] regard further integration with them as a threat to their own economic viability and prosperity (Abbott 1991).

Unrelated catastrophes have, to be sure, crippled the economies of Guyana, Jamaica, and Trinidad. But there is also a more general trend. Larger Third World lands are disadvantaged *simply by being larger*. Small states enjoy more manœuvrability and are often better placed to profit from strategic location. Small size and global impotence justify hanging on to residual colonial ties that residents find more beneficial than being an appendage of some larger near neighbour.

Flying in the face of the global cult of sovereignty, the folk of Anguilla and Montserrat, the Virgin Islands and the Dutch Windwards, are enormously better off in terms of individual livelihood and freedom of movement than those in sovereign Caribbean states of comparable size (Antigua, St. Kitts, the Windwards, Curaçao and Aruba).

RESEARCH AGENDA

Certain queries remain unresolved – matters often touched on in specific island studies that sound a common Leeward chord. One is a need for detailed records of land-holding, tenurial systems, inheritance patterns, and family histories for all the islands. For most larger teritories such records are well collected and collated; Barbados and Jamaica, Martinique and Guadeloupe are models of what might be learned. One problem is that data available since emancipation are generally inferior to those before; it is a bitter reality that records are best kept in armies and prisons, as these islands essentially were during slavery.

Likewise little known are local responses to the oppressive hegemony perpetuated after emancipation – oppression at such variance to initial expectations. Several chapters in this book stress specific modes of resistance and accommodation. But to understand how people in general dealt with economic and social constraints, our focus must broaden from particular eventful crises to day-to-day patterns of aggravation and negotiation between rulers and ruled, white and black, employers and labourers.

Family-land traditions exemplify issues of tenure and obligation where private and collective ownership, freehold and leasehold and share-cropping, social and symbolic uses of land often overlapped. In the Leewards, where many are off-island episodically or permanently, the role of absentee owners and others who share rights in land is critical, as Barbuda and Anguilla have recently shown. Emigrants often innovate, fund, or implement resource development. On the other hand, the confusion of tenures where heirs are widely scattered, as in Nevis and Montserrat, may exacerbate neglect and abandonment by preventing or long delaying decisions about maintenance and production.

Education, religion, family life, and the work place have played a role in forming social identities in the Leewards in ways that are little known. The mix of folk and formal patterns of schooling and attachment varies from place to place but is of signal import where economic decline and emigration have frayed local and regional institutions. Larger islands do not lack these syncretic complexities, but in the Leewards they pervade every aspect of life. The autobiographical fictions of Jamaica Kincaid, for example, vividly convey a mix of British, American, Afro-Caribbean, Antiguan, and family influences quite different in assumptions about composite identity from those conveyed in, say, George Lamming's larger Barbados or V. S. Naipaul's ethnically heterogeneous Trinidad.

Along with a keener apprehension of everyday life, we need clues to popular understanding of the whole post-emancipation period. How did ordinary people, as distinct from officials and popular spokesmen, view the changes and continuities they perceived in their lives? How far did they conceive their options to be constrained by local circumstances, forge links overseas, seek wider identities within the Leewards and beyond? Intermarriage and inter-island movement suggest an emergent eastern Caribbean identity. But insights into the nature and extent of such patterns must await the collection and analysis of extensive oral accounts.

Those concerned with the Leewards must also come to terms with the area's ineluctable diversity. For so long resolutely themselves, these islands are not now apt to become more alike. Not only do some – notably Barbuda and Anguilla – explicitly stress differences from larger neighbours. But it is also the Leewards' common nature that each of their uniquenesses persists and even magnifies. The Organization of Eastern Caribbean States encourages members to pursue their own developmental goals and objectives. 'Consequently, there is now more (not less) divergence and disparity among the members.' Indeed, members have given up any pretence of seeking uniformity of taxation and fiscal policies (Abbott 1991:337).

Although diversity is a hallmark of the Leewards, in one respect these islands are much alike: their vulnerability to external influence, benign or malign. Whether formally autonomous or not, the Leewards are too small and impotent to resist global piracy, tourism, banking, drug dealing, or reformist panaceas. No other part of the Caribbean feels at once so remote from, yet so dependent on, the developed world. Influential outsiders encourage local eccentricities. What other semi-abandoned cast-offs in the 1990s can match Anguilla's Royal visitation, the Virgin Islands' paradise hideaways (Laurence Rockefeller's St. John, Richard Branson's Necker), Barbuda's delusory refuge for llamas? The Leewards pay the price as they reap the rewards of being the last and least remnants of imperial enterprise.

REFERENCES

Abbott, George C. 1991. 'Integration and Viability in the Caribbean'. *Journal of Commonwealth & Comparative Politics* 29:327-45.

Bell, Kenneth N., and W. P. Morrell. 1928. *Select Documents on British Colonial Policy, 1830–1860*. Oxford: Clarendon Press.

Chamberlin, Russell. 1983. *Loot! The Heritage of Plunder*. London: Thames and Hudson.

Duclos, B. Havard. 1956. *MABES: Pilot Economic Project for Grouping the Islands around St. Martin (Anguilla, St. Barthelémy, St. Eustatius, Saba)*. Port-of-Spain: Caribbean Commission.

Horsman, Reginald. 1981. *Race and Manifest Destiny: The Origins of American Racial Anglo-Saxonism*. Cambridge, Mass.: Harvard University Press.

Lowenthal, David. 1985. 'Mobility and Identity in the Island Pacific'. *Pacific Viewpoint* 26:316-26.

Lowenthal, David, and Colin G. Clarke. 1979. 'Common Lands, Common Aims: The Distinctive Barbudan Community'. In *Peasants, Plantations and Rural Communities in the Caribbean*, Malcolm Cross and Arnaud Marks (eds.), 142-59. Guildford, Department of Sociology, University of Surrey.

______. 1980. 'Island Orphans: Barbuda and the Rest'. *Journal of Commonwealth & Comparative Politics* 18:293-307.

Ragatz, Lowell Joseph. 1928 [1963]. *The Fall of the Planter Class in the British Caribbean, 1763-1833: A Study in Social and Economic History*. New York: Octagon Books.

Williams, Eric. 1961. *Massa Day Done: A Masterpiece of Political and Sociological Analysis*. Port-of-Spain: P.N.M. Publishing Co.

Notes on Contributors

Riva Berleant-Schiller is Professor of Anthropology at the University of Connecticut. Her recent work on the Leeward Islands includes *Antigua and Barbuda* (1995), jointly written with Susan Lowes, and 'Merging Domains and Women's Roles in Barbuda and Dominica' (with Bill Maurer), in *Women and Change in the Caribbean*, edited by Janet Momsen (1993).

Jean Besson is Lecturer in Anthropology at Goldsmiths' College, University of London. She edited with Janet Momsen *Land and Development in the Caribbean* (1987), and has written extensively on family land, kinship, and land tenure in Jamaica and elsewhere in the Caribbean.

Gad Heuman teaches in the Department of History and is a member of the Centre for Caribbean Studies at the University of Warwick. His publications include *Between Black and White* (1981) and a study of the Morant Bay Rebellion in Jamaica, *The Killing Time* (1994). He has edited books on slave resistance and on labour in the Caribbean and is co-editor of the journal *Slavery & Abolition*.

Barry W. Higman is Professor of History at the University of the West Indies, Mona, Jamaica. He has published books on the comparative history of slave populations in the British Caribbean and on the geographic aspects of slave societies.

David Lowenthal is Professor Emeritus of Geography at University College London. He is author of *West Indian Societies* (1972) and co-editor (with Lambros Comitas) of *West Indian Perspectives* (1973). With Colin Clarke he confuted the myth of slave-breeding in Barbuda and in vain supported that island's claim to autonomy at the 1981 Antigua-Barbuda constitutional conference.

Susan Lowes received her doctorate in anthropology from Columbia University and has written many articles and papers on issues of race and class in the West Indies after emancipation. She has for a number of years been director of Monthly Review Press in New York City.

Karen Fog Olwig teaches at the Institute of Anthropology, University of Copenhagen. She is the author of *Cultural Adaptations and Resistance on St. John: Three Centuries of Afro-Caribbean Life* (1985), and *Global Culture, Local Identity: Continuity and Change in the Afro-Caribbean Community of Nevis* (1993).

Elizabeth Thomas-Hope is at the Centre of Environment and Development at the University of the West Indies, Mona, Jamaica. She has written *Explanation in Caribbean Migration* (1992), and edited *Perspectives on Caribbean Regional Identity* (1984). She has specialized in West Indian migration.

George F. Tyson is a public historian specializing in Virgin Islands and Caribbean history. A resident of St. Croix, US Virgin Islands, he has written and edited several books and articles, including *Toussaint L'Ouverture* (1973). He is co-author of *Slavery in the Danish West Indies: A Bibliography* (1994), and *The Kamina Folk: Slavery and Slave Life in the Danish West Indies* (1994). He is currently working on a study of the plantation system in the Danish West Indies.

Index